WALK, CLIMB, OR FLY

WALK, CLIMB, OR FLY

SURVIVING AND THRIVING IN THE WORKPLACE WILDERNESS

LEIGH DURST

LIONCREST
PUBLISHING

WALK, CLIMB, OR FLY
Surviving and Thriving in the Workplace Wilderness

ISBN   978-1-5445-0200-7 *Hardcover*
   978-1-5445-0199-4 *Paperback*
   978-1-5445-0198-7 *Ebook*

THIS BOOK IS
DEDICATED TO

For Brent, Michelle, and Josh

*Thank you for loving me, embracing my wings, and believing
in me. You are such precious, beautiful gifts from God, and
I am so proud to share this journey with you.*

*For my Mama and the Don. Thanks for believing in me and teaching
me about faith, grace, and the importance of spreading my wings.*

CONTENTS

ADDITIONAL
APPRECIATION

I want to thank the following people for their encouragement, validation, support, patience, pushes, prayers, and cheerleading.

Thanks first to my loving family: to my husband Brent, daughter Michelle, and son Joshua. You are the absolute best people I know. You have made my life so rich and rewarding. Thank you for embracing me in my entirety and for your sacrificial support. I love you so much. To my Mom and her Don: You made this book possible. Thanks for your support, generosity, and wisdom! To Momma, "Krickie," and our extended family—love, love, love you.

To Cindy Campbell, who saw it all first on the back of a napkin: thanks for being my sounding board, testing ground, and an incredible Flying friend. To Ann Handley, who has walked many miles with me: thank you for helping me find my voice, for the writing encouragement, the nudges, and all the laughter. To Nancy Duarte, an inspiration, a mighty woman, a shining beacon, a great encouragement, and soul sister. Thank you for everything.

To Ken Lingad, a good man, a steadfast friend, champion, advocate, and voice of reason who has given to me sacrificially and with love and kindness: thanks to you and the 1680PR team crew, including Elijah Rawlings, for all the incredible support, advocacy, and polish!

To Dr. Kristina Johnson, PhD: thanks for helping me trust God and my gut, and your incredible validation, input, and wisdom. To Brandon

Johnson, a lover of all people: you are a contagious world changer and atmosphere shifter!

To my Flyer bestie Kelly Goto, my sister-friend and partner in crime for over twenty years: we fly *free* and the best is yet to come! To my Walker bestie Michelle Kenny, my lifelong friend: I just love you! To Poppy Crum, a fellow Flyer and brilliant buddy: Tag! You're it!

To the Scribe team, Zach Obront, Ellie Cole, Meghan McCracken, and team: bless you for knowing how to manage (and edit down) this flapping, honking goose.

Heartfelt thanks also to my extended Walking, Climbing, and Flying tribe in no specific order: Nicole Lockwood, Kristie Wells, Chris Heuer, Tove Bormes, Lisa Priappi, Darin Durst, "Whurley," David Armano, Monique Morrow, Neal Joseph, Parry Aftab, Sherol Chen, Jesse West, Lori Smith, Diane Bryhn, Denice Crowell, Lauren Vargas, Ekaterina Walter, Skip and Janiece Rizzo, Esteban Contreras, Jeff Pane, Jay Iorio, Karen McCabe, Bob Labelle, and Brenda Bethke—your encouragement, input, help, and support made all the difference.

Finally, thanks to the managers and mentors that were instrumental in helping me learn, grow, and spread my wings while I became more grounded: Jim McCann, Chris McCann, Bill Bowers, Larry Simpson, Mike Adatto, Tom DeGarmo, Cat Ciric, Patricia Funderburk-Ware, Dr. Susan Rogacz—thank you from the bottom of my heart for helping embrace my own design.

INTRODUCTION
THE WORKPLACE AS A WILDERNESS

While most of us spend decades preparing for a job or career, we spend comparatively little time preparing for the professional journey we will face each day. For many, entry into a profession or career feels like being air dropped into a jungle—2017 Jumanji style. We receive minimal training and instruction for the "Workplace Wildernesses" we will face. The lucky few are fortunate enough to find a manager or mentor that may serve as a kind of trail guide for part of the professional journey. For the rest of us, there's no map to guide us—and most of us are left to ourselves to find our way.

As we journey forward, it's up to us to navigate effectively, secure the right job "fit," select the right career path, develop our skills and abilities, and strive to meet demands and expectations laid out before us. We must rely on our smarts, skills, and resourcefulness as we journey forward and learn to survive. Given time, we learn the lay of the land, develop an understanding of the pecking order, the process for decision-making, and figure out the political undercurrents, as well as the spoken and unspoken "rules" that surround us. Through trial and error, we eventually acclimate to the cultures of the environments within which we serve, pressing forward to establish and manage relationship dynamics, forming relationships and strategic alliances that can fuel our progress. We learn to establish and assert boundaries and learn how to identify and take advantage of opportunities to learn, grow, and advance.

In truth, for many of us, navigating the twists, turns, and obstacles of the professional territory we face isn't easy. While your formal education (if you are blessed to have had one) may have helped you cultivate your natural talent and develop skills that are incredibly useful, there's often little to prepare you for the vast, foreign landscape you will traverse over the course of your career. While it may be full of opportunity, challenge, and excitement, it can also be an environment that proves to be surprisingly difficult, and at times, harsh or hostile. Any seasoned professional will warn you that finding your way in the Workplace Wilderness can be hard. Yet, surprisingly, very few of us have been conditioned to prepare ourselves for this journey by asking—and answering—thought-provoking questions like this:

- What kind of work energizes, motivates, and gratifies me?
- What are my natural strengths—and what makes me special?
- What do I really love to do, and how can I leverage this in my profession?
- How am I designed to function in a work setting?
- What kinds of environments help me deliver at maximum potential?
- What is my personal definition of the word "success," and how do I quantify it?
- Where should my professional path lead me?

Some of us take a road less traveled, in the form of self-employment, and others opt for traditional employment. We are shown a workstation or cubicle and told how lucky we are to have been chosen, as we are given a list of things to do. Energized by new challenges and motivated to prove ourselves, we dive in headfirst, striving to meet and exceed expectations and do our best to work with the rules, perform well. We are encouraged to advance through the ranks, to be flexible and take on more responsibility. As we become busier, it becomes easier to switch on "career autopilot," placing hopes and dreams on the back-burner—at the mercy of the corporate machine as we become preoccupied with managing demands and complicated requests, navigating workplace dynamics, and the 24/7 "opportunity" to respond to email, text messages, calls, and more.

SURVIVING, NOT THRIVING

Unfortunately, our busy work life and autopilot mode can steer us off-course like a poorly connected GPS, directing us down a path we may not otherwise conscientiously choose for ourselves. We may not just end up in the wrong place: for many in the Workplace Wilderness, it becomes difficult to maintain a reasonable "work/life balance." Perhaps this is why a recent Gallup poll indicated that 23 percent of workers skate dangerously around the edge of burnout, with another 44 percent reporting burnout "sometimes." It's no wonder people don't feel better about this thing called "work"—or that they question whether they are meant for more. Digging into the numbers can feel a bit like falling down the proverbial rabbit hole. Consider the following recent statistics:

- Eighty-five percent of employees worldwide are disengaged in their jobs, with 53 percent of US workers classified as "not engaged." (Gallup)

- Only 5 percent of employees feel they have the right fit, high engagement, and have worked ten or more years at the same organization. (Gallup)

- In 2017, 61 percent of Americans cited work as the most common source of stress. (American Psychological Association)

- Seventy-six percent of U.S. employees surveyed say stress at work has had a negative impact on their personal relationships and 66 percent say they have lost sleep due to work stress. (Korn Ferry)

- Fifty-six percent of U.K. employees admit to suffering from stress, 36 percent from anxiety, and 25 percent from depression. Forty-six percent of employees cite work as the main cause of their mental health problems. (BHSF)

While employers struggle to redefine and reengineer the modern workplace, the real key to reversing job disengagement is *unlikely* to be engineered by the institutions we serve. While we can certainly wait for them to come up with a magic solution, we often underestimate the power that *people* collectively have—as essential players in the workplace ecosystem—to reverse negative trends and patterns in the workplace. In reality, your ability to move into a more positive relationship with this thing called "work" starts with your willingness to take the helm of your professional journey and manage that journey with determination and sensitivity to how you—and others—are designed.

Armed with a greater sense of determination and purpose, you can develop a clearer vision of the future you wish to create—one that's consciously aligned with your own sense of purpose, values, beliefs, needs, and priorities. You can approach work differently as you embrace your place and part in your chosen field, industry, and workplace, and work in a way that is more energizing. You can also become more sensitive others and work in an adaptive manner to unlock potential, more effectively collaborate, and drive meaningful, gratifying, and remarkable results.

FINDING A BETTER WAY TO WORK

In my journey through the Workplace Wilderness, I successfully tolerated the unusually high demands of my job because I genuinely enjoyed what I did for a living. As an in-demand business consultant, for years I skated around (and off) the edge of burnout by working the *wrong* way. Like a frog placed in a pot of tepid water over a hot stove, I didn't recognize the escalating heat until the water began to bubble, and then it was too late. I gradually became burned out and frustrated, and then I got sick—physically sick, and sick of work, of myself, and of people in my workplace.

When I finally hit my peak of dissatisfaction and frustration, I realized that somehow, the majority of my attention and effort had become wrapped up in how to survive the "necessary evil" of work, rather than aligning my work to how I was designed to function—or to things that filled me with energy, a sense of purpose, and gratification. When I woke up to the truth, it seemed futile to continue this way: I didn't just want to spend my life *surviving a job*; I wanted to *thrive in my work*—and in my *life*. I knew in my heart there had to be a better way to handle this thing called work, and a better means of managing myself and others. So, I set out to find it.

My Quest

It was 2001, and I was a management consultant for a firm known at the time as one of the "Big Five" consulting firms. After a decade of pioneering in my field, I had worked for almost every imaginable type of company, from startups to the Fortune 100, non-profits, and government agencies, across industries and geographies from high tech to healthcare. My experiences with such a broad array of companies had given me great perspective on different types of work cultures. I also managed diverse work teams—often working with teams split into different geographic areas. As an individual who was tasked with managing projects that ushered in a high degree of people, process, and technology change, the work was also very high-pressure.

To bolster my success, over the years I had taken more than my share of training courses, from leadership and management training, to courses and workshops covering communications, contract negotiation, conflict resolution, and much more. I was psychologically profiled, discovered my strengths, and learned about emotional intelligence. I discovered different leadership styles, temperaments, as well as personality types. In the immediate term, I found most of my training incredibly insightful for better understanding myself and others.

However, in the longer-term, I found it difficult to *apply* what I'd learned to improve the way I *interfaced with others*—especially in the midst of complicated workplace dynamics. I also found it difficult to memorize and internalize all that I'd learned, and because I *had a job already*—I didn't have time to carry around a book as a point of reference to help me figure things out! My work in particular required me to quickly assess the environments I faced and figure out how to lead and motivate people. As I attempted to leverage my training, I found myself consistently frustrated about how to recall what I'd learned and make it actionable in my daily work life to "plug in" better with other people.

In time, I realized I needed something different: a better way to understand and adapt to the various people I encountered at work, and a simple, actionable methodology that would pack neatly into my scattered brain, to be easily unpacked when I needed it most. I longed for a simple guide book that would help me navigate the Workplace Wildernesses I faced, and not just to support my client work! On a personal level, I was often frustrated at work, tired of feeling perpetually misapplied, misunderstood, marginalized, and under-utilized. I became purposefully determined to:

- Leverage my talents and abilities in a way that was energizing, efficient, and effective

- Mesh with people in ways that brought out the best in others

- Help management understand me better and improve my "fit" in my workplace

- Better position myself for success, advancement, and growth

- Walk away at the end of the day feeling more gratified, satisfied, and balanced

A New Methodology

In my search for a solution, I devoured self-help, business, and management books. I raided online knowledge repositories. I took a myriad of self-tests, quizzes, and exercises. In 2002, I was somewhat shocked to find more than thirty-two different personality typing methodologies on the market. Today, there are more than forty. One aligned me to one of four archetypes and sixteen sub-archetypes. Another method scored me against thirteen different personality types, while another painted me a color. Most assigned me with labels that I was hard-pressed to recall, such as an element, color, descriptor, acronym, renaissance royalty title, spirit animal, and more.

In the end, while I found some frameworks more useful than others, there was something good to be extracted from many of the methodologies I explored. However, the problem remained that when the book or coursework was over, I was mostly left with the same frustrations I had all along. While these personality, leadership, and temperament frameworks "told me a lot about me," they didn't seem to offer practical, actionable, and memorable insight that helped me readily work with *other people* better! One book in particular outlined forty-five different personality archetypes! I remember wondering who in their right mind could remember it all. It felt like my search for a more memorable and actionable framework kept leading me to dead ends.

My job put me in a unique position to compare behaviors, cultures, and people across some very diverse work environments, from enterprise companies to startups, public sector to non-profits. In comparison, these organizations—many of which were household names—were markedly different. Yet, I was constantly amazed at the remarkable parallels in workplace dynamics and cultures I noted. This was especially true as it related to the incredible parallels I saw, related to how people functioned at work. I found this so fascinating that studying workplace and interpersonal dynamics became a side hobby for me.

I focused rapt attention on how different people got things done, examining how people handled tasks, interacted, and communicated. I observed social behavior and how people managed relationships with others. Because I sat at the helm of many initiatives that introduced significant change within these organizations, I also had the opportunity to observe people performing under pressure—people that juggled many tasks, faced reorganizations, and grappled with uncertainty or transitions. I watched how they handled the emotions that arose (stress, fear, territorialism, burnout, feeling overwhelmed, etc.), noting how the pressure often revealed the best and worst character traits of people.

I didn't just watch. I also listened to the explicit things people said as I tried to weigh the implicit meanings behind their messages and behaviors. I asked many questions to better understand people's perspectives, which were not just shaped by their backgrounds but the context within which they viewed themselves professionally. I met with people to discuss attitudes, fears, concerns, and actions, and helped them plan how they'd respond, seize opportunity, support their fellow workers, and ensure success in the midst of change.

In addition to being exposed to diverse companies and cultures, I was fortunate to have a job that allowed me to spend time with people at all organizational ranks, from the cubicle to the corner office and even the boardroom. This provided me with a wealth of insight into how people manage work tasks, process and handle pressure, demands, and relationships. I observed the dynamics in both harmonious and disharmonious groups—groups that shared a sense of mission and purpose, and groups with division and cultures marked by rumor, gossip, and other bad behavior.

THE BIRTH OF OPERATIONAL STYLES THEORY

As I began to identify trends related to the different ways people operate at work, a new theory began to take shape. My friend and colleague, Cindy, was the first person with whom I shared my ideas. We were in a New Jersey diner, in the middle of a nasty snow storm in the winter of 2002. We were both battling brutal winter colds, huddled in a booth with flushed faces and red noses, as we slurped down chicken soup, commiserating about the project within which we were both immersed. The project was fraught with drama, poor communication, and chaos—a veritable case-study on management and interpersonal dynamics gone wrong.

Thinking out loud, I attempted to explain what I had been observing. I pulled out a napkin and sketched out my first stab at articulating my ideas, which later became "Operational Styles Theory," or "OST." My simple, back-of-the-napkin sketch resonated with Cindy, who grappled with many of the same issues I did. From that time on, she served as a confidential sounding board, and a supportive proponent for my ideas and this book.

With my first supporter on board, I continued to observe people and map out my theory in more detail, porting initial concept into an outline, and eventually into a slide presentation. I later created some visuals and charts, which served as the foundational materials for this book. More importantly, I leveraged the insights I gathered to modify the way I worked—the way I managed relationships and myself within my workplace. I was blown away by the incredibly positive and incredibly rapid results garnered by the introduction of a few, relatively simple changes in my approach. These included dramatically improved interpersonal relationships, better communications, relationships, better teamwork, and faster results—with less drama and stress! It was like the sky parted and the sun shone bright from above!

I soon learned that my little theory wasn't just helpful for me. As I moved on to other projects and other employers, I encountered countless colleagues, coworkers, clients, and friends that felt just as frustrated and disillusioned as I had been. They were dealing with difficult people and situations. They needed to better manage workplace dynamics and navigate troubled career waters. They struggled to manage difficult people and troubled teams. They didn't feel properly aligned and/or felt stuck and were seeking answers. When I began to share my simple, street-smart theory and how it had helped me, I half-expected polite dismissals, eye rolling...perhaps some snickering in response. However, I was instead met with very strong interest and positive response as well as requests for *more* information.

I was pleasantly surprised to discover how receptive people were to the ideas I shared and the delight many expressed over how my simple "from the trenches" theory resonated against the unique situations they faced. I was delighted to hear how OST helped people pinpoint the issues they struggled with and offered solutions to help them better navigate the challenges they faced within their workplaces. It was so gratifying to hear that my little theory was doing for others what it had done for me, and I was amazed to have many colleagues request copies of my materials to share with their teams at work. Without fail, every single colleague I shared my theory with asked when I was *writing a book* on the topic.

I hadn't set out to write a book. Having a framework that helped me understand people better and work better with others was something I did for *myself*. It had made me a better manager, a better servant-leader, and a better person, one that was more at peace and driving toward meaningful success. Learning more about myself and others, and embracing the way I was made to function, also had the net effect of motivating great change in my own life. In time, I stepped out to start my independent consulting business, an experience that has offered the most exhilarating, satisfying, and rewarding experiences of my life. I became gainfully employed and had moved into a thriving, fruitful place.

But writing a book? Really? Who was I to write a book?

My dear friend, Ann Handley, CCO of Marketing Profs and author of the best-selling books *Content Rules* and *Everybody Writes,* encouraged me as a writer, and became a trusted confidant and sounding board, as well as a periodic nudge-giver. Ann once suggested I name this book *The Book I Never Meant to Write.* I immediately countered with another snarky title suggestion, "How about, *The Book I Am Terrified to Write?*" This wasn't a joke: I was dealing with fear and a fair dose of imposter syndrome. Beyond the typical insecurities one might have, the origin of the ideas and the subject matter in this book felt intensely personal to me. As a result, putting my little street-wise, non-academic theory "out there" for everyone to see felt akin to exposing my sensitive underbelly to a waiting crowd who was not only scowling but also armed with ping pong paddles!

My fear, in retrospect, was the reason I managed to talk at least two interested publishers *out* of publishing this book—publishers *who came to me* after hearing about this theory from other best-selling authors that were applying OST successfully themselves. Among other things, I grappled with timing and "readiness." To those friends that brought these opportunities to me, I apologize. It took years to run out of excuses.

One day, I stumbled upon an article that highlighted the history of one of the most popular personality typing methodologies on the market today. This particular methodology (which I am intentionally not going to name) is purported to be taken by two million people each year, driving $2 billion in annual revenues. Originally developed by two women with no academic affiliation who shared an interest in human behavior—it was birthed from a desire to develop an instrument that would help people understand and appreciate human differences. While the methodology was later deemed problematic by psychological and academic circles, it continues to be leveraged today by an extensive list of Fortune 1000 companies, non-profits, governments, and other organizations. It is also credited with helping many people and organizations, including many people I know. In fact, I can hardly go one day on Facebook without seeing someone posting about it in personal and professional circles, and a host of colleagues swear by it. I have also leveraged this methodology myself, though it was one that I struggled with.

I found it fascinating that this popular methodology, under which I had also been trained, started as a non-academic theory, like mine. This discovery further shifted my perspective about sharing my own ideas more broadly. I realized that even as a non-academic and street-smart theory, my insight was informed by more than twenty years of business experience. If what I'd discovered had the potential to help others, there really wasn't a good reason *not* to share it with the world. I had never met anyone who had a negative response or bad experience with OST. It seemed there was little to lose by "putting it out there" and potentially much to be gained from the standpoint of helping people! So, while it took some time to find the courage to lay my heart out on these pages, here we go...

OPERATIONAL STYLES THEORY

Over the decades I've spent working with organizations of every size across almost every imaginable industry sector, I have found that people naturally align to one of three distinct patterns that I call "operational styles," which I will outline in this book.

Unlike personality types, operational styles address how you view your job, how you view yourself within a work context, how you prefer to get things done, and how you build and leverage relationships within a *work context*. Everyone has a dominant operational style, and our styles are meant to complement each other to drive productive outcomes. Developing an understanding of operational styles is relatively easy. Embracing and appreciating the way you—and others—are naturally designed to function can not only help you leverage your strengths but also adapt to work better with others. This can dramatically improve the way you approach your work, relationships, and collaborations.

On a personal level, embracing your style and working "by design" can be instrumental in realigning people to work that is more energizing, motivating, and fulfilling, resulting in a better job "fit" and a greater sense of satisfaction and gratification. On a workplace/relational level, as we learn to quickly identify the operational styles of others and adjust or adapt the way we work with them, we can more easily establish bridges of understanding that improve communication, partnership, collaboration, and results. This can dramatically improve relationships with management, peers, and direct reports. In short, OST helps people work with greater awareness and empathy, unlocking individual and group potential to drive productivity, profitability, positive morale, and more!

THE OPERATIONAL STYLES FRAMEWORK

In short, this book identifies the three primary operational styles that dominate every workplace: Walkers, Climbers, and Flyers. It articulates how each style is critical for business success and how our styles are meant to work harmoniously together. It describes how individuals with different styles *tend to* view themselves, their jobs, and leverage relationships to get things done at work. It also explores the inherent strengths and potential pitfalls that can exist for each operational style, and addresses how style dynamics impact work relationships and productivity. The street-smart mental model provided in this book can help anyone—from any walk of life—regardless of gender, race, age, or position in the corporate or non-corporate "ladder" better navigate the Workplace Wilderness. As you apply the principles in this book, you will discover and embrace how you and others in your workplace are designed to function and how to drive greater individual, team, and business success. Leveraging the insight, tips, and tools in this book, you can begin to move from career survival to a thriving professional existence.

This book is organized into a four-step framework, featuring exercises, self-audits, stories, tips, and challenges that will help you adopt new perspective, self-awareness, and understanding. We'll help you assess your current state, retrace your steps to assess your journey-to-date, identify and validate your operational style, learn how to recognize the styles of others, and work adaptively as you negotiate tough terrain. Finally, we'll help you thoughtfully engage in any needed career course correction, so you can navigate to a more gratifying, satisfying, and meaningful professional destination.

This book will challenge your thinking, attitudes, and behavior, and help you become more aware of your strengths, weaknesses, and personal power. You'll also develop a renewed understanding and appreciation for what you—and others around you—bring to the table, in terms of strengths, skills, and capabilities. Armed with this new appreciation for your potential and the possibilities around you, you will be empowered to work within your workplace ecosystem to leverage your strengths, build better relationships, mitigate weakness, and become more purposefully engaged in your work. I hope it helps you as it has helped me.

PART ONE

GETTING YOUR BEARINGS

CHAPTER 1
YOU ARE HERE

MY JOURNEY TO BURNOUT

I was in a Caribbean luxury resort, and even though my hotel room window was open and it was sweltering outside, I was lying in bed, freezing under a pile of blankets. I was so sick, I could barely move. My body was aching and wracked with fever. So much for my vacation.

I had flown down to Saint Thomas for a much-needed break after a period of intense work as a senior management consultant. I'd just wrapped up two challenging projects in different states, commuting each week to both from my home in Virginia. I was burned out and ready for ten days of all-inclusive relaxation at a five-star resort.

My life as a management consultant—sedentary and filled with stress—was taking a toll. I had been an athlete in college and an A-level beach volleyball player who rarely got sick, but in the last month, I'd been in the urgent care twice with severe bronchitis. For months, I'd been burning the candle at both ends, surviving on room service, airport meals, and vending-machine fare: Diet Cokes, Mrs. Fields cookies, trail mix, and when desperate, those salty, fluorescent-orange crackers with fake cheese or peanut butter in the middle.

I know, yuck.

My excursion to the Virgin Islands was supposed to give me time to heal and recharge. I was going to lounge on beaches, scuba and snorkel, consume vast amounts of tropical fruit and healthy food, and sit on the beach sipping fruity adult beverages. Because it was very hard to forecast my work schedule, it was a last-minute get away. None of my friends could join me, so I had made the bold choice of going solo for the very first time. Taking off alone didn't bother me at all; I was happily independent and I just wanted to rest. However, lying there in my hotel room, shivering, dizzy, and weak, I became aware of how alone I really was. I realized that as much as I hated to admit it, I needed help. So, I called down to the front desk and asked for a referral to a doctor. The next morning, with a 103-degree fever, I dragged myself into the nearest clinic.

"You have walking pneumonia," the doctor said. "I want to admit you to the hospital."

"I can't go into the hospital," I coughed. "I'm on vacation!"

She looked at me sympathetically. "Honey, on this vacation, you need IV fluids, antibiotics, rest, and professional care."

Choking back tears, I insisted that I would behave and rest in my expensive, all-inclusive, *non-refundable* resort. I promised I would consume large pitchers of water, take my medicine, be diligent with my inhaler, and check into the ER if my condition worsened. The doctor finally gave up trying to convince me otherwise.

"I think this is a very bad idea," she said, writing notes in her chart. She gave me two bags of IV fluids and injected a large syringe of antibiotics into my flank. Handing me a prescription for more antibiotics, she wished me luck. I was so exhausted, I really don't remember making my way to the pharmacy. After handing over the script, I went outside to wait at a café, falling asleep face-first on the table like a drunk. I jerked awake thirty minutes later, sitting up with a napkin stuck to my face as tourists stared. Clutching my pills and a case of water, I finally made it back to the hotel, where I slept for thirty-six hours.

After three days of seeing a "Do Not Disturb" sign on my door and remembering my request for a doctor, the hotel staff became concerned and started calling and knocking. When they saw my condition, they ferried up soup, fruit, and more fluids. After several days, I started to improve. Sleep became more sporadic and, with a clearer mind, I grappled with some nagging questions:

Is this the kind of life I want?

Is the price I'm paying really worth it?

Is this all there is?

When my fever finally broke and I became well enough to venture out, only eighteen hours remained of my vacation. I jumped on a ferry to Saint John and then cruised the island's winding roads in a badly abused rental—a green Suzuki Samurai, stopping in beautiful towns, beaches, and shops along the way. I eventually stopped at a cove and curled up in the warm sand. The ocean in front of me was spectacular: citrine green at the shoreline, melting into a deep, comforting turquoise blue that stretched to the horizon. Surrounded by arching palms, I took it all in. Overwhelmed by beauty, color, and possibility, juxtaposed by the realization that I'd spent thousands of dollars for a single day on that beautiful beach, my eyes welled. Taking it all in, all I could think was, "Something's got to change."

Everyone thought I had such a great life. I had a successful career, a good paycheck, a nice home, a new car, and I had enjoyed some very nice vacations. While I counted my blessings, I was absolutely miserable inside, and I wore my fatigue like an ugly Christmas sweater. I had little peace, no balance, and a lack of fulfillment. I didn't feel valued for my contributions at work and I had become machine-like in my obsession with it. My job was incredibly demanding and for four years, I'd been engaged in nearly full-time travel. I came home long enough to dry clean my clothes, water my dying plants, and make travel arrangements. My relationships were suffering, along with my health. While I had obtained much of what popular culture says one needs to be successful, I couldn't silence the nagging sense that I was missing out on the most important things in life.

I reflected on how I got there and awakened to the certainty that staying my present course could be the end of me.

LIFE ON AUTOPILOT

Maybe your story is different than mine and you're not presently in an overly demanding job that requires a crazy level of sacrifice or full-time travel.

However, like many others, you may be experiencing challenges at work or feeling a lack of satisfaction and gratification from your labor. You may be troubled by unhealthy work relationships, face unreasonable demands, or obstacles that seem insurmountable. Maybe you carry a lingering sense that you are made for something different but lack the courage to make a change, or you just don't know where to start. Perhaps the things you care about most are missing from your life, as they were with me.

How I got to my state of exhaustion is a complicated story—but it happened to me the way it does with most people: It occurred *gradually*, over a period of years. My professional journey was shaped by an iterative sequence of compromises and decisions that slowly-but-surely took me off course. My choices were driven by a poor understanding of who I am, how I'm designed to function, what I need to feel energized and gratified, and a twisted idea of what success should look like. As I veered deeper into the jungle of my own professional wilderness, I became lost, tired, frustrated, and a little bitter—feelings that are not uncommon to many in the modern workforce today. To make things worse, I was so incredibly busy I barely had time to have a personal life, much less embark on a journey to career course correction. Merely thinking about how to fix my professional life overwhelmed me. As a result, I persisted in a kind of professional half-life, running on an odd form of autopilot.

Career autopilot is, unfortunately, the popular default setting for many professionals, and, like a bad GPS, it often leads people in a very wrong direction. Ironically, however, most of us are not conditioned to purposefully and intentionally steward our career journeys. While most of us spend years preparing to enter the workforce, we spend comparatively little time preparing for how we will approach our professional life and thrive. Most of us are conditioned from an early age to accept societal, cultural, and professional mores that influence our ideas about success and the way we approach our careers. Parents, teachers, authority figures, and popular culture proffer their own ideas and formulas, imposing their own biases and cookie-cutter methods for attaining success. In time, our exposure to these influences impacts the way we think, what we believe, and the things we value. It also influences the education and training we receive, the profession we choose, the ways we relate to others, the career choices we make, and our ideas about what success should look like.

The modern workplace conditions us in a similar manner. In truth, many of our present expectations of our employers are shaped by modern business conventions formed during the Industrial Revolution, which is when most modern management systems began to take shape. These systems were designed purposefully to focus individuals to be productive and to produce reliably, consistently, and profitably. In addition to better organizing people and tasks, modern management processes sought to reduce individual expression as well as experimentation with the end product, creating better uniformity of outcomes. This thinking not only produced assembly lines and organizational silos that narrowed and compartmentalized jobs and functions, it significantly impacted culture by introducing things like the "nine-to-five" workday, three meals per day, lunch at noon, established break times, paid holidays, sick leave, and paid vacations and pensions. In short, it contributed many of the organizational artifacts and rules that remain active in the workplace today. Collectively, this has shaped the comparatively *unnatural* order of the Workplace Wilderness we *natural* humans must traverse! It is a foreign place we all share—though we each deal with our own territories complete with their own ecosystems that support the larger environment.

I was happily surprised to find these dynamics artfully addressed in a 2018 *Quartz* article entitled "There's a Biological Reason You're Bored at Work," by Daniel M. Cable, Professor of Organizational Behavior at London Business School and author of *Alive at Work: The Neuroscience of Helping Your People Love What They Do*. Cable asserts that during the Industrial Revolution, organizations intentionally deactivated a critical the part of employees' brains called the "seeking system." According to Cable, "Our seeking systems create the natural impulse to explore our worlds, learn about our environments, and extract meaning from circumstances. When we follow the urges of our seeking system, it releases dopamine—a neurotransmitter linked to motivation and pleasure—that makes us want to explore more." Cable states that our seeking system is why animals in captivity prefer to search for food rather than to have it delivered. He attributes the activation of our seeking systems to making us feel more motivated, purposeful, zestful, and alive!

Cable explained that the rules imposed by the Industrial Revolution intentionally *deactivate* the seeking system of employees, to activate instead their "fear systems, which narrows their perception and encourages their submission." As Cable describes it, the rationale for more "scientific methods" of management like this were considered rational, efficient, and designed to help ensure employees "did only what they were told to do."

Cable attributes the deactivation of our seeking system at work to depressive symptoms and disengagement from work. He further argues that, in an era of rapid change, innovation, and competition, as well as an era marked by more flexible methods and tools for working, a new manner of working is in order. He goes on to issue a rousing call to activate the seeking systems of employees, and also lays out some ways to do this in his book, which I recommend.

Daniel's work resonated with me, validating many of my assertions and suspicions. After decades of immersion in nearly every kind of business, I had already come to believe that the rules of the Industrial Age, as well as the cookie-cutter formulas imposed on us for career success, can *work against us.* When people are not encouraged to explore, learn, experiment, and extract meaning from the world, they often, intentionally or unintentionally, either tune out or switch on the "career autopilot." Both actions result in failure to consciously and purposefully steward our professional journeys, and often create pressure to work in ways that can undermine individual potential and purpose. This causes a loss of motivation, a drop-off in energy and vitality, and in the long term, can result in exhaustion, disillusionment, disengagement, and even burnout. I believe this is a central reason for the incredible levels of workplace disengagement we are seeing today in the modern workplace. While problems have taken years to manifest on a broad scale, we're now paying the price for shutting off our seeking systems, and the results are overwhelmingly evidenced in workplace statistics, across demographics.

THE STRUGGLE IS REAL

Why did you pick up this book? Perhaps you are dealing with burnout, like I was, or feel as if you've gone off course. Maybe you picked it up in the name of finding some tips that will help you derive a greater sense of fulfillment from your labor. Perhaps you were seeking ways to manage your career journey or the people who report to you. You may be interested in securing a job that fits you better, or in finding ways to better align your work to things that energize you. Whatever the reason—and wherever you are in your career—I believe this book can help.

In the end, it doesn't matter if you feel like roadkill on the highway to success or have approached the summit of a successful career—whether you are just starting or have a well-established, professional reputation. It doesn't matter if you are in the lower ranks or the top dog. This book offers helpful insight on how to switch off career autopilot and better navigate your Workplace Wilderness and the relationships within it to drive better communication, collaboration, meaningful outcomes, and a more satisfying, gratifying professional existence.

Our workplaces have become increasingly challenging and demanding. The technological advancements of the past decade have brought amazing new capabilities to workers, making it possible to work anytime, anywhere. However, the internet, mobile, the cloud, 24/7 email access, web meetings, instant messaging, and other technologies make it harder than ever before to maintain a divide between our work and personal lives. Beyond technology, our cultural boundaries around work have also shifted, as more and more of us work remotely, during non-traditional hours and/or bring work home in the evenings and on weekends. There's not just more work—people work more.

In the United States alone, the parents of baby boomers managed to work a nine-to-five job, and managed to retire with pension and Social Security at around age sixty-five. Today, the scene is less optimistic, with Social Security in the United States in crisis, the erosion of pension plans, exponential inflation, and rising costs. Chances are, if you're reading this, like me, you are *not* independently wealthy. You need to work in order to eat, live, pay bills, and keep a roof over your head and plan for retirement.

If you're in the United States, you need healthcare benefits. You may even have a family for which to provide. Like me, perhaps you feel concerned for the future. In light of this pressure, it's easy for work to feel more like a necessary evil than a purposeful adventure.

Statistically speaking, a large majority of workers today are struggling. While the problems that plague global workers are complicated, I tend to break down challenges into what I call the "Big Bs."

Boss

Problems with "the boss" are frequently cited as one of the most common sources of workplace stress. "Boss-related" complaints frequently involve trust issues, frustration over a lack of recognition and/or appreciation, a manager's inability to manage well, motivate and/or establish clear goals. Lack of engagement, micromanagement, poor communication, being hypercritical, and taking credit for work were included among other complaints commonly found. A study conducted in December of 2017 by Ultimate Software and the Center for Generational Kinetics, surveyed more than 2,000 US employees and revealed that for 93 percent of employees, trust in their direct boss is essential to workplace satisfaction—and tied to an employee's ability to put forth "best efforts." While studies directly correlate employee engagement and positive business outcomes with the quality of relationship between managers and employees, studies also show that management problems are very common. Gallup reports that one-in-two U.S. employees have left their job to get away from a manager at some point in their career. A 2018 Korn Ferry study found that the largest source of workplace stress (at 35 percent) was reported to be the boss. A recent Monster.com "Boss Day" survey that revealed three out of four Americans has have had a toxic boss, 35 percent of professionals were driven to quit by horrible bosses, and another 15 percent were strongly considering leaving.

Boredom

Typically accompanied by feelings of apathy, indifference, disinterest, and disengagement, bored workers feel unchallenged, unstimulated, and unmotivated. A Korn Ferry survey of 5,000 workers looking for a job in 2018 revealed the top reason for the job search as boredom, with 33 percent of respondents selecting "I'm bored, need new challenge" as their motivation for moving on. In a 2017 survey, Robert Half conducted a small survey on boredom at work, and found that employees report being bored at work 10.5 hours per week, whereas managers think their employees may be bored 6 hours per week. Boredom was also cited in Daniel Cable's aforementioned *Quartz* article, "There's a Neurological Reason You May be Bored at Work" as tied to the shutting off of your "seeking system" resulting in a cut-off of the benefits of that system, including dopamine release and feeling "alive."

Bereft (of Purpose)

When you look at the numbers, boredom and a desire for a greater sense of purpose seem to be esoterically related. For example, in 2018, Covestro reported that 68 percent of executives believe their employees would be more engaged in their work and perform at higher levels if they had opportunities to be *challenged* by working on "purpose projects." Research suggests that millennials in particular express more desire for "purpose-driven" work and feel more strongly about the responsibility of companies to positively contribute to solving social problems. Also, in 2018, Covestro reported that roughly 70 percent of executives surveyed have a strong, five-year increase in the number of workers who want the opportunity for more social purpose in their work. People don't just crave exploration—they crave meaning and purpose in work.

Boundaries

According to Gallup, the average full-time worker collectively spends more than 2,000 hours per year with coworkers. We celebrate birthdays and anniversaries together, and go on corporate retreats and happy hours with bosses and colleagues. This, combined with the modern advancements of the tech-enabled workplace, are effective at twisting the boundaries between work and personal life. In the UK, a 2018 study by Working Families and Bright Horizons reports that 72 percent of workers bring work home in the evenings and on weekends. A lack of boundaries may take the form of employee overwork or taking on tasks that don't align with the individual's responsibility, capacity, or job function. Boundary issues may result in bosses asking for work or favors outside of established parameters or even work hours. Ethical boundary violations are also a rising concern. While the types of violations abound, a lack of respect is always felt when one's boundaries are violated. The 2018 Workplace Distraction Report by Udemy suggests that a lack of boundaries, tools, and instruction to enforce boundaries contribute to damaging workplace distraction. Research suggests that 60–80 percent of all difficulties in organizations stem from strained relationships that are exacerbated by a lack of boundaries.

Bullying

Bullying is typically associated with feelings of harassment, ridicule, antagonism, mistreatment, coercion, disrespect, or being pressured to perform or behave in a way that feels inappropriate. In 2018, Radius Global Market research announced the results of the first "Bullying in the Workplace" study, with key findings that nearly half of American workers, or 77 million workers, have been bullied at work. The 2017 study found that 81 percent of respondents had witnessed bullying in person, and the most common form of mistreatment reported was being ridiculed or reprimanded in front of other staff (29 percent). Other types of harassment categorized by the study included harassment over looks or body type (23 percent), work attire (23 percent), pressure to take on a specific task (23 percent), or coercion to work extra hours (22 percent). One in five reported subtle or overt sexual harassment, and 44 percent of the problems remain either unaddressed or unresolved.

Buried

Typically described as feeling consistently overburdened, overworked, overwhelmed, stressed, disrespected, unappreciated, dumped upon, and/or improperly supported in one's duties, feeling "buried" often results in problems in balancing work against the other demands of life, impacting employee health and relationships. US-based West Monroe Partners surveyed managers and found that 44 percent of managers frequently feel overwhelmed at work. The Execu|Search group released a 2018 Hiring

Outlook Study in early 2018 that found that, while 54 percent of professional career choices are motivated by seeking work/life balance, 45 percent of US professionals feel their company does not promote a healthy work/life balance. In a 2018 Korn Ferry study, 76 percent of 2000 workers surveyed said stress at work had a negative impact on them, with more than three-quarters of respondents saying they've lost sleep due to work stress. In the UK, Bright Horizons and Working Families states that the lack of work/life balance in organizations *disadvantages working parents and damages family life*, with only 35 percent of parents finishing work on time each day, and the majority staying late or working at home and on weekends.

Burnout

The World Health Organization classifies burnout as a "state of vital exhaustion" that results from chronic workplace stress. In truth, burnout is really one extreme of a stress continuum, which starts with feeling burdened, overwhelmed, and buried, and worsens over time. Burned out individuals typically feel exhausted, fatigued, depleted, mentally blocked, unfocused, irritable, and detached, experiencing concentration difficulties and disrupted sleep. A recent 2018 Gallup study of nearly 7,500 full-time employees revealed that 23 percent felt burned out at work very often or always, and 44 percent reported feeling burned out sometimes. This equates to 67 percent of the workforce grappling with burnout—and those rates are even higher in high-tech sectors! Burnout comes with a high personal and organizational cost. Burned out employees are 63 percent more likely to call in sick, 2.6 times as likely to be seeking a different job, and 23 percent more likely to visit an emergency room. Gallup reports that job burnout accounts for an estimated $125 billion to $190 billion in healthcare spending each year and is attributed to type 2 diabetes, coronary heart disease, gastrointestinal issues, high cholesterol, and death for those under age forty-five.

Been Lookin' for a Job

Between the gig economy, company downsizing, and personal choice, you may be looking for something new. You may already be employed and seeking a new opportunity for a variety of reasons. You may have already jumped the wagon in your search. You may already be unemployed or recently laid off, which can be accompanied by fear, anxiety, and depression. Whatever the case, you stand with a motley crew! In 2018, Gallup found that 51 percent of today's workers are looking for a new job or actively watching openings. In comparison, a 2017 study survey of 17,000 US workers conducted by the non-profit group Mental Health America and the Fass Foundation revealed that a whopping 71 percent of surveyed US workers are looking to change employers! The same report states that 71 percent of people surveyed admitted to speaking poorly about their companies, bosses, or coworkers to others.

Busy

We're all familiar with the terms "time-starved," "time pressure," "over-scheduled," and "overworked." We live within a cult of busy-ness, often feeling like we are "pressed for time." While many people are legitimately busy, working multiple jobs to care for themselves, family, and loved ones, our Western "cult of busyness" is partially culture-driven. Being busy can also be regarded as a "status claim." While busyness is also an outcome of our digital age and having 24/7 access to everything, it can also be an excuse we cling to, in order to avoid things we'd rather not focus on. According to the Bureau of Labor Statistics (2017 and 2018 data), we'll spend about 25 percent of our lives working. Further, about 82 percent of employed persons work an average work day. In 2017, theaverage American worked 44 hours per week, or 8.56 hours per day. Part time workers worked an average of 5.67 hours per week. Gallup reports that US workers work an average 43.6 hour work week, or 8.2 hours per week. However, this is only part of the story. In the United we worked 38.1 hours per week in 1980, and an average of 43 weeks per year. In 2017 (the most recent available data) at 44 hours per week, we work an average of 43 weeks per year. This equates to more than 173 additional hours worked per year. According to EU data, the average EU work week is 40.3 hours per week. Further, in an analysis of full-time workers, workers in the United Kingdom work the longest work week, at

42.3 hours per week. Cyprus followed at 41.7 hours per week, followed by Austria, Greece, and Poland.

Bread and Benefits

Whether you are looking for higher pay or a job with better or more flexible perks, "bread and benefits" upgrades motivate many to pursue greener pastures. Robert Half reports that 44 percent of workers would leave their job for better pay, while a survey conducted in 2018 by Yoh found that most Americans would accept a job offer for better benefits or perks. A survey conducted by Zenefits of employees in 2018 said that "work perks" are just as important as health insurance, life insurance, and other traditional benefits. The same study claimed that poor benefits are causing 42 percent of employees to consider leaving their jobs, while 55 percent have already left jobs because they found better benefit offerings elsewhere.

Bothered

There's really not a better way to say it: if you feel restless, disquieted, suspicious that something is off, or incomplete in your work, you are feeling bothered. There are many bothersome things in the workplace—some of them may already be listed above. You may be bothered by relationships in your workplace (incredibly common) or deal with difficult people (insert another "b-word" here). You might feel like you have the wrong job fit, feel an unaddressed need, or misalignment with the values or practices of your organization. You might also carry the nagging sense that perhaps you're meant to be doing something different—or you just hate your job. Perhaps you long for a greater sense of purpose.

The Other B Words

Maybe you feel like your workplace is **broken**, plagued by internal conflict, or poor management that can't be fixed. Perhaps you just want might want a **better** job or improvements in your current position. You may feel **blocked** and unable to find a clear path to a more optimistic professional existence. Whether you are **bored, buried, bullied, burned out, bothered**, or you have **been lookin' for a job**; if you feel **beat**, can't **bear** going to work in the morning, feel **barred** from getting ahead; if you struggle with **bad, belittling, boorish** coworkers or subordinates inside your company; or if you grapple with feeling motivated, frustrated, anxious, underutilized, or underappreciated; if you harbor feelings of resentment, anger, and **bitterness**—you are not alone! In fact, you stand with a very large **band** of people. I'll stop with the B-words now.

In the end, we all face an array of challenges that plague the workplace today—even those of us who are fairly satisfied in our professional experiences. Work has been tough since people started building shelters, pulling rocks from the ground, and getting scratched up by thorns while clearing fields. However, while it will always be hard on some level, work does not have to be a "necessary evil" we merely endure. It is possible for anyone at any career stage to better navigate their own professional terrain. It is possible to better align your work with how you are designed to function and to employ a greater level of empathy, understanding, and adaptivity as you work with others to drive better results. It is possible to take the helm of your professional journey to move purposefully into a more hospitable destination that is marked by a greater sense of well-being. Further, it's possible to share the freedom you obtain with others.

So, if you feel ready to press through on this challenging journey, let's get started! As you move ahead, there will be a number of exercises that may require more writing space than this book affords. Feel free to pull out paper, a journal, or notebook—or open a word-processing document to record your thoughts. You can also find many of the exercises in this book on the website in a printable form at www.walkclimborfly.com.

GETTING YOUR BEARINGS

EXERCISE 1
TIME SPENT AT WORK

HOW MUCH TIME DO YOU SPEND IN WORK MODE?

Take a minute to think about the time you spend in work mode. This is not just the time you spend in the office. Consider the time you spend commuting, the time you spend prepping for work, working after-hours, and even traveling for work! Take some time to calculate your average day, week and year. Because this can get a bit complicated, we've created and Time Spent at Work Calculator at **www.walkclimborfly.com** to help you quickly calculate how much time you spend in work, sleep and leave mode, and how much of your "waking time" is spent working!

In truth, there is no magic formula that will tell you whether your work mode percentages are too high or too low. You can also skew your numbers by sleeping less, which is far from healthy. According to the Sleep Foundation, adults need an average of 7-9 hours of sleep per night to be healthy. In truth, the proper amount of time that should be spent in work mode is entirely dependent on your age, individual design, needs, goals, priorities, preferences, and commitments. Many of us also experience peaks and valleys in our work demands. For example, if you are in accounting, your peak busy time will be stacked around tax deadlines. It's important to factor those things in.

Time is obviously not the only factor you'll need to weigh in evaluating the quality and depth of your investment in work. Where this becomes useful, however, is having a concise understanding of the percent of your waking *time you spend working*, juxtaposed to *how work leaves you feeling*. Which brings us to the next exercise.

EXERCISE 2
HOW WORK MAKES YOU FEEL

Now that you've quantified the percentage of your waking time spent in work mode, let's talk about the outcomes. How does work make you feel?

Answer the questions below with *focus on your professional life or job*—not your personal life as a whole. While the two are intimately related, we're dealing primarily with work for the purpose of these exercises.

A. BRAINSTORMING

Write down the first word that comes to mind when you think about your job/work/career. Write down any other additional adjectives that rise to your attention when you think of work, even if the words that come to mind seem to compete or conflict with each other. There are no wrong answers. Do a "brain dump" until you're out of steam, which should take a few minutes.

Examples: Exhausted, frustrated, depressed, angry, interested, hopeful, challenged, overtaxed, disgruntled, poorly paid, overdemanding, stimulated, stressed.

B. ORGANIZE AND PRIORITIZE

Now, take a minute to organize your thinking by categorizing your descriptive words as negative, neutral or positive. List your words within the columns below and prioritize the words, in order of strength of feeling. Last, *circle* the word or words that best summarize the way you feel about your job, work, or career, today. The examples below, while not exhaustive, may help.

NEGATIVE/DYING	NEUTRAL/SURVIVNG	POSITIVE/THRIVING
Examples:	*Examples:*	*Examples:*
• *Dissatisfied*	• *Uncertain*	• *Satisfied*
• *Frustrated*	• *Satiated*	• *Gratified*
• *Depleted*	• *Utilized*	• *Energized*
• *Used*	• *Compensated*	• *Rewarded*
• *Bored*	• *Persevering*	• *Challenged*
• *Hopeless*	• *Neutral*	• *Purposeful*
• *Depressed*	• *Acclimated*	• *Content*
• *Enraged/Angry*	• *Juggling*	• *Joyful*
• *Burned Out*	• *Playing the Game*	• *Rested*
• *Giving Up*	• *Finding My Way*	• *Engaged*
• *Miserable*	• *Indifferent*	• *Optimistic*

NEGATIVE/DYING	NEUTRAL/SURVIVNG	POSITIVE/THRIVING

C. SURVIVING OR THRIVING?

Finally, looking at your results and factoring in how you most feel about work, take a minute to plot your position on the "surviving-to-thriving continuum" below. Consider the number and weight of the negative, neutral and positive words you wrote down. Where are you today? Place a marker on the line below:

DYING   SURVIVING   THRIVING

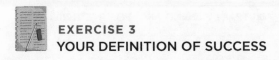

EXERCISE 3
YOUR DEFINITION OF SUCCESS

HOW DO YOU DEFINE SUCCESS?

Now, take a moment to write down how you currently define the word "success." Consider all the elements you consider critically important, such as pay, benefits, vacation time, and other perks, professional mobility, advancement, influence, networking, monetary gain, work/life balance, and any other things you associate with success or the attainment of it. Write a definition of success that you could stand up and share in a room full of trusted colleagues.

CHAPTER 2
RETRACING YOUR STEPS

BACKTRACKING

When I returned from the Virgin Islands, frustrated by a near total lack of professional mentoring and support, I decided it was time to be the pilot of my own professional journey and steer myself to a better place. To get started, I applied my consulting skills to conduct a classic SWOT analysis on myself. That is, I analyzed my Strengths, Weaknesses, Opportunities, and Threats.

Some of my *strengths* included intelligence, experience, broad skills, strategic vision, problem solving ability, creativity, and deep knowledge of operations, business, and technology. Some *weaknesses* included a tendency to overwhelm people with information, talking too much without listening, trying too hard to gain the acceptance of others, retrofitting myself into positions that were entirely wrong for me, people-pleasing, and exhibiting poor boundaries, resulting in workaholism and poor self-care.

I also spent some time thinking about how I got to this place of burn-out. I began to retrace my steps and professional journey. As I did, I began to recall past positions and projects that had energized me. As I mentally reconnected with the work I loved to do—things that fueled my sense of self-worth and identity—I began to see how I'd gotten off track over time. Interestingly, as I backtracked to review the professional path I'd followed, it took me back much farther than I expected!

One of the patterns from my past that emerged was one of entrepreneurialism. I was an enterprising kid from a very young age. It started with lemonade stands where I sold artwork to the neighbors at age five. However, my first real business enterprise came together when I was seven years old and living in Loveland, Colorado. That summer, we gathered with neighborhood friends to watch the annual Fourth of July fireworks show at Loveland Lake, where thousands of people come each year to picnic, boat, and relax each year. The evening was clear and warm. The sky was cloudless, and trillions of stars shone in the dusk, reflecting against the midnight-blue water of the lake. Couples and families sat on a checkerboard of blankets looking skyward.

Our family and friends had set up camp on a spot that was a bit of a hike from the snack shack. When my group wanted popcorn, I was selected as the "snack Sherpa" who would make the trek. This was a very big job for a seven-year old. On my first mission, I marched proudly through the throng with a fist full of dollars, making a determined path for treats. "Six bags of popcorn, please," I asked the vendor. When he pushed the bags across the counter, I realized they were too bulky for my little arms to carry. Spotting a shallow box that formerly held cases of soda, I convinced the guy at the counter to donate it to me as snack luggage.

As I carried my box of popcorn and a few candy bars back to our blankets, people kept stopping me, asking if they could buy my popcorn. I told everyone it was for my family, but one man offered me twenty-five cents a bag. The snack shack was selling the popcorn for ten cents a bag. So, I made a new plan, sold all my popcorn to strangers, went back to buy more, and headed back to my family and friends. On my return the second time, I encountered a chorus of shouts and additional requests from others, who saw my first transaction. I felt like a hawker at a stadium ball game. Before I made it all the way to my family's side of the lake, I had already made over one dollar, and realizing the opportunity before me, I didn't even light a sparkler. Under the watchful eye of my parents, I secured a small loan from my dad, and ran back to the vendor.

"If you let me buy popcorn from you," I said breathlessly, "I can go around and sell it and bring the money back." He thought this was cute and rewarded my ingenuity with ten bags of popcorn, which was about all

I could carry in my box. He also told me I could come to the back door to circumvent the line. I started selling, learning as I went how to make change. It was challenging and overwhelming, but I held my own as my parents watched from a distance. After an hour, I recruited a neighborhood kid to help me. I paid her ten cents a bag and kept five cents per bag from her proceeds. The snack man gave us grape sodas to keep us fueled. We sold twenty-five cent bags of popcorn for two hours—we even did a few candy runs. I didn't even notice the fireworks because we were running around so much. Because we were cute kids, we also earned tips. This went on for only a few hours, but it felt like a lifetime.

In the end, I made over twenty-five dollars. For me, this entrepreneurial undertaking was a high I'll never forget. I remember my dad driving me home on the back of his Yamaha touring bike at almost eleven at night. I basked in his sense of pride in me. I felt like a million bucks, giddy over my idea and my accomplishment, and drunk with fatigue. When we got home, I went down like a bag of rocks and slept soundly. I woke the next morning amped and on a total high.

That feeling of satisfaction that comes from a job well done was ingrained in me that night. As I grew up, I did odd jobs for cash and started babysitting when I was only thirteen, developing a veritable babysitting empire that employed other friends. I also started my first graphic design business in high school with my best friend, which was featured in the local paper.

The recollection of these accomplishments came flooding back, like water on the parched ground of my soul. Recalling my first enterprise became a touchstone, but it came with some sadness. I realized that I had lost that unfettered feeling of accomplishment and gratification that I'd enjoyed in other work positions—even as an adult. I had lost sight of doing work that was creative and entrepreneurial. As I considered the journey forward, I began asking, "What inspires me?" "What energizes me?" and "What am I designed for?"

WHAT INSPIRES YOU?

What will inspire and energize me will be different than the things that feel good to you. This is one part a reflection of our individuality, and another part a reflection of our operational styles, which you'll learn about very soon. It's relatively easy to lose our grasp on the things that fill us with inspiration, energy, and a sense of well-being. Further, this almost always happens gradually, resulting in a misalignment between the work we do and the work we may be *meant* to do.

When I looked back at my journey, I realized I had gotten off course by compromising the things I loved in the name of other things. For example, I craved acceptance and validation, and as a result, I began to gravitate to jobs where I was "needed" rather than maintaining a purposeful focus on doing work that inspired and energized me. This went on for over a decade. I weathered the changes and demands that were placed on me fairly well because I loved a challenge; I was pretty flexible, resourceful, and hungry to learn anything I didn't know.

However, I eventually arrived at a place where being in demand constantly was sucking the life out of me. Flexibly adapting to so many roles was beginning to break me. My work no longer paid off with a sense of *exhausted gratification*—like the feeling I had that night riding home on my Dad's bike, or the exhilaration of pioneering I had enjoyed later on. I was, without question, exhausted—but gratification eluded me. I became depleted and had more and more trouble recovering after expending my energy. I got to a point where I no longer slept well. I got sick. I gained weight and couldn't lose it. The rewards no longer seemed worth the sacrifice, and joy became elusive. The price I was paying was too high for the result. By working against my design and my purpose, I'd given until I had almost nothing left!

Whether you are spent or not, like me, there may well be some important things you have lost sight of along the way in your professional journey. In the woods, when you get off course and need to find your way, it can be beneficial to retrace your steps. In like manner, taking the time to look back and ask yourself some hard questions about how your work aligns energetically with activities you enjoy, work that you are great at, and/or your sense of purpose, can help you find your way forward. Rediscovering the things that make you special and fill you with energy can be helpful in course-correcting on your professional journey.

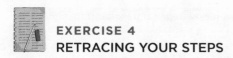

EXERCISE 4
RETRACING YOUR STEPS

Take a moment now to look back at your path, to date. Consider the ground you've covered, the forces that influenced your journey and your decision-making. Retracing your steps can often reveal identifying patterns and trends, and help you make important realizations. You can even find and reclaim things that you may have lost along the way.

WHAT ENERGIZES YOU?

At a high level, look back at the things you loved to do and the things you were good at, at different ages. Take note of how things shifted over time as your interests changed and morphed and look for significant events, patterns, or themes.

A. ENERGIZING ACTIVITIES & PURSUITS

What did you love to do as a child, youth and young adult? What were you really good at? What made you special or unique? How has this changed over time?

AGE 0–10	AGE 10–20	AGE 20–30	AGE 30+
Examples:	Examples:	Examples:	Examples:
• Artist	• Art/Design	• Graphic Design	• Design (side)
• Piano/Singing	• Singing/Piano	• Singing/Band	• Less singing
• Play Outside	• Athletics	• Athletics/League	• Workout
• Watching TV	• Movies	• Film/TV Work	• Go to movies
• Building Forts	• Home Décor	• Building Stores	• Build sites/apps
• Entrepreneur	• Entrepreneur	• Startups	• Consult startups
• Reading	• Writing	• Writing	• Blog/Articles
	• Entrepreneur	• Entrepreneur	• Entrepreneur
	• Reading	• Reading	• Reading

B. GOALS & ASPIRATIONS

Did you ever have a strong desire to "be" something as an adult? Did you aspire to a certain achievement? Did you ever feel a sense of having a purpose or a calling? Perhaps you have a professional "bucket list." Write down the things that come to mind, which may be very specific or a more esoteric desire or a sense or longing you've carried for years. How did you respond to these desires? Did you act? Did they change or morph into something else? Did you lose sight of anything important? What impulses linger today?

SOMEDAY I WANT TO...	HOW DID YOU RESPOND?
Examples: • *Set up my own photography studio and pursue professional photography* • *Teach and mentor students*	• *On hold (still) Having trouble affording the studio – not likely to make a living this way.* • *Volunteer 1x per month with Junior Achievement*

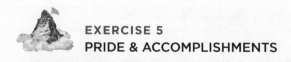

EXERCISE 5
PRIDE & ACCOMPLISHMENTS

A. YOUR GREATEST MOMENTS

Now, think about your greatest accomplishments, starting as far back as you can remember. What were some of the best and most gratifying moments of your life? What made them so great? How did those accomplishments influence your future? Write down everything that stands out—it doesn't just have to be work-related.

ACCOMPLISHMENT	YEAR/AGE	HOW IT MADE YOU FEEL
Example: *Started my own business selling popcorn on the 4th of July and made $25.*	*7.5 years*	• *Proud of myself* • *Made parents proud* • *Felt smart, accepted, ingenious, empowered, supported by family, excited, exhausted, prosperous, competent and appreciated.*

USING THE PAST TO GAIN PERSPECTIVE

My struggle to find my professional fit was, for years, compounded by the fact that one of the companies for whom I worked was fraught with turmoil. I can't count the different teams I served on. I survived at least three rounds of corporate downsizing because I was smart, resourceful, scrappy, and a producer. At one point, I was the last person standing out of a twenty-person team, which was brutal. In the mix, I was shuffled through a myriad of managers—few of which managed me long enough to get to know me well.

Shortly after I developed Operational Styles Theory, I transitioned to a new boss, an executive vice president who was a very successful guy and was cut from the same cloth as most of the executives in my organization. We had worked together before and shared a mutual admiration and respect for each other. When I joined his team, after four years of full-time travel, I explained my need to assert some better boundaries in my work, reducing travel and hours. He helped me in securing a local project.

Unfortunately, that particular local project turned out to be a hornet's nest of contention and personnel issues. I kept my head down and did my job, eventually rising to the top without calling too much attention to myself or burdening my new manager with what might be perceived as drama. I kept him posted at a high level on the critical news, helped the project management team handle the issues, and eight months later I walked away, proud of what we accomplished, leaving our company smelling like a rose and boasting a tidy profit.

My review came shortly thereafter. It was very positive. Once the pleasantries were over, I attempted to address lingering concerns over how issues on the prior project were handled. I finally explained what transpired on the project in greater depth. I expressed concern over the impact it had on staff, and our firm's culture in contrast to policy. I highlighted the increasing demands and burnout that were rampant, and how situations like this compounded those issues. While my ideas were thoughtfully laid out, it was clear that my boss wasn't prepared to have this discussion. While it felt like a reasonable time to raise these concerns, he responded by underscoring how fortunate I was to have been given a local project within which to "rest." This was my first surprise: There hadn't been much rest, just a much shorter commute. He then added, *"Maybe you are just high maintenance."*

High maintenance! It felt like he'd landed a blow in my midsection, knocking the wind out of me. My mind raced as I retraced my steps: I had survived six painful reorganizations and three rounds of downsizing, as I was tossed like a rugby ball from manager to manager for the better part of four years. I didn't complain. I billed 105 percent of my time to client work on average. I attained sales in the millions, and after joining his team, vanished for eight months to quietly suffer through a horrible project, taking serious abuse yet demonstrating the highest level of professionalism and shielding our client from any *hint* of drama. This was the first time I'd complained or laid a deeper reality on him. His accusation managed to negate every bit of positive feedback I had received. I was thrown for a loop. The call ended shortly thereafter, and I hung up, crushed.

I carried his comment around with me for weeks, like some kind of scarlet letter, reliving the conversation and beating myself up. I was discouraged by the lack of acknowledgement of my feedback and plight. Then, I got angry. *Why did this comment bother me so much?* I began to dig deep. Thinking about it one night, I realized that part of the reason his comment cut so deep was that my own father had assigned me with a very *similar label* as a child.

I had always been a bit of a Daddy's girl. My father was a highly intelligent, introverted, hard-charging engineer. He liked quiet contemplation, playing classical guitar, listening to music, working on cars, and doing "his thing." I was an extroverted, talkative, imaginative kid who talked constantly, craved interaction and attention, and assistance with my many projects. When I pushed things too far, my dad would frequently exclaim, *"Man! You are a pain in the ass!"*

Now, it wasn't like I consciously thought about my dad saying that to me all the time. One day, however, the remembrance of it just surfaced in my mind. I found myself surprised to realize how this had stuck with me. My dad left our family when I was in my teens, so I suppose that label, combined with the abandonment, had a deeper impact than I realized. I don't need to get into the psychology of that. Sufficed to say, separating my dad's label from my manager's comment was instrumental in taking the edge off things.

Next, I began to very objectively consider his remark. Sitting in an honest place and aware of my pitfalls, there was actually some truth to the idea that I could be high maintenance. At times, I did require periods of more intense engagement. However, this served an important purpose, and at this point in my career, I was an adult who managed that tendency fairly well. As I truthfully and objectively questioned whether I had been high maintenance, going back to consider all our interactions. The answer was *no*.

I realized his comment was triggered by attempts to assert healthier boundaries for myself! Beyond asking for a local project (the first one in four years), it was the first time I'd tried to do this. This was not only the right thing to do, it was the healthy thing to do. However, this made him feel uncomfortable, and pressing the issue likely *did* feel high maintenance to him. I began to feel strength well up inside me as I realized I had finally shut off autopilot to take over my own professional destiny and set healthier boundaries. This was just pushback that comes from doing the right thing!

When I figured this out, my manager's accusation lost all power over me. Over the months that ensued, I was inspired to more introspection. While I did end up going back to full-time travel after that, I made some serious changes in the way I worked. I placed less emphasis on receiving validation from the corporate machine and more emphasis on maintaining better boundaries. While I sensed my time with my firm was short, I was determined to end things well—to go out as a victor with her head held high, instead of feeling like a victim. This strengthened my resolve to begin to work a different way.

Six months later, in a half-yearly review with the same manager, my manager surprised me with an unsolicited and uncharacteristically humble apology.

"Listen," he said, "Six months ago, in our review, I called you 'high maintenance.'"

"Yes," I grimaced, "I remember."

"Well, I was wrong," he said. "I should have never said that."

I almost keeled over in my chair.

He continued: "That was patently unfair, Leigh, and I'm sorry. You have had a lot thrown at you, and you have handled yourself with professionalism and grace. You are FAR from high maintenance."

I swallowed hard as a lump rose in my throat and tears rose to my eyes as he continued, "You have done an outstanding job and conducted yourself with the utmost professionalism in really difficult situations. You are really an asset to this firm."

"Thank you," I said, trying not to cry. "This means a lot to me."

His apology was water on the desert of my soul. While his comment had long before lost its power over me, his apology was healing and restored the trust between us. The very nature of it further underscored that I was on the right track and had arrived at a place where my understanding of my shortcomings no longer outweighed a confident acceptance of my strengths and abilities.

My purpose in sharing this story is to underscore this point: Part of becoming a better steward of your professional journey requires a greater and more honest level of ownership of the truth about yourself. Reconnecting with the past can help you rediscover hopes, dreams, and the energizing accomplishments you may have forgotten along the path to "success." It can also help you identify things that trigger you—like the teasing label my dad assigned me at young age—that have a lingering impact today. Retracing your steps can help you come to terms with your history, identify things you've lost along the way, and provide you with perspective to see the future more clearly.

ENCOURAGERS

Comedian Dave Chappelle was interviewed on Inside the Actor's Studio in 2006 with James Lipton. He spoke about the fact that, at age nineteen, he was offered his first acting contract for a Hollywood movie. His father took him aside to discuss his career choice. As Dave described the story, the discussion went something like this:

"Listen," his dad said, "to be an actor is a lonely life. Everybody wants to make it, and you might not make it."

"Well, that depends on what making it is, Dad," Chappelle said.

"What do you mean?" asked his dad.

"We'll, you're a teacher. If I could make a teacher's salary doing comedy, I think that's better than being a teacher," answered Chapelle.

"If you keep that attitude, I think you should go," his father laughed, but becoming suddenly serious, he said, "but name your price in the beginning. If it ever gets more expensive than the price of your name, get out of there!"

Chapelle's father realized his son had his priorities straight and empowered him to be a steward of his own professional path—even if his choice didn't fall within his father's own comfort zone. Many of us have lacked that kind of support in our lifetime—the unselfish ability of a parent or even a manager to empower us to work within our area of calling and passion, or someone who encouraged us to "count the cost" of pursuing our dreams. It is significant that later in his career, the price did become too high for Chapelle, leading to a withdrawal from the entertainment industry, a move to Africa, and a later relocation to a farm in Ohio, where he raises his family today.

Chappelle's father's reaction is, unfortunately, rare. The majority of well-intentioned people we meet embrace that we must follow a certain formula to be successful in life. Squeezing past societally imposed expectations and taking ownership of your professional journey can be a lonely and difficult path to follow. This is especially true if you're attempting to rebound after taking some hits on the path to success—or course-correcting later in life after being blown off course for years. These things can lead to discouragement.

Discouragement can lead to blindness to what's possible, so don't give in to it! Even if you find yourself in a proverbial desert, remember that even when resources seem scarce, hope lies in unexpected places. In a real desert, certain plants provide hydration; it's possible to find water, signs of life, and sources of food. Even in the harshest climates, you can find abundance if you know where and how to look. Taking optimistic ownership of your professional journey—especially when knowing "the price of your name" can help you survive the rough patches and navigate to a more fruitful and hospitable place.

EXERCISE 6
YOUR ENCOURAGERS

As we retrace our steps, it's important to understand how our paths have been positively influenced by others along the way. We can call these people, like Dave Chapelle's Dad, "Encouragers." Look back to identify the Encouragers in your life. Who cheered you on? Who had your back? Who saw something in you that you didn't recognize yourself? Who helped you cultivate your gifts? Who gave you permission to make a bold choice, spoke encouraging words, gave you a pat on the back, or a nudge in the right direction? No person is inconsequential!

A. WHO ENCOURAGED YOU?

NAME	RELATION/ROLE	POSITIVE ACTIONS	IMPACT & FEELINGS
Example: Mrs. Hobbs	Art Teacher	Encouraged me to start my first graphics business.	Worthy, capable and confident. Supported my dreams and made me believe I was capable.
NAME	RELATION/ROLE	POSITIVE ACTIONS	IMPACT & FEELINGS

B. SAY THANKS!

Consider writing a brief note of thanks to each person who encouraged you in your journey, summarizing the impact they had on you. This can be a wonderful way to repay someone for their investment in you. Even if that person is no longer around to receive your note, consider leaving a tribute on social media! It can be cathartic and encouraging to others to describe in detail how another person's positive investment in you mattered!

DISCOURAGERS & DREAM KILLERS

Some of us have had it easier than others. Some people have had few, if any, Encouragers and more than their share of discouragement. One of sadder stories I've listened to is the story of Bradley. Brad grew up in a family of seven on mid-size family farm in the southwest. His mom stayed at home with the children, working hard each day to nurture a large garden, make home-cooked meals, and tend to chores and farm work. The kids grew up with their fair share of chores too—walking fields and pulling weeds, driving tractors, stacking hay bales, feeding the livestock, shucking beans and corn. As the eldest child, Brad was bright, inquisitive, and mischievous. When he wasn't at school or baling hay or feeding livestock, he spent his spare time tinkering on engines, riding dirt bikes, and inventing.

On the surface, they seemed like a normal family, but they lived a hellish reality. A deacon in the local community church by day, Brad's father was a demon at home—a man prone to extreme, abusive rages that left his family living in terror. When his father got angry, the family scattered to various hiding places. Brad was frequently the target of his anger. He had a regular hiding place in the hayloft. Brad's dad was physically abusive and frequently lost control in a blind rage. Once, in a "discipline" session at the age of five, Brad's father picked him up by the back of his neck and rammed his head repeatedly into the basement's cement block foundation until he was unconscious. He then kicked him repeatedly as he laid on the floor. Brad woke up alone, in the dark, lying on the old floor of that basement, aching and covered with emerging bruises. This is just one example of the unbelievable physical abuse he endured.

Beyond the physical abuse, the words his father uttered to his son made an indelible impact on Brad's soul. "You'll never amount to anything" was a curse that tormented Brad into adulthood. The minute he turned eighteen, Bradley got a job and left home. Despite his father's words, he excelled as a skilled laborer, making his way quickly to the top of his trade in manufacturing. In the early years, Brad loved what he did. Impressed by his abilities and intelligence, many bosses and colleagues encouraged him to pursue an engineering degree.

However, Brad never felt empowered to become an engineer. It felt intangible to him. His father's conditioning had blocked his path and altered his course, putting him into survival mode at a young age. He had trouble believing he was meant for more. At thirty-five, Brad found himself having hit the ceiling in his ability to advance further in his profession. He had to face the demons of his past as he considered his future. As he attempted to define what was next for himself, a critical aspect of moving forward involved confronting the abuse he faced—addressing and canceling out the labels, lies, and curses his father had spoken over him as a boy.

It is my sincere hope that you have not suffered like Bradley did. However, simply looking at statistics, it's likely that many readers of this book are survivors of some form of abuse or trauma. If you are an abuse survivor, it is my hope that you are receiving counsel that can help you heal and cancel out the lies you've been told about your identity, worth, and the future for which you are destined. If you are dealing with past trauma or abuse, it may be a good idea to engage a trusted friend, qualified psychologist, or counselor who can offer wise counsel as you go through the potentially triggering exercises in this book.

In addition to the Encouragers, it's also important to look back to identify and address the people who have served to discourage and kill your dreams, just like Brad did. Discouragers are significant people in your life who may have failed to recognize your gifts, talents, desires and/or the things that make you *special*. Discouragers offer misguided advice, even when driven by good intentions, that is very often tainted by their own dysfunction, experiences, successes, failures, and fears. As a result, they tend to channel any lack of support or abuse they themselves have received to others.

For example: I was a creative kid who wanted nothing more than to be an artist. One day, when I was about eight years old—I professed passionately to my grandfather that I wanted to become an artist just like him. My granddad, an accomplished commercial artist himself, recoiled and said sternly, "*If you become an artist, you'll always be poor.*"

"*Poor.*"

He spit it out with contempt: "*You will always be poor.*"

Now, I was very young, but that simple conversation made an indelible impact on me, like a gust of wind that shifted my course, blurred my creative vision, and told me I'd couldn't be successful in pursuing my passion.

I didn't understand, as a child, that my granddad's statement reflected his own insecurities over being less successful than he wanted to be. Regardless of his intention, however, what he said was incredibly discouraging. I sought affirmation and encouragement. His emphatic warning (which wouldn't be the first) told me that my passion and skill would never be enough. Effectively it influenced me to believe I should value the pursuit of money more than my heart's desires!

At a certain point, Discouragers cross the divide to become Dream Killers. A Dream Killer is any individual that blocks the path of opportunity or destiny for selfish reasons. The behavior of a Dream Killer is always one of denial and redirection. They may discourage, berate, or outright block your path and/or force you down an alternative path to which you are not well suited. Dream Killers will often lie to you about who you are and what you're capable of doing, proclaiming "truths" over you that can undermine your confidence and damage your self-esteem. Dream Killers are abusers who often use others for selfish means, keeping them around to suit their needs, living vicariously through others, berating, discouraging, taking advantage, and attempting to dictate and dominate a person's path. They live in fear that the success of others undermines their own chances at success.

Dream Killers are like selfish, brooding trolls that refuse passage into a fruitful, promised land and gobble up your potential. They may take many forms in your life: bosses, colleagues, mentors—or even friends, relatives, parents, educators, and religious leaders. They can be ever-present characters or people who appeared at a crossroad or critical season of life. Regardless of timing and form, Dream Killers destroy dreams and ambitions by blocking pathways of opportunity. For example, Brad's father was a Dream Killer who literally pounded in the message that he would never amount to anything and robbed him of the confidence he needed to pursue an engineering degree.

Examining what has inspired and energized us, and who encouraged us along the way—is a good thing. However, taking a hard look at the impact of Discouragers and Dream Killers is equally important. To face the future, it's important to brush off the dust of the past and pick up the important pieces of our identities that lay writhing on the path in the aftermath of abuse, mistreatment, and failure. It's important to identify the injuries and heal on this journey—because in doing so, we can avoid repeat performances, course-correct, and head toward a much better destination!

EXERCISE 7
DISCOURAGERS AND DREAM KILLERS

A. WHO INHIBITED YOU?

Take a minute to reflect upon the Discouragers and Dream Killers who have influenced your path. List them here. Note that it isn't uncommon to find that some of the same people that encouraged you to have, at some level, also proved to be discouraging. So, it's perfectly fine to list someone as both an Encourager and Discourager. Circle the name of your Dream Killers and identify the dream(s) they killed.

NAME	RELATION/ ROLE	NEGATIVE ACTIONS	IMPACT ON PATH & FEELINGS
Example: George	Grandpa	"Don't be a designer, you will always be poor"	Taught to respect money over passion. Believed skills were not good enough. Being wealthy is most important. Don't do what you love.

B. LABELS, LIES & CURSES

Very frequently, Discouragers and Dream Killers superimpose names, labels, lies, and even curses on our identities that may be far from accurate, but can settle into our being as "truth." Take a minute to write down and mentally confront any names, labels, and lies that have been superimposed upon your identity. Weigh the truth of these labels. Cross out and renounce things that are untrue. *Note: This may help you recall other Discouragers and/or Dream Killers!*

Example: "You will never amount to anything."

A Well-Intentioned Case of Both

As mentioned, some people may fall into both camps, serving in different areas as Encourager or Discourager by succeeding in one place but influencing attitudes and/or behaviors that work against us in others. For example, I grew up with really loving parents who earnestly believed I could do anything and supported me in all my enterprises. Their support for me was matched only by their expectations of me. If I got a B in a class, it should have been an A. When I received an A, they would want to know what prevented me from having an A+. I believe they recognized that I was a bright kid who didn't always apply herself, and the pressure was well-intentioned: they wanted me to do my best. However, I sometimes interpreted this pressure as an indication that I wasn't good enough. When I didn't perform as well as they thought I should, I also perceived that there was a lack of acceptance or love, even though this was not necessarily the case.

The support/expectation dynamic for me was a double-sided coin. My parents, without question, fueled my dreams. They also influenced a performance-based mentality that carried through my life, and influenced my career path. Like my grandfather, my parents meant well; they were trying to prepare me for a successful life, based on their own understanding of how to do so. Many of us deal with these kinds of dynamics, and it's good to be aware of them and how the forces at play have influenced, and continue to influence, your course, decision making, thinking, and self-perception, as well as the way you define success.

PICKING UP THE PRECIOUS PIECES

How did the exercises in this chapter impact you? Did you discover anything? Did you make any connections? In retracing our steps, we can often rediscover important pieces of ourselves that we've lost along the way. These may include:

- Passions we loved to pursue

- Accomplishments that filled us with a sense of worth

- Energizing activities that made us feel alive

- Dreams we wanted to fulfill
- Things that made us feel special
- The "fun" parts of our character
- Truth about who we are

In laying it all out, we can take up the things that fill us with energy and joy, and put to rest the damaging voices of the past. Going forward on this journey, you get to choose the voices that shape your future. You get to decide what you'll carry forward as a part of your legacy.

I hope you will take the time you need to seriously consider your responses to each exercise. Pay close attention to the activities and accomplishments that have filled you with a sense of accomplishment, gratification, satisfaction, a greater sense of self-worth, and accomplishment, as these are very likely tied to your design. While it might seem unlikely, it's possible that some of these things could play an essential, energizing role in helping you reaching a place where you can thrive, professionally. Grasp ahold of those precious things and put them in your proverbial pocket! We'll come back to them later.

Next, we'll help you discover your own design and the rich resources you have at your disposal to thrive within your Workplace Wilderness.

PART TWO

DISCOVERING YOUR DESIGN

CHAPTER 3
WHAT ARE OPERATIONAL STYLES?

Operational Styles Theory (OST) asserts that every person you meet has a single, dominant operational style. Unlike personality typing methodologies, operational styles address people within the "lens" of work, and characterize the following:

- Your perception of your job, work, or career
- How you view yourself within a work context
- How you prefer to get things done
- How you leverage others to achieve your goals
- What motivates and energizes you

Operational styles are like patterns that define how individuals are designed to function at work. Just like any real-world design pattern, laid on top of an operational style, you may see a number of "embellishments" or variables. These may include a person's background, history, attitudes, behaviors, choices, role, profession, personality, context, and conditions. At face value, this "layering effect" can make individuals with a shared operational style seem different. However, with a little observation and practice, it becomes easier to deconstruct the layers to identify the pattern underneath—determining a person's operational style with relative ease.

THE THREE OPERATIONAL STYLES

The three primary operational styles are **Walkers, Climbers,** and **Flyers**. While we're going to delve into each style in much deeper detail, *at a very high level*, you can think of the three styles as follows:

 **Walkers are the reason things run.** Walkers have a well-defined lane of expertise, a critical depth of specialized knowledge, skill, and ability, and often, a wealth of operational know-how. Walkers know the "lay of the land" inside an organization incredibly well. They are usually present in jobs for a longer period of time. Also, while a Walker tends to view their work as an important *component* of life, a Walker's job or work is not typically something that solely defines the Walker's identity.

 **Climbers are the focused drivers.** They operate from a focused set of goals and objectives and excel at aligning and driving organizations against these to hit desired milestones and achieve desired outcomes. Like their real-world counterparts, Climbers approach work with a somewhat intense, methodical focus, and know how to leverage power, influence, and authority to advance to the "summit." A Climber tends to view his or her job as a "stepping stone to something greater" and will acknowledge a relatively strong tie between work and a sense of self-worth.

 **Flyers are the future-builders.** They carry broad, unique vision and perspective that establishes future direction, inspires innovation and invention, and drives the evolution of the organizations within which they serve. Flyers have an almost prophetic ability see and sense the future and work in ways that are multidisciplinary and boundary-crossing. For Flyers, work is critical to identity and a critical component of a higher mission, calling, or purpose.

EVERY PERSON HAS A DOMINANT STYLE

Every individual has a single, dominant operational style that can usually be determined with relative ease. I'm often asked if people can be "a mix" of "more than one style." I'm also asked if people can switch from one style to another over time. The short answer to both questions is "No." In fifteen years of practicing OST, I have never seen someone who has legitimately presented as having more than one style. Further, I have never seen an instance of an individual switching from having one dominant style to having another. People who initially believe they are a mix of styles typically narrow down to a single style as they better understand OST. While I have found people who have expressed a *desire* to switch styles, I've noted these individuals are often dealing with internal conflict related to their professional identities. We'll talk about this more, later in the book.

NO STYLE IS SUPERIOR TO ANOTHER

Because each style is critically needed in business, there isn't one style that is superior to another. Each style is critically suited to manage aspects of business. For example, the high-level perspective of the Flyer helps the organization see beyond boundaries, to identify opportunities for the future. The strong ability of a Climber to prioritize, focus, and drive can help an organization measurably progress against established objectives and realize goals. The deep expertise, specialized knowledge, and proficiency of the Walker helps create a smooth-running operation with repeatable processes and operational excellence without which an organization would fail. The presence of all three styles contribute to a balanced organization that thinks big, progresses effectively toward the future, and runs productively, reliably, and efficiently.

STYLES ARE EQUALLY, UPWARDLY MOBILE

An individual's operational style does not determine a person's level of upward mobility. Operational styles can be found at every level and within any department within an organization. Climbers are often selected for "fast track" positions to management, simply because their methods for getting things done tend to be appreciated in formalized management circles—especially within large corporations. However, this propensity for Climbers to rise to management doesn't impact or limit the upward mobility of other styles. Further, Climbers are not always managers, *nor* are they always good managers. In truth, I have known Walkers, Climbers, and Flyers at every level of an organization's hierarchy. I have worked with C-level Walkers, Climbers, and Flyers, and I have mentored more than my share of individuals with each style in various levels of organizations.

STYLES AND POSITION GRAVITATION

Just as there is no rule that aligns different operational styles into a company's management hierarchy, there is no "rule" that aligns certain operational styles to specific positions, roles, or functions. Walkers, Climbers, and Flyers can take on any position they desire. However, I have noted some trends in *position gravitation* between operational styles that are noted in the individual chapters on each Operational Style. For example, I have found a stronger bias of Climbers in sales-heavy organizations, where they are energized by challenge, incentive-based pay, and deal making. In contrast, it may be more common to find Flyers in consulting, creative services, and development roles. You may find Walkers, who have highly focused core competencies that often require a depth of expertise or training, working in specialized positions like human resources, accounting, marketing, operations, IT, and other areas. We'll discuss this in more depth as you read along.

OPERATIONAL STYLES VS. PERSONALITY TYPES

You may be one of the millions of people who have already taken one of the many personality tests or self-quizzes available on the market today. As mentioned, there are many books available on temperament styles, leadership styles, and personality-types for commercial and consumer use. I conducted an informal count of the different methodologies on the market a few months ago and counted over forty in under an hour. That number does not include the myriad of simple self-quizzes that you may have seen on sites like Facebook or BuzzFeed that will tell you what *Downton Abbey* character you are, or what the colors or images you select say about your psyche.

Some modern tests are formally administered, while others are broadly available. Many are available free or for a nominal fee online. You may be a fan of popular methods like the Myers-Briggs Personality Type Indicator (MBTI), or the Enneagram, or Strengths Finder. From the serious and clinical to the simple and playful, these quizzes, self-tests, and assessments—workshops, training, and full certification courses options range dramatically in size, scope, and range in terms of scientific and academic acceptance.

Temperament and personality-typing methodologies tend to focus on people's larger emotional makeup—how they perceive, process, and interact with the world around them. While methodologies vary in terms of academic acceptance, these methodologies typically examine and dissect an individual's deeper psychological or cognitive constructs through complex analysis and what can sometimes (but not always) be based on scientific, research-based examination.

Operational Styles Theory focuses on people's perspectives, expectations, and relationship with this thing we call *work*. OST offers a simplified way of looking at people within the workplace. Rather than scientific dissection and examination, OST offers a simplified framework for looking at yourself, professionally, and the people in your workplace. Recognizing operational styles is a lot like trying to recognize an apple based on simple attributes like shape, color, smell, size, or taste. Generally speaking, because there are only three types of distinctly different OST apples, identifying someone's operational style doesn't require complex dissection or core analysis. OST doesn't seek to dismiss or replace other methodologies for understanding yourself, others, or your world; it merely offers a simplified lens for better understanding people in a work-related context.

While OST is simpler than many methodologies, it is hardly one-dimensional. It considers how people view themselves within the context of work, how they prefer to get things done, how they leverage the insights and expertise of others to achieve their goals, and how they respond to the natural tensions and conflicts that arise in the workplace. In particular, style dynamics play an incredibly profound role in the workplace. While the three primary operational styles are designed to work harmoniously together, there are common patterns of conflict that occur when styles clash. This can create predictable patterns of interpersonal conflict, disharmony, and stress that compromise productivity, relationship integrity, and workplace morale. We'll talk more about this in chapter 13.

As mentioned in the introduction, I developed OST in response to a critical drawback I noted with many of the personality typing, temperament, and leadership style methodologies on the market today. Over the years, I studied many, and I always gleaned some useful insight from the courses, workshops, and trainings I attended; however, I found it difficult to apply what I learned to improve the way I worked with others. Working as a management consultant tasked with driving change, I always found it hard to leverage the insights I'd gained to *quickly* assess and build understanding with others—or to use what I'd learned to adjust how I worked with others to drive better outcomes.

Early on, I feared I was just an odd duck and a bad student. Then I began meeting other professionals with the same concerns I had. Some, like me, thought that perhaps they had missed some key information or that they'd absorbed course materials with too much self-focus. Others complained with frustration that they had trouble recalling and applying what they had learned. Many complained that while the frameworks and methodologies they studied seemed interesting, they proved too complicated for practical, daily use, and were hard to internalize or commit to memory. OST seeks to help remedy these issues.

THE PURPOSE OF OST

OST offers a simple mental model for the workplace that can help you work with greater insight, understanding, and empathy. Designed to commit more readily to memory, OST insights are easy to recall when you need them most—which is typically under pressure! The OST framework will help you better understand and embrace your own operational design, manage your weaknesses, and arrest unproductive thinking. This can help you radically improve the way you work and help you better understand and work with others.

OST also provides people with a method that allows them to quickly assess, understand, and adapt to work with others more effectively.

However, the mission of OST extends beyond *style recognition*. My earnest hope is that, in practicing OST, people will be conditioned to build bridges of understanding with others, getting to know individuals in the workplace, recognizing their gifts, and working with greater empathy.

Building bridges of understanding in the workplace is powerful: Understanding others opens the door to working with greater empathy, strengthens interpersonal relationships, improves communication, and establishes common ground for more effective collaboration and better results. Working with greater empathy naturally shifts self-driven focus to an emphasis on creating "mutual wins" that benefit all collaborators and the larger workplace ecosystem. This can shift interests, create better alignment between teams, and encourage people to work with a higher level of ownership, accountability, and responsibility.

In short, it's a better way to work! Collectively, OST seeks to help people:

- Steward their careers in a more confident, empowered way
- Work "by design" to leverage their natural abilities
- Manage potential areas of weakness
- Recognize triggers and arrest negative thinking that can cause them to stumble
- Align work to activities that are more prone to motivate and energize
- Recognize favorable, supportive work cultures and secure a better job "fit"
- Better understand and work adaptively with people
- Establish common ground for better communication and collaboration
- Build better relationships with management, peers, and direct reports
- Demonstrate a higher level of personal ownership, accountability, and responsibility

- Establish mutually-beneficial outcomes that benefit the workplace ecosystem

- Wield their power to lead and manage well, as a force for good

- Embrace a sense of purpose, goals, vision, and dreams for the future

- Extract a greater sense of satisfaction and gratification from hard work

CHAPTER 4
IDENTIFYING YOUR OPERATIONAL STYLE

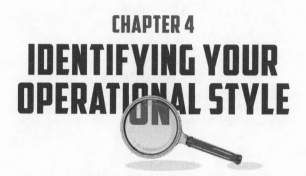

You don't need certification or special training to identify your operational style or the style of someone you work with. In the long-run, you shouldn't have to rely on this book to do so, either. Style identification is a simple matter of aligning a person to a dominant style through trait mapping. It is best supported by internalizing an understanding of the three operational style archetypes presented in this book. Identifying your own style requires honesty and self-awareness. Identifying someone else's style requires observation, inquiry, and sometimes, a little research. In both cases, the goal is to identify behavior patterns that align a person to a dominant operational style as quickly as possible.

SHARED NEEDS & DESIRES

Before delving into the traits that align to Walkers, Climbers, and Flyers, it's important to acknowledge the needs and desires that apply to people *in general*. In 1943, Abraham Maslow articulated his "hierarchy of human needs" in a paper called "A Theory of Human Motivation," which continues to be popular today. The hierarchy categorized human needs into five categories: Physiological, Safety, Social, Esteem, and Self-Actualization. When we consider our relationship with work, in like manner, there are some universal needs and desires that may apply to anyone. While I'm not going to delve deeply into this or Maslow's Hierarchy, here is a list of needs aligned to Maslow's Hierarchy of Needs that might resonate with you:

SELF-ACTUALIZATION
A job that is challenging, meaningful, and purposeful, the ability to problem-solve, make a difference, impact the world for good, reach potential, achieve, and advance

ESTEEM-RELATED
Interesting job with sufficient title or authority, the provision of necessary resources, the feeling of being needed, useful, rewarded, and gratified

SOCIALLY-RELATED
A job that provides a sense of community, a sense of belonging, the feeling of being cared for, and respected

SAFETY
Job security, safe working conditions, benefits, the ability to save for the future

PHYSIOLOGICAL
A job with sufficient pay, income to pay bills and buy food, a physical means to get to work

While the needs and desires listed above may apply to everyone, some people may place more value on some attributes than others and/or feel less need for work-related esteem or self-actualization.

STYLE-SPECIFIC TRAITS

The three operational styles—Walkers, Climbers, and Flyers—are characterized by a set of commonly found, *potentially distinguishing traits*. Understanding these traits and their alignment with each operational style can help you more quickly identify your own style, as well as the operational styles of others. Style traits are divided into two categories: pros and pitfalls.

Pros represent a spectrum of commonly found natural capabilities, strengths, or talents that are typically embodied by a person with a specific operational style.

Pitfalls represent potential *characteristics* that combine with certain situational or emotional triggers, to become negative, career limiting, or problematic.

For example, one key trait of a Flyer is being a *natural change agent* (PRO). This can be incredibly positive, under the right conditions. However, Flyers must be aware that their inclination to challenge the status quo and tendency to "stir things up" can also create an *uneasy work environment,* where *people feel uncomfortable or threatened* (PITFALLS). We'll talk about how this works later in the book. For now, it's most important to understand that each style comes with a set of potentially distinguishing traits, and how an individual aligns to those traits helps indicate a person's dominant operational style.

Recognizing your *own* operational style may prove to be tricky. This is a natural outcome of the battle we all fight between perception and reality, wherein we must recognize the difference between how we perceive ourselves, how we *want* to be perceived, and how we *are* perceived by others. Style recognition requires objectivity and honesty to break through our natural perceptions and defenses. The rewards for our honesty are found in the form of important revelations that can help us on the professional journey ahead. As we prepare to delve more deeply into each operational style and help you identify your dominant style, here are several important considerations related to style traits:

Style Traits Are "Potentially Distinguishing"

It is not necessary for *all* the traits defined for an operational style to apply to you. You may have one, or you may have many. When asking if a trait applies to you, go with your gut as a rule of thumb—it's usually correct. If you're find yourself "on the fence," as to whether a trait applies, take a break and come back to it.

It's Normal to Embody Traits Across Several Styles

It isn't uncommon for an individual to possess traits across several styles. However, a stronger clustering of traits aligned to one style typically emerges. For example, I know a Walker who strongly associates work with her identity and mission, which is a strong Flyer trait. She works at a non-profit, a type of organization that tends to draw people that are more missionally-minded. Otherwise, she checks out very strongly as a Walker.

Traits Manifest Differently in Individuals

How traits manifest can vary with each individual. However, with time and practice, it becomes easier to recognize these differences. For example, depending on where you are in your career progression and maturity, traits may be active or dormant. For example, a more senior Climber that has minimized many weaknesses or pitfalls may seem very different than a Climber who is new in her career and hasn't learned how to manage her weaknesses well. A person's work context and/or emotional condition also influences the traits that may be evident. For example, a person that is feeling disgruntled, insecure, or angry, may have more active pitfalls. Some traits can manifest differently based on personality characteristics, morals, and other factors. For example, an introverted Flyer may behave differently than an extroverted Flyer.

Recognizing Weakness Tends to Be Easier

While I'd love to say that we're all great at identifying and acknowledging the strengths in ourselves and others, it seems to be human nature to pick out weaknesses more easily. Perhaps this is due to human nature and our tendency to sense weakness in others and/or to view others with a critical eye. Even so, it's important to look past the negative and do our best to be objective in finding and acknowledging positive traits and strengths in ourselves and others!

Clustering Is Key

The key to style recognition is always to look for a *clustering of traits that* align a person to a particular style. Specifically, what's important are the traits (Pros and Pitfalls) that "absolutely or mostly apply" to you. However, it's also important to take a look at the Pro traits that "absolutely do not apply" to you, as a large number of negative responses clustering in the Pro area may indicate misalignment with that operational style. Pitfalls that do not apply don't really count, because negative response could merely mean a pitfall is not active or problematic.

Narrowing Is Natural

Sometimes, the process of style identification is clear and straightforward. However, often the process is one of narrowing down, as there are many factors that can skew self-assessment results. As a result of these factors, you might find what seems to be an alignment to two styles. The chapters on each style provide more context and detail on Walkers, Climbers, and Flyers that can help you narrow down to identify your dominant operational style.

FACTORS THAT SKEW ANSWERS & RESULTS

As you prepare to take the "Self Assessments" provided in Chapters five, six and seven, it's important to understand how results can be skewed:

Self-Perception

People often respond to tests in a way that reflects how they want to be perceived, rather than how they actually are. They may feel insecure admitting the truth or skew answers due to denial. They may also have received coaching that labels certain behaviors as "bad" and other behaviors as desirable, which can influence responses. When people select answers based on what they perceive as a "better answer" rather than the answer most closely aligned to how they actually are, it will skew the result and cause confusion.

Age & Experience

The amount of work experience and history you have can impact your self-assessment results. For example, if your answers are only based on your exposure to a *single job*, you may not have a high level of professional self-awareness Further, a person's generational alignment can influence results. For example, there is a lot of research that suggests that millennials have a strong association to the sense of being world changers and attachment to work with meaning and "purpose." This may have an impact of skewing responses toward the operational style of Flyer. However, it's important to remember hopes and desires are different than reality. Having a *desire* to do something is radically different than actually doing that thing on a steady, regular basis.

Type of Employment

Self-employed individuals and individuals who may work alone all or part of the time (e.g. psychologist, counselor, or consultant) may also score higher as a Flyer or Climber. This is partially because of the entrepreneurial forces at play that can naturally broaden an individual's lane of focus and/or require an individual to wear many hats and fulfill many roles, and become skilled in focus, prioritization, and hitting milestones. Further, it is common for self-employed individuals to have less separation between their professional and personal identities, and to have different social dynamics at work. Factors like this can skew self-assessment results, and underscores the need to read the chapters on Walkers, Climbers, and Flyers for additional context.

Associations

Individuals who work in an environment with a very strong bias toward a single operational style, or who work for a manager with a strong operational style, may internalize the characteristics of the workplace or manager. For example, if you work in a hard-charging, Climber-driven sales environment, you may identify or embrace more Climber traits than if you worked somewhere else. If you work in a heavy, compliance-driven organization that is steeped in process, you might score in a way that results in more Walker traits resonating with you. Regardless of your associations, it's important to really focus on asking whether the traits align to *your organization—or to your own natural tendencies.* It's also important to make sure you are responding based on your broader, professional history, to avoid skewing answers due to association.

Culture

The culture within which you were raised and/or are currently immersed can impact the way operational style traits manifest and skew your self-assessment results. On an individual level, people that have been raised in other cultures embrace different sets of cultural norms, values, etiquette and/or carry different perceptions about acceptable and non-acceptable behaviors. This is especially true outside of Western nations. However, even within Western cultures, values, manners, and cultural norms vary across nations, geographic regions, and ethnicities. It's important to consider how your cultural biases may impact your perceptions and how this impacts how your style traits manifest, as this may also impact your scoring.

I have personally lived abroad and have experience working with people from an array of different countries and cultures. I have witnessed operational styles at work in individuals from both Western and non-Western nations, and have noted differences in how traits manifest. Unfortunately, due to practical limitations, it isn't feasible to address different cultural norms in this book, which primarily addresses individuals living and working in or with Western business cultures.

Pigeonholing

I've heard people say that they don't want to be "pigeonholed" (assigned to having a dominant style), because they perceive this as somehow limiting. The purpose of OST isn't to pigeonhole anyone. Honing in on your *dominant* operational style—and embracing it—is actually liberating in many ways, giving you the freedom to be yourself, and the skills to work more effectively with others. Just because you follow an operational style pattern doesn't mean you are the same as anyone else, or that your heart's desires are off-limits to you. Our traits, features, and characteristics manifest in different ways—shooting through the facets of our unique makeup as unique reflections of ourselves. Having a dominant operational style doesn't limit anyone. We have freedom to do what we love, love what we do, and pursue any path we choose.

A STYLE DISCOVERY EXAMPLE

I always thought my good friend, Marie, was a Walker, though it was hard to tell for sure because we don't live in the same city and have never worked together. This summer, she came to visit, and she went through the self-assessment. As I suspected, her responses indicated she was a Walker. However, there was a surprising scattering of Climber traits as well as a significant Flyer marker that piqued my interest, so I began asking some questions to learn more.

First, we talked about the Climber traits in detail. It turns out, the relationship she'd formed with her Climber manager was incredibly strong. In discussion, it became clear that some of the traits she identified as her own were actually traits that are embodied by her manager. She admitted that if he were not in the picture, she might approach things differently, as she had in past positions. In this area, her results were skewed by *association* not just because of her close relationship with her boss, but because she made the mistake of answering based on her *present job only*.

Marie had also identified as having a job that fueled her identity and that was part of her purpose in life. This is a significant marker for a Flyer. Growing up in an economically disadvantaged environment, Marie had worked her way to the top of her field without any support from her family or a formal college education. She had risen steadily over the years by working hard, delivering well, and building a strong reputation. She was proud of what she had accomplished, and that pride rightfully fueled part of her identity as a person. However, she admitted that her identity, in reality, was fueled by many other things—including her role as a wife, mother, volunteer leader, athlete, and coach—outside of work. When pressed, she said "My work doesn't really define me"—which is a Walker response.

When I asked *how* Marie's work tied to her purpose, she admitted that while the accomplishment of overcoming and establishing a good career for herself partially fueled her identity, she didn't feel her job was necessarily a calling or a mission for her. Putting it in her own words, "While I feel blessed to mostly love my job—work is work...it's one significant part of my life. However, if I didn't need to work, I probably wouldn't do it." This was insightful, as it's unlikely that a Flyer would make such a statement, in a job he or she loved. A true Flyer might be inclined to continue working even if it wasn't necessary.

Finally, she also expressed concern about being a Walker, saying that it didn't seem as "exciting or important" as the other styles. However, when we went through how a Walker functions, she admitted that she misunderstood the style entirely and realized that being a Walker didn't subtract any passion, purpose, excellence, or leadership Marie brought to the table. In fact, Marie began to better appreciate the power of her operational style—and how it bolstered her in her position in her company, and with her boss. On almost all other fronts (role, career history, purpose, management, collaboration, communication, and risk), Marie scored as a Walker with a great deal of love and passion for what she does for a living.

UP NEXT:
IDENTIFYING YOUR STLE

At the beginning of chapters 5, 6 and 7, you will find a list of potentially identifying traits that align to each operational style. These are formatted into a checklist and divided into two columns, one that contains pros (left), and the other that contains corresponding pitfalls (right). You can use these as a kind of Self-Assessment.

1. Before reading each chapter, follow the directions provided to mark the traits that are "absolutely or mostly like" you, or "absolutely or mostly unlike" you.

    - Be as honest and objective as possible
    - Don't over think the questions
    - Go with your gut—it's often correct
    - Choose your answers based on:
        ○ How you are in a *work-setting* only
        ○ *Your entire professional history*—not just your present job.

2. If you have a mixed reaction or get stuck:
    - Look at the corresponding pitfall for additional context, thinking of it as the "other side" of the proverbial trait "coin"
    - Simply leave the box blank if you can't decide

3. Once you have completed the Self-Assessment:
   - Follow the instructions and record your score
   - Read the chapter to gather additional context

   Note: It's fine to take all three self-assessments before reading the chapter materials. *However, it is very important to read the chapters to adequately understand each style and validate your responses.* The trait lists provide simplified, one-line summaries for consideration purposes. They were created as "cheat sheets" to help point people in the right direction" as they try to attempting identify their own operational style, or the style of someone else. However, the trait lists *don't* present the level of detail, explanation or context the chapter materials cover. Reading the chapter contents will help you better identify your style, and provide clarity in the event your scores suggest you may align to more than one style.

4. Once you have completed the checklist for all three styles, compare your scores.
   - The assessment that has the *highest number of positive responses overall* is most likely to be your dominant operational style.
   - Comparatively, if you look at the *pros only*, a higher number of negative responses compared to positive pro responses may indicate that style is unlikely to be your dominant operational style.

If you have difficulty identifying your dominant operational style, be patient. Reading the chapters should help. However, sometimes it takes time to hone-in on your dominant operational style. If you get really stuck, obtaining some additional, objective feedback from others can often be helpful. Consider providing a copy of the self-assessment to two-or-three colleagues, and ask them to complete the checklist *for you*, as a point of validation. For optimal results, have them provide their completed responses to a trusted peer who can give them back to you in an anonymized manner. This will give your colleagues a greater level of comfort in providing very honest feedback. You can then compare their responses and scores with your own.

CHAPTER 5
WALKERS

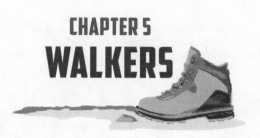

WALKER
TRAITS & SELF-ASSESSMENT

Traits that are common in individuals with this operational style are listed below. Place a checkmark (☑) in the box next to each trait below that is "absolutely or mostly like me." Place an "x" mark (☒) in the box next to every trait that is "absolutely or mostly not like me." Leave anything you are not sure about blank. Answer objectively based on how you are in a *work-setting only* and *across your entire career*—not just your current job!

WALKER PROS	WALKER PITFALLS
VIEW OF JOB/WORK	
☐ Job is an important and meaningful component of a larger existence	☐ Potential for some individuals to adopt an indifferent stance—"work as means to an end" mindset
☐ Identity and self-worth are garnered from a wider spectrum of roles, activities, and accomplishments beyond work	
☐ Job does not *particularly* align to sense of higher purpose, mission, or calling (unless employed by a cause-oriented organization)	

EMPLOYMENT/CAREER PROGRESSION

- [ ] Career progression from job-to-job is logical and relatively easy to follow

- [ ] Prone to maintaining employment for a longer period of time, contributing to longevity and preservation of intellectual capital
- [ ] May stay with a job or position as a "safe choice" which can compromise growth, innovation and/or productivity

- [ ] Job typically requires and aligns with formal education, training, and certification
- [ ] Doesn't like to be told how to "do my job," especially by anyone perceived as an "unqualified expert"

- [ ] Motivated and energized by efficiency and productivity—ensuring area of responsibility is managed properly
- [ ] Frustrated by an environment of chaos, disorder, and/or lack of structure

- [ ] Stronger propensity to demonstrate clear boundaries at work and/or maintain "work/life balance"
- [ ] Prone to become disgruntled if balance and boundaries are perpetually disrupte

- [ ] Values periodic engagement with management as well as scheduled reviews, feedback, goal setting, and rewards

FOCUS/PURPOSE

- [ ] "Reason Things Run"— establishes systems and frameworks for productivity and efficiency (tools, process, policy, guidelines, structure)
- [ ] May place too much emphasis on process, rules, policies, or guidelines, hindering individual or organizational progress

- [ ] Specialist with well-defined expertise—mastery of core operational function critical to business
- [ ] May be hesitant to expand or go beyond current area to grow and pursue new opportunities

- [ ] Core competency, area of specialization, or job are easy for others to understand and describe
- [ ] Job, role, tasking are often misunderstood and/or underestimated by others, resulting in unrealistic expectations

- [ ] Often serves as a "go-to" person for practical knowledge, information, permissions, procedures, support, etc.
- [ ] May become a "single-point-of-failure" if proper transparency or knowledge transfer fails to occur

☐ Excels at managing complex tasks, details, procedures, communications, and handoffs with many stakeholders and dependencies	☐ Prone to become buried when tasks, schedules, or dependencies collide—may feel "dumped on"
☐ Tends to develop a wealth of insight into the organization (personnel, key decisions, business history, interworking, scandal) over time	☐ Longevity with an organization can increase attachment to "status quo" and fuel change resistance
☐ Tends to have a grounding effect on an organization, establishing operational and social roots that create staying power	☐ May establish an engrained way of doing things that is hard to change

MANAGEMENT

☐ Prefers to have a clearly defined role, area of responsibility ("territory"), and parameters within which to work	☐ May respond defensively, protectively, or negatively when someone encroaches on assigned territory
☐ Demonstrates strong ownership over assigned area of responsibility	☐ May be reticent to allow others "in"—becoming unnecessarily protective
☐ Prefers to work with "accountable autonomy," having freedom to manage assigned area	☐ May not be ready for autonomy— may not be properly accountable or transparent in activities
☐ Natural propensity to efficiently manage and coordinate areas where detail, process, and accuracy are critical	☐ Perception of "efficient" may not align with the perceptions or sentiments of others
☐ Emphasis on having the necessary/ required tools and resources in place to manage assigned area properly	☐ May allow or intentionally slow productivity, or reduce output to underscore/escalate the need for required tools, resources, etc.
☐ Asserts boundaries to create balance and maintain a manageable, predictable schedule and workload	☐ May demonstrate a lack of flexibility with boundaries, which can frustrate management and peers
☐ Role or function may have dependencies with other departments, involving deadlines, handoffs, and schedules	☐ Failure to properly manage incoming requests, and unanticipated "surprises" can have cascading impacts

MANAGEMENT *(continued)*

☐ Requires the ability to forecast or anticipate what's ahead (schedule, meetings, workload, requests, etc.) to maintain balance	☐ Lack of ability to forecast ahead tends to create anxiety and stress
☐ Maintains a "juggling act" that is predicated on rhythm, predictability, and timing	☐ Disruption in rhythm, predictability, timing can throw off balance and cause anger or frustration
	☐ May "punish" individuals that habitually upset balance, disrupt schedules, demonstrate insensitivity

CHANGE & RISK

☐ Prefers environments with a lower level of volatility and change	☐ May operate within a "comfort zone" and/or be more closed to new possibilities
☐ Supports well-informed and well-orchestrated change with proper introduction and support	☐ Prone to change resistance without a clear understanding of scope, nature, timing, and impacts to assigned area
☐ Lower propensity to take risks—prefers to have defined parameters and policies around risk areas	☐ Propensity to miss opportunities due to discomfort with taking risks
☐ Resourceful in overcoming obstacles, streamlining, and making improvements within area(s) of responsibility	☐ Resourceful "work-arounds" and/or "Band Aid" fixes can become problematic, especially if not widely understood
☐ Prone to "whip things into shape," identifying and proactively making changes and improvements to areas under purview	☐ Propensity to make "silo-based" improvements with benefits that do not extend to, or negatively impact, other stakeholders

COMMUNICATION & COLLABORATION

☐ Reasonably open communicator—provides information that is relevant to the situation at hand	☐ May withhold information from others when threatened or insecure
☐ Offers deep subject-matter or skills-based expertise (and with longevity—a wealth of operational insight) that can be critically important	☐ May be reticent to contribute to discussions that address topics or areas outside of purview "not my area"

COMMUNICATION & COLLABORATION *(continued)*

	☐ May underestimate the valuable and critical nature of their professional insight and/or support
☐ Potential mastery of a core operational function critical to business operations—knows it like no other	☐ May become myopic—too narrowly focused on own role/function/area—"silo bound"
☐ Prefers to engage in visioning/brainstorming in a manner that is relevant to assigned area or knowledge in "manageable spurts"	☐ May be exhausted and overwhelmed by too much intense discussion, ideation, or brainstorming
☐ Works best with people who demonstrate respect and appreciation for role, job, process, rules, and opinions	☐ Tendency to "shut down" when feedback, input, insight are summarily disregarded or ignored
☐ Prone to "go the extra mile" during busy seasons or critical periods of activity as a key contributor	☐ May be reticent to give additional support when "outside the job description," especially for sustained time period

RELATIONSHIPS

☐ Establishes relationships that bolster productivity and fuel ability to perform "super human tasks" (in team environments)	☐ May form cliques where "outsiders" are not welcome, and/or favoritism occurs
☐ Contributes to social environment and helps create a sense of community or "family"	☐ Propensity for close personal relationships to cloud judgement and/or contribute to a lack of appropriate professional boundaries
☐ Social connections form the backbone of "the grapevine," through which positive news and information spread to motivate employees	☐ News or gossip shared through "grapevine," connections can spread, magnifying rumor, escalating conflict, and fueling workplace "drama"
☐ Often active in organizing celebratory, social, team, or volunteering events at work	☐ Social organizing may disrupt assigned duties

RELATIONSHIPS *(continued)*

☐ Expresses thoughts/feelings openly with persons within established "circle of trust" (a safe-zone for self-expression)	☐ May be reticent to share thoughts/feelings openly with management
☐ Typically demonstrates good interpersonal boundaries	☐ May be reasonably guarded—slow to warm up to people and/or build trust

SCORING

Tally your positive (☑) and (☒) negative responses for both the pro and pitfall columns.

☑ Absolutely or ___ Mostly Like Me	☑ Absolutely or ___ Mostly Like Me
☒ Absolutely or ___ Mostly *Not* Like Me	☒ Absolutely or ___ Mostly *Not* Like Me
___ No Answer	___ No Answer

Note: A higher ratio of negative-to-positive responses in the "PRO" column may indicate this style is not your dominant style.

Calculate your total score by adding your positive ☑ responses in the pros and pitfall columns.

_____ **Total Score** *(out of 82 traits)*

WALKER FUNDAMENTALS

The Reason Things Run

Walkers are best described as the individuals who keep an organization running smoothly. They typically possess a depth of focused expertise and a breadth of operational knowledge which deepens over time. Very often, but not always, Walkers have specialized knowledge, training, and/or expertise that may require training, certification, licensing, or credentials. They tend to be detail-oriented and task-focused, though the tasks they manage may be highly complex and involve many interdependencies. They also tend to balance a very neatly stacked "apple cart" of responsibilities, managing so efficiently it becomes easy for others to underestimate the complexities of their job or function inside an organization. Walkers excel at entering an environment and identifying ways to drive efficiencies and streamline operations or process.

Position Gravitation

While Walkers can work anywhere within an organization, you will likely find a predominance of Walkers in areas that require very specific skill sets and expertise, such as human resources, accounting, contracts, legal, administration, IT, marketing, finance, accounting, market research, and analytics. I have also seen Walkers actively employed in customer service, call centers, operations, training departments, project and program management, and other areas. Walkers can work in any kind of company and may even be self-employed.

Work & Identity

In contrast to Climbers and Flyers, Walkers tend to view their jobs as a *component* of a larger existence. While work may be a very significant and important part of life, the job or career typically does not play a definitive role in establishing a Walker's sense of identity. While the Walker's sense of self-worth may be *partially fueled* by professional accomplishment, typically their sense of identity is garnered from a wider spectrum of roles, activities, and accomplishments. Walkers often exhibit a high level of ownership and responsibility over the areas they are assigned, and tend to take role and function seriously. They are energized by establishing order to ensure critical responsibilities are managed reliably, consistently, and properly.

Work & Purpose

Unless the job itself is tied to a Walker's sense of mission, calling, or purpose, Walkers won't usually associate the job, work, or career as essential to fulfilling a higher purpose or calling. A job, in many cases, may just be a job—even if it's one they like. In the many compartments of a Walker's existence, however, you may often find purpose-driven activities or pursuits. For example, outside of work, you may find a Walker donating time by coaching sports, mentoring, volunteering, being active in religious, civic, or social organizations, and other activities. "Missionally minded" Walkers, who possess a stronger sense of mission, calling, or purpose may professionally gravitate to jobs that *do align* to causes they care about, such as non-profits, religious or political organizations, and/or organizations that support a social cause or mission. In these cases, Walkers are more likely to associate their job with a mission, calling, or higher purpose when asked.

Deep Insight & Experience

Walkers typically have a specialized and well-defined area or "lane" of expertise that isn't usually difficult to name, describe, or categorize. This area of specialization often requires some form of training and/or education. In some professions, the Walker's ability to practice within their field may be dictated by the receipt of ongoing training, testing, licensing, and/or certification. This not only keeps the Walker sharp but can deepen their level of expertise and usefulness to their employer. While there are many fields where this may apply, a few examples include healthcare, teaching, tax and accounting firms, IT, cosmetology, machining, medicine, and other fields. As a result of this specialized, deep expertise, Walkers are often considered specialists and/or become "go-to" resources for subject-matter expertise. Regardless of the type of position, Walkers tend to excel in areas where there's a great deal of complexity and detail to be managed.

Whether a Walker's lane of expertise is narrower or wider will depend on the job, type of work, training, experience, employment history, and job responsibilities. For example, the specialization and competencies of an independent business owner who owns and operates a retail business are likely to be much broader than an assistant manager at a department store. Generally speaking, broad or narrow, Walkers tend to stay within their lane of expertise for the duration of their professional careers with minimal (e.g. career change) exception, broadening the path as they grow in knowledge, skill, and experience.

Walkers are most effective when their job leverages their deep, specialized knowledge, which may be topical and/or functional in nature. Topical expertise may be, for example, focused on understanding the law, risk, or compliance. Functional expertise may extend to people like HR managers, or even Microsoft-certified programmers who work in IT or operations, or certified Project Management Professionals (PMPs) who specialize in program and project management, and work across departments. Some Walkers work more independently (e.g. consultant, counselor, business owner). For example, I once met a Walker who worked for a large publisher. His job was to develop outlines for book authors, and he worked in a nearly completely self-sustaining manner within a large organization. He loved the work and his autonomy. As an introvert, he really didn't engage with co-workers in his job.

Dig deep with a Walker and you are likely to find a virtual gold mine of insight, information, and understanding that extends beyond the Walker's topical or functional "deep well" of specialized knowledge. Seasoned Walkers—especially those who have been employed with an organization for a longer-period of time—typically possess a *wealth* of operational knowledge and insight. Walkers that have persisted through different seasons of leadership and organizational change, participating in an array of initiatives often understand the evolution of the company well. In relaying this understanding, they can often explain why problems exist, why decisions were made, what has worked—and what has failed—in the past. They may even have the "inside track" on business happenings, have "dirt" on coworkers or leadership, and/or "know where the bodies are buried" related to scandal inside the enterprise. Because Walkers in team roles tend to be very interconnected across the enterprise, they also tend to develop a solid understanding of what's happening in other departments, and may also have access to privileged or sensitive information, which may or may not be shared within circles of trust.

Employment Cycle

A Walker's career progression often looks like a smooth, bell-shaped curve. They start gradually and build momentum, progressing methodically from position to position through their careers at a steady, even pace. Walkers are more likely to stay with a company for a longer time period than Flyers or Climbers. The logical progression of the Walker from one job or position to the next typically makes it easy to "follow the path" of a Walker's career progression. In fact, one telltale sign of a Walker is what I call the "*clear path through the career grass.*" There's not just a defined "lane of expertise," but the progression from one job to the next forms the footsteps of the trail— like a path through tall grass—which is usually easy to follow. While it may not be common, exceptions occur, such as interruptions like career changes, extended absences, or other significant employment events. For example, I knew a Walker whose husband was a senior executive in a high-tech firm. She was also gainfully employed in high tech, but when they started a family, she made the move to stay home with her children for almost five years before returning to the workforce.

A Stabilizing, Grounding Force

Walkers keep their feet on firm ground and excel at creating order and establishing frameworks (tools, process, policy, and routines) that create the foundation for efficient productivity. This makes Walkers a stabilizing, grounding force within an organization. They prefer to have a well-defined territory and are more content in focused positions with clearly defined responsibilities, priorities, and directives. While they may manage areas or tasks that are sensitive, Walkers typically prefer environments with a lower level of volatility, where the parameters for risk taking are well-defined and managed, and policies and expectations are clear. Collectively, the Walker's grounding effect is boosted by the social networks and circles of trust they establish. The Walker's social network helps bring a sense of community to the workplace that bolsters productivity and supports social activity, discussion, and human connection.

Accountable Autonomy

Walkers in early career stages typically respond well to hands-on managers who provide clear and consistent direction, as well as coaching and reliable follow up. Establishing a defined role, clear responsibilities, parameters within which to work, and providing the authority to oversee it, helps establish the Walker's territory. This is critical to a Walker's sense of well-being, as clearly defining boundaries can be likened to giving the

Walker a map to work from so they can anticipate and respond to the terrain ahead. As mentioned, Walkers prefer to have clear understanding of "who owns what" and often demonstrate a very high level of ownership over their assigned territories (role, duties, and responsibilities). This can (but doesn't always) lead to an inclination to become protective or territorial over their assigned areas.

While "green" or early-career Walkers may need more oversight, seasoned Walkers are likely to crave a wider berth within which to function. Walkers very often prefer to work in a manner that provides them a sufficient level of autonomy to manage their area, schedule, relationships, demands, and outputs. This typically works well, as long as they remain reasonably accountable to management for the assignments, tasks, deadlines, and deliverables within their purview. Walkers find having a level of autonomy energizing and motivating, fueling their ability to be efficient and self-running. An appropriate amount of autonomy also signifies they have earned the trust of management, which is also energizing.

Time Management

Walkers also tend to be more reliable and predictable in their time management than Climbers or Flyers, and it is typically easy to predict a Walker's schedule. They generally prefer to establish a manageable schedule and work day/week that allows them to juggle the other commitments of life. In some types of roles or positions (e.g. part-time, self-employed, independent, or a job that requires extensive travel or unusual hours) the Walker's schedule may not fit a traditional nine-to-five day. However, typically, a Walker's schedule, work arrangements, and time commitments will be arranged to accommodate activities and commitments outside of work.

Depending on the line of work, it is very common for there to be periods of peak activity or "busy seasons" that require more time, focus, and effort. A few examples of this might include: processing and distributing payroll; conducting annual reviews; budgeting season; tax season; managing an event or a campaign launch; dealing with flu season (for a doctor or nurse); midterm grading (teacher/professor); and/or fulfilling a big order on a deadline. For the most part, busy seasons are viewed as a natural part of a

Walker's job, and they are usually fine going the extra mile, as long things can be reasonably predicted and the work falls within their job descriptions.

Boundaries

While it's possible for a Walker to lapse into a workaholic-type existence marked by a lot of overtime or overwork, it is generally true that preserving work/life boundaries and maintaining a life outside of work are critical to a Walker's sense of well-being. While there are certainly exceptions to this, Walkers generally demonstrate a greater need and aptitude for establishing work/life balance.

As a result, *work boundaries* are also important to Walkers. As mentioned, Walkers typically prefer to have a well-established understanding of the boundaries within which they will work—such as a job, role, function, reporting relationship, authority, assigned tasks and deliverables, areas of ownership, and performance expectations. They may also demonstrate a desire to have a regular schedule. Along with setting the boundaries for territory, Walkers also want to establish clarity about how they will work with others and ensure the ground rules and responsibilities are understood, even if only informally. Depending on the job, a Walker's boundaries may involve establishing policies, protocols, procedures, rules, and/or guidelines that make it easier to interface with other people, the workload easier to manage, and help ensure handoffs are complete and deadlines are hit, protecting the Walker's schedule. For the Walker, boundaries help create order and the ability to anticipate what's coming, which supports a better ability to *balance* workload.

Balance

Balance is also important to the Walker. For a Walker, establishing balance is a bit like properly packing a hiker's backpack. It involves the distribution of burden and weight (e.g. workload and task distribution), minimizing discomfort (e.g. establishing a manageable schedule), loading items in the proper order (e.g. organization and prioritization of tasks), and maintaining ready, easy access to what's most important (e.g. tools, flexibility, routine, and process). Establishing balance at work is important to the Walker because they typically manage areas and tasks that involve a lot of details that often have cross-organizational and departmental dependencies. As mentioned, because Walkers tend to balance their responsibilities admirably, often with a kind of quiet proficiency, it's very common for others to underestimate and/or fail to appreciate the demands and complexities of the Walker's job. This can result in assumptions, requests, and demands that are unreasonable.

Systems & Structure

In the process of managing their assigned territories, Walkers establish *systems* that help get work done that serve their needs, as well as a potentially broad array of stakeholders. Walker systems leverage people, process, technology, and policy, establishing order, workflow, repeatable processes, and making tasks and collaboration more efficient—fueling productivity and quality of outcomes. The quality and type of structure that is put in place—and how much structure is created—will depend on the individual, the scope of the area they manage, and the way the area or individual interfaces with other stakeholders and/or departments.

While a Walker may not consider themselves a "systems thinker," Walkers typically have a natural ability to make things more efficient, and are inclined to adjust and improve existing processes to optimize the way things get done. New-hire Walkers will often spend the initial weeks assessing the existing structure and/or putting new or improved structure in place before the real productivity begins. This may include procuring needed tools, establishing processes, communications, guidelines around their assigned area, organizing the work area, getting a handle on the resources at their disposal, making sure the technology systems are properly set up, examining any rules and policies, and getting to know direct reports as needed. Walkers will also meet key stakeholders in an attempt to understand their systems and establish functional working relationships.

Collectively, whether extensive or limited, formal or informal, Walker systems help drive efficiency and establish the groundwork for productivity inside the organization. Formalized, robust, well-documented and operationalized multi-stakeholder structures are often put in place to support the broader organization. For example, Katie was hired as the Director of HR for a startup company. When she took over this role, they had a simple payroll solution that would not scale as they hired more employees and moved from rudimentary benefits to a more competitive offering. Katie worked with the CFO and CEO to establish a comprehensive Human Resources infrastructure. Her first action was to procure a new payroll provider and establish a new internal process for hours tracking and payroll management. She then secured a new benefits provider and administrator, developing a plan and communications to migrate all employees to the new system. She not only documented the new process, but she also created the first employee handbook, an onboarding process, and first-day orientation materials for new hires, and organized the employee records system. She also established an employee intranet site that streamlined time tracking, enabled communications, and self-service for benefits enrollment, expense submission, and more. Finally, she conducted training for her team and management to help them understand the HR and payroll process, from hiring to badging to time reporting, benefits enrollment, and payroll from A to Z.

At times, Walker systems may seem *less* organized, more informal, homegrown, and possibly confusing to understand. For example, Glenn is a senior researcher and the de-facto go-to person for any data that may be helpful in understanding customer behavior at a Fortune 1000 corporation. A data scientist, Glenn is regularly immersed in analysis, conducting extensive "deep-dives" into complex data, compiling his analysis into spreadsheets, enterprise systems, and dashboards. There are office-wide jokes about the condition of Glenn's office, nicknamed "the Vortex." It looks like a bomb went off. It is notoriously messy, with stacks of paper everywhere, leaving just enough room to cradle his Star Trek coffee mug. Glenn's boss shudders to think about how he'd go through his office if he ever left—but he has been with the company for twelve years and is a data rock star. While Glenn's filing system is unintelligible to everyone else, his output for the organization is well-organized. When asked, Glenn can find useful and highly accurate facts on almost anything with incredible speed. He isn't just a great analyst; he has a unique ability to connect data to tell stories that open people to new realities. His analysis organized intranet dashboards with the help of an organized assistant. Like other Walkers, Glenn stands as a veritable fountain of critical knowledge, and his system of organization works well for him and his employer.

Fixes & Workarounds

Walkers frequently encounter problems and roadblocks when attempting to establish efficient procedures to get things done. When this happens, they often prove to be resourceful at developing work-arounds and creative solutions to circumvent obstacles in the name of productivity. The challenge is that, like the more informal Walker systems, these workarounds may not always be well-understood by management and can pose later challenges.

For example, my team was once brought in to streamline the HR operation of a very large, Walker-driven, government organization. They were passionate and dedicated to their jobs and pushed a lot of paper in addition to managing outdated "legacy" computer systems. When we arrived on scene, it became clear that the leadership in charge did not understand how the Walker systems functioned as well as they thought. Behind the scenes, to avoid manual labor, like printing out documents and re-entering data into a different system, the resident Walkers had put an array of programming scripts in place that were "pulling data" from one legacy system to another. Over the years, the number of scripts had grown exponentially. What we learned about the Walker systems and fixes had a big impact on our project requirements, which had to do with updating their computer system, and migrating the old data into the new system. If we hadn't discovered all the scripts, we may have had problems with our systems implementation. Fortunately, it wasn't our first rodeo: we discovered these Band-Aid fixes early on and adjusted. However, I have encountered incidents where issues like this caused major problems on similar projects.

Walker fixes or Band-Aid solutions may be systems-related, tools-related, or process-related. They may impact one or more people, have large or small implications, and involve detail or minutia. Collectively, it's important for managers to encourage Walkers to document their systems and process for getting things done, as well as the fixes they put in place so that others understand them, to the extent possible. This can help prevent a single individual from becoming a "single point of failure" during a resignation, key transition of a person from one job to another, or extended absence.

RELATIONSHIPS

Walkers that work in team-based environments typically establish strong relationships that may extend across departments and/or the organization. Walker relationships play two important roles at work:

1. They create a sense of community for the Walker that adds variety.
2. They help the Walker work more efficiently and productively across departments.

Collectively, the Walker network not only helps the Walker get things done, but it fuels an understanding of how the broader organization works. On a personal level, the Walker's network also breaks the monotony of work and serves as a safety zone for the free expression of opinions, thoughts, and information. As a result, Walker networks tend to form the backbone of the "grapevine" through which news travels inside the organization. Discussions within the grapevine often center on business events, leadership decisions, departmental happenings, personal news, general "buzz" and, very often, gossip.

Co-workers that find themselves embraced within a Walker's "trusted circle" will gain access not only to the Walker's deep well of knowledge and operational insight, but to the insight afforded through the grapevine related to departmental and organizational morale. While Walkers generally feel free to share inside the grapevine and within their own "circles of trust," they may be more reticent to speak freely or candidly with management or people who fall outside the trusted networks. Walkers tend to be more guarded when communicating outside of these networks. When they do share, it's important for them to feel heard and respected. When Walkers feel they are being disregarded or ignored, trust is eroded.

WORKING WITH & MANAGING WALKERS

Again, it's important to remember when working with Walkers that they deeply value clarity, order, structure, boundaries, balance, and respect. The

Walker's workload tends to be carefully balanced, with contingencies that impact other departments and stakeholders across the enterprise. Unanticipated requests, favors, and increased workload often have a cascading impact on other work, which can be problematic, especially if they impact tight schedules, deadlines, or processes that impact other departments. People who fail to appreciate the complexity of the Walker's job are often guilty of making unreasonable requests or disruptive inquiries. Recognizing all this is important as you manage and/or work with a Walker. While a lot of what you'll find here is simply good advice for working with anyone, the admonitions here are especially true for working with and managing Walkers:

Building & Maintaining Trust

Like Flyers flock and Climbers cluster, Walkers tend to congregate. The inner sanctum of a Walker's social clique is typically comprised of other Walkers. However, Walkers also have extended circles of trust that may include a select number of trusted Climbers or Flyers. Walkers are highly relational and sensitive to breaches of trust and loyalty. As a result, they may be less prone to trust newcomers or individuals perceived as "outsiders." Some actions that will help build trust and establish the confidence of the Walker include:

- Demonstrating respect and support for the complexity of the Walker's job

- Advocating for a Walker's concerns, especially when it matters most

- Actively listening and helping ensure the Walker has a voice

- Supporting and respecting the Walker's system(s), rules, and protocols

- Helping ensure Walkers are properly included in key discussions

- Flagging a Walker when something arises that may impact their area

- Asking for consultative input from the Walker to inform decisions when needed

- Choosing your approach and timing wisely, to avoid becoming a burden

- Offering clear and concise communication; making requests and expectations clear

On a one-on-one basis, establishing confidentiality with a Walker is an important way to protect a relationship. It's important to know when the information a Walker has shared with you is confidential, or whether (and how) it may be shared. A Walker may be very sensitive to having something they have shared with you relayed to upper management or another colleague. In general, asking permission to share their thoughts or comments is advisable. In turn, establishing confidentiality parameters for *yourself* is also a good idea, as anything shared may easily find its way into the Walker Grapevine.

The Power of a Good Approach

Walkers carry a whole lot of proverbial gear, neatly and efficiently packed, and do not want to be blindsided, sent on a goose chase, knocked off course, or distracted from the path they are on. Again, it's easy to upset a Walker's apple cart by approaching the *wrong* way, by under or overestimating the impact of your requests or demands, or by making an unreasonable or disruptive last-minute request. Making too many of these will alienate you from a Walker, especially if the requests or demands are a result of poor planning or management on your part. When you screw up, a thoughtful apology usually goes a long way. However, forgiveness is typically given, predicated on the assumption there won't be a repeat offense.

In approaching a Walker with a request, remember that any initial resistance you may encounter should be taken in stride, as the Walker may not be able to break free immediately to help you out. Choose your approach and timing with care. To understand the context (demands, schedules, extenuating circumstances, and situation at hand) the Walker is grappling with, pay attention and listen well! Because they draw from a deep well of knowledge and expertise, they typically offer insight after some deliberation and thought. As specialists and subject matter experts, that take time to provide input; being disregarded, or having admonitions, warnings, ideas, cautions, or exhortations ignored, will very often offend and potentially result in bigger problems. When Walkers feel disrespected or disregarded, they may be resistant to future invitations to provide input, collaborate, or share.

Walkers respond positively to people who try to work respectfully within their defined boundaries. They appreciate people who follow directions, funnel work through the proper channels, work within established protocols, communicate clearly, and hand off accurate and complete information on time. As mentioned, they are typically very helpful and reasonable and responsive to reasonable requests, especially when given time and with advance notice. They press hard during busy seasons, are typically helpful "in a pinch" and can offer sympathetic and sacrificial assistance when it matters. When faced with a challenge, Walkers excel in examining the facts and offering helpful suggestions and ideas and practical support.

Timing is Everything

Demonstrating sensitivity to the Walker's schedule and demands is important, especially as disruptions tend to have a "trickle down" effect, impacting multiple schedules, departments, and stakeholders. Asking the Walker about his or her preferred method of communication can be helpful. Further, asking if there are any deadlines or commitments you need to be sensitive to, or what days and times are the best to work together, can help you work around their demands with greater sensitivity, while building respect and trust.

In the "cubicle farms" that seem to dominate the modern workplace, it can be hard to shut out distractions. In general, it's good to be careful about the "walk up" approach for impromptu discussion. If you must approach a Walker informally or in an impromptu manner, be sure to ask first if it's a good time. If it is, clarify how much time they have to give you and stay within it. Otherwise, use email to ask questions, being sure to specify when there is an urgent need. If you need to have a discussion, schedule coffee, a lunch, or set up short, efficient meetings when needed. Use the time efficiently, stick to the agenda, and establish next steps. "Bunny trails" (going off topic) are distracting to Walkers, who much prefer not to waste time, and to stick to an established outline. Stay focused in your communication.

The Art of Inclusion

Walkers like to be properly included but hate feeling overwhelmed or sucked in to a project or initiative to the point where other commitments suffer. Walkers don't want to be included on *everything* but can become angry or resentful when *excluded*. Unless a Walker has dedicated time reserved to support a project, it can be very helpful to find ways to focus his or her involvement to minimize interruptions.

When engaging with a Walker, it's important to recognize that Walkers like to feel grounded and rooted in facts, and understanding how these relate to the territory for which they are responsible. Explaining the "lay of the land" can be very helpful in identifying how a Walker should be involved in a project or initiative. When you need a Walker's input or involvement on a project, it's important to think through how, when, and at what points you will need the Walker's input. Using this information, you can lay out a plan for inclusion and meet with the Walker to "map out" your recommended approach. In that meeting, provide an explanation of the project or initiative, and present the key drivers and priorities that make it necessary. Explain your needs and pose your recommendations about how the Walker might best participate—demonstrating your interest in "minimizing disruptions" in the Walker's best interest.

In general, I have found dictating how a Walker will engage in a project or collaboration to be a slippery slope. While managers can certainly direct how Walkers will participate, a consultative approach often works better—especially in a peer setting. Providing guidance and asking for input can allow the Walker to choose points of engagement where they can provide the most value. This will also help preserve the Walker's time and motivate ongoing participation. Rather than dictating meeting attendance, it may be better to highlight the most important meetings, giving the Walker the power to attend all, or opt-out of some. Once you've mutually agreed on how the Walker will be involved, finalize the plan.

This inclusion process works well for everyone. Collaborators walk away with a commitment from the Walker to participate and understand how they will engage. The Walker leaves with clarity about the project or issue, the key points at which they will be asked to provide input, the tasks they will be assigned, and the meetings they'll attend—and a firm sense of what's coming. At each point of interaction, follow up with a quick summary and next steps. This will reinforce that you're tuned in and help the Walker anticipate what's next. This iterative, focused way of inclusively working helps maximize Walker participation and input without demanding too much.

Upsetting a Walker

While Walkers are usually flexible, you may find them irritated or upset by certain behaviors. In addition to having their boundaries violated or the balance upset, Walkers are sensitive to exclusion and disrespect. Some other behaviors that may anger the Walker include:

- Ambiguity, being left hanging, poor direction and communication
- Individuals who demand support instead of asking for it
- Individuals who dictate action instead of asking for input
- Patterns of interruption without regard for workload or schedule
- Patterns of laziness and/or incomplete hand-offs that create more work or rework
- People who fail to listen or follow clear direction
- People who perpetually circumvent "the process" to ask for favors, help, or "rescue"
- Not being consulted on decisions that impact them or their areas of responsibility
- Being left out of discussions regarding their areas of responsibility
- People who posture as if they understand a Walker's area, when they do not
- Being forced to comply with direction that feels ill-informed
- Requests that disrupt the schedule or their ability to meet other obligations
- Breaches of trust or confidence

- Behavior that feels dismissive or disrespectful

- Big ideas and a lot of talk with no follow-through or action

Depending on the authority and rank of the offender and the mental state of the Walker, responses to offenses may vary. Sometimes, Walkers will go insular to think through or process things. Walkers generally respect the chain-of-command and are reticent to push back on requests that come "from above." When offenses are committed by people outside of the chain of authority, offenders may be met with a variety of responses, from direct pushback to verbal scolding to an outright refusal to cooperate. Many have admirably pragmatic ways of neutralizing offenders.

Walkers may intentionally delay response or even give an offender the silent treatment for a period of time. While some Walkers may be direct in expressing objections, other Walkers may also resort to passive-resistance or passive-aggressive responses. I have seen offended Walkers intentionally dodge calls, and brush off repeat offenders. I have been privy to situations where Walkers have made repeat offenders resubmit paperwork in the name of their original requests "getting lost due to late submission." I have watched Walkers deny requests, and/or "back-burner" requests or projects in a punitive manner, just to make a statement. Depending on the serious-ness of an offense, an offender may be ousted from a "circle of trust" for a serious violation. There won't typically be an explanation, just an eviction. They may also escalate chronic problems to the attention of management.

Walkers may feel threatened when others encroach on their territory. This is specifically true when someone—even someone in authority—attempts to better understand the Walker's area or system, inquire about an event that transpired, or recommend ways to streamline operations to boost productivity. Walkers can be especially sensitive to criticism and input from people who they don't consider "qualified" to tell them what to do, such as individuals that do not have a comparable depth of specialized knowledge that rivals their own. To motivate receptivity, a positive attitude, and willingness to collaborate, it's critical to establish trust and work in an assuring way that minimizes perceived threats.

Dealing With Change & Uncertainty

Generally speaking, Walkers typically support well-conceived, planned, managed, and executed ideas, discussions, or projects. This is especially true if the work at hand is going to make the company operate more efficiently. However, it's important to remember that out of all the operational styles, Walkers tend to be the most prone to resist change. Most experienced Walkers have seen enough change—from reorganizations to process changes to poor systems configurations—to know it's not always good or productive. This often results in a highly skeptical view of change, as well as a general distrust for (and potential hostility to) *agents* of change.

In most cases, Walkers that initially resist cooperation or collaboration have an array of legitimate concerns. Many respond out of general uncertainty, fear, or discomfort. Walkers generally do not like ambiguity because it makes them feel less grounded and unprepared to handle daily terrain. They want to understand why change is being made and whether it is properly informed. As a result, they may hesitate to engage out of a lack of understanding of what's expected of them, or concern that a project or activity will upset the balance in their area and undermine the systems and structure they have put in place.

Change skepticism and resistance is often more pronounced in individuals with more experience and work history. In worst-case scenarios, trail-weary Walkers that have been impacted by many different kinds of organizational shifts and "bad change" can become disgruntled and pessimistic. When approached for help or support, they may actively resist and in some cases, attempt to subvert change. One of the ways they do this is to leverage the grapevine as a channel for the airing of grievances. This has the potential to spread fear, concern, and ill will across the organization and can work to undermine key improvement initiatives.

Walker concerns can usually be resolved by providing clear direction—and practicing the art of inclusion, as previously described. When facing organizational, operational, or procedural change, a Walker's immediate desire will be to fully grasp the *reasons and drivers of change*. In addition, a Walker will want to understand the *scope and nature of the change, the timing for the change,* and the *short-, mid-, and long-term impacts*. The Walker will also want to understand *how they are expected to participate* and *to antic-ipate interruptions and delays*, especially when they impact the Walker's assigned area.

Because Walkers respect the chain of command, it is particularly effective to have both direct management and leadership communicate rationale for a change initiative, as well as associated details, very clearly and authoritatively. Details such as the timeline, ownership of tasks, timing, process, stakeholders, and expected outcomes provide the clarity that can help a Walker feel more secure. It also helps ensure they understand their role, involvement, and timing, as outlined above. Further, during periods of change, it's important that management provide proactive communication and support. Proactively addressing Walker concerns while confronting resistance, or can't-do thinking, will help ensure positive contribution and good outcomes.

It's important to take change-related concerns and resistance in stride and maintain positive assumptions. The Walker's level of deep, operational expertise is invaluable in defining future needs as well as driving *well-informed* change. Engaged Walkers may not only provide important input, they can also help encourage the participation of others, drive momentum and progress, spread the word to promote the effort (this is where the grape-vine becomes handy), and partner with you to create and celebrate success.

Management Relationships

Without question, the happiest Walkers I know enjoy strong, established, trust-based relationships with their direct managers. Better managers understand and respect the Walker's need for balance and boundaries, as well as the need for an appropriate level of freedom to "own" their territo-ries. In short, great managers of Walkers:

- Excel at building strong, trust-based relationships
- Champion the expertise the Walker brings to the table
- Establish a clear understanding of the Walker's responsibilities
- Periodically touch base on goals, results, and next steps

- Remain open, approachable, and available to provide support
- Support prioritization and make performance metrics clear
- Provide stronger supervision where needed, and auto-nomy where earned
- Ensure that Walker systems are documented and understood sufficiently
- Hold the Walker accountable for promises, actions, and behaviors
- Minimize interruption to help preserve balance and boundaries
- Don't assume they know everything about the Walker's area(s) of responsibility
- Break down barriers to help the Walker work more efficiently
- Help ensure the Walker has a voice and a place at the table
- Demonstrate authentic respect, loyalty, and keep promises
- Push, stretch, broaden, and challenge people to grow and advance
- Provide proactive and constructive feedback
- Recognize, acknowledge, and reward hard work and contributions

Trust & Sharing

Managers that build trust with Walker direct reports can develop effective, loyal, and powerful partnerships that can last for years. Walkers appreciate strong managers who are accessible, transparent, advocates for their success, and good communicators. Walker managers appreciate the ability to glean from the Walker's deep knowledge and insight, and benefit from the Walker's organization, order, and productivity. Depending on the depth of trust that is built, managers may also benefit from the Walker's natural "tie" to the corporate grapevine, and may enjoy more candor in the relationship as well as the ability to attain insight into the organization's undercurrent of concerns, discussions, and morale. In building trust, it's important to remember that Walker circles of trust are layered—like a jawbreaker. The core, "inner circle" relationships are marked by the most trust, candor, and personal sharing. The "outer circle" relationships may have a more limited set of benefits. Remember that Walkers can take time to warm to individuals, and while it may not readily show, trust can be hard-earned and take time to build.

When relationships are not strong, Walkers may feel uncomfortable expressing needs, requests, and thoughts to management. As mentioned, most Walkers will shut down if they feel like their input falls on deaf ears or is readily disregarded. To avoid this, it's important to demonstrate how you have listened and address what the Walker has shared in your responses. Finding even one connected Walker within a team who is willing to speak openly can produce a goldmine of insight for managers.

For example, I know a Walker named Carina who is a licensed clinical psychotherapist in a major healthcare company. Having built a strong level of trust with her management, she feels a level of comfort openly sharing cares and concerns. Because of this, Carina has become an informal spokesperson for the many Walkers with whom she works. Her workplace is a Walker-dominant environment, with a number of Walker/Climber managers. In the course of daily work, she assimilates the concerns and feedback of colleagues. When asked—or when there is a real concern – Carina excels at diplomatically relaying information to leadership in a tactful and objective way. They, in turn, handle what she shares with sensitivity and confidence, and use the "intelligence" she provides to improve working relationships and morale, speaking to the concerns of employees and acting when needed.

Again, the larger majority of Walkers feel most comfortable sharing within trusted networks and are more reserved outside their own circles of trust. Beyond trust building, when breaking through with a Walker becomes difficult, there are ways to gather feedback from Walkers who are reticent to share. Gathering anonymous, 360-degree feedback from employees and conducting surveys can be very useful to obtaining insight. Using that feedback to demonstrate sensitivity, modify your approach and make improvements that can help build trust that can fuel relationships.

Advancement & Rewards

Walkers like to be prepared for the path ahead and to know what's coming with regard to advancement and rewards. It's important to recognize that Walkers often select their jobs with an eye toward staying awhile, and they are prone to take the performance reviews process seriously. Walkers also aspire to maintain appropriate work/life balance while producing good results. With an eye toward productivity, they are keenly interested in being able to anticipate and forecast what will be on the path ahead, in terms of rewards, advancements and benefits.

The desire to know what's in store starts with having a clear understanding of employee compensation packages including medical, dental, and vision benefits, paid time off and leave policies, stock options, stock purchase and profit-sharing plans, tuition reimbursement, 401(k) and pension plans, and other benefits. It continues with the development of a solid understanding of an organization's review process, including timing, activities, process, and how rewards and promotions are managed.

Most Walkers place value on the formal review processes, including the recognition and celebration of performance awards, key milestones, and achievement. Many Walkers are willing participants in annual goal setting, planning, and performance reviews. These individuals are also more likely to participate in the formal process as well as in programs related to professional development, coaching, and mentoring. At the same time, there is a contingency of Walkers who may view the performance review process as an overblown exercise in which they participate because they must. These individuals typically prefer a more informal, down-to-earth review approach—such as a quick heart-to-heart with a manager that produces some good feedback and a clear understanding of whether they will receive a raise, bonus, additional compensation, promotion, and/or increased resources.

Whether the process is formal or informal, it's important to back up feedback with specific examples of incidents to help the Walker process input and feedback. It's also important to "check-in" on performance issues and establish and follow up on plans to address areas of weakness. On a day-to-day basis, Walkers also appreciate sincere displays of appreciation and recognition and rewards for going the extra mile.

Walkers are motivated by rewards that are measurable and commensurate with their contributions and performance. This is especially true regarding raises, commissions, bonuses, and promotions. Walkers are generally unimpressed by promotions in title only. It is of paramount importance to a Walker to ensure they have the necessary resources to perform the job well. In fact, they may take offense to being asked to accept more responsibility in exchange for a mere change in title. Many Walkers require ongoing training or certification related to their area of expertise. To the Walker, however, such training is not a perk or reward—it's a requirement of the job and expected that the organization will properly support necessary training and certification, as well as professional memberships. Collectively speaking, when rewards are withheld, or a Walker perceives the company is withholding or breaking promises (especially if this is done consistently), it is likely to produce anger and, potentially, backlash. Neglect, poor management or managerial relations, and lack of support or reward will lower morale and employee engagement, increasing the risk of attrition.

When Walkers Leave

Depending on a Walker's level of engagement, skill, and dedication to their role, there can be a high cost of attrition when they decide to depart from an organization. Beyond the simple loss of a resource, seasoned Walkers tend to leave gaps that are felt far and wide. The loss is felt due to an absence of specialized expertise, the deficit of deep insight into the interworking of the organization, as well as a loss in the workplace "community." Depending on the Walker's specialty, longevity with the company, and other factors, it can be hard to find a replacement that feels like an equal and can take over seamlessly. Very often, Walkers who depart leave big shoes to fill. This is one reason why managers should take steps to ensure proactively that a "lynchpin" Walker doesn't become a single point-of-failure who may leave a company in the lurch. Having the Walker instead share and document their knowledge and processes for the benefit of the team as an ongoing responsibility is recommended. It's also wise to conduct on-the-job knowledge transfer with replacement staff prior to the departure of a Walker, if possible. In fact, it is almost always worth keeping a Walker around to conduct knowledge transfer to a replacement staffer—even if it costs a bit more to do so, as it pays off in continuity and future productivity.

CHAPTER 6
CLIMBERS

 CLIMBER
TRAITS & SELF-ASSESSMENT

Traits that are common in individuals with this operational style are listed below. Place a checkmark (☑) in the box next to each trait below that is "absolutely or mostly like me." Place an "x" mark (☒) in the box next to every trait that is "absolutely or mostly not like me." Leave anything you are not sure about blank. Answer objectively based on how you are in a *work-setting only* and *across your entire career*—not just your current job!

CLIMBER PROS	CLIMBER PITFALLS
VIEW OF JOB/WORK	
☐ Tends to view job as a stepping stone to something greater	☐ Focus on leverage, advancement, and "push to the finish line" can undermine the quality of the journey
☐ Job isn't necessarily a part of a "higher calling" or purpose (unless working for cause-oriented organizations)	
☐ Progress, advancement are directly tied to self-esteem and sense of well-being	☐ Lack of progression or advancement can lead to low self-esteem, insecurity, anxiety, and depression

EMPLOYMENT/CAREER PROGRESSION

☐ Career progression may reveal leaps, jumps, shifts in direction that may require explanation	
☐ Gravitates to roles involving management, coordination, oversight (deals, projects, programs, people, and teams)	☐ May maneuver to obtain higher-profile positions for personal/professional gain
☐ Highly ambitious goals or plans for professional advancement	☐ Drive and determination can compromise relationships and override best interest of organization
☐ Motivated and energized when advancing and growing in authority, power, influence, or material gain	☐ Prone to leave for a better opportunity or upgrade
☐ Stays with organization as long as there is promise of advancement and opportunity	☐ Desire for advancement may create managerial, interpersonal, interdisciplinary, social, and political conflicts

FOCUS/PURPOSE

☐ Focused driver—helps organization hit key milestones, achieve goals and objectives	☐ Prone to cut off or shut down people with ideas or objectives that threaten to undermine or distract from own agenda
☐ Aligns organizational agenda and imperatives to personal agenda to drive focus, decisions, and activities	☐ Refrains from sharing too much about agenda, goals, and objectives—hard to build understanding and establish common ground
☐ Strong emphasis on goals, objectives, and associated tasks	☐ Reticence and/or difficulty focusing on anything that does not align to own established priorities
☐ Strong prioritization and negotiation kills	☐ Prioritization and negotiation may also be swayed by personal motives
☐ Excels in filtering out "extraneous" detail to define paths to action	☐ May choose to ignore critical details or warnings from others that may have consequences
☐ Strong self-preservation instinct	☐ May be reticent to admit mistakes or wrongdoing and/or face ethical challenges

FOCUS/PURPOSE (continued)

☐ Natural ability to conceive, negotiate, and facilitate deals and partnerships that help the organization	☐ May attempt to secure personal benefit from deals, relationships, or partnerships

MANAGEMENT

☐ Natural ability to "manage up" well with senior leadership	☐ May develop a reputation for "kissing up" or "brown nosing"
☐ Naturally inclined to "speak the language" of executive leadership	☐ May have problems "managing across" with peers or "managing down" with direct reports
☐ Politically savvy—knows how to leverage people and situations— works situations to own benefit	☐ May have a "utilitarian" view of people or "use" people as resources to help achieve goals
☐ May be earmarked or selected for fast-track to leadership or management positions	☐ May advance too rapidly without developing needed people and leadership skills
☐ Emphasis on building power, influence, and authority	☐ May demonstrate ruthless ambition leading to shrewd actions and/or questionable ethics
☐ Propensity to steer, guide, and/or direct activities, individuals, teams	☐ May take over and/or come across as authoritarian or dictator-like
☐ Natural inclination and talent for distributing workload through delegation— becomes stronger with experience	☐ May seem unwilling to do "do the work" or as "dumping" on others
☐ May demonstrate natural charisma, charm, persuasive ability that motivates people to action	☐ May attempt to bypass rules or assume "rules don't apply to me"— taking them seriously only if breakage could result in professional harm
☐ Potential to be a strong advocate, champion, and proponent for "goal aligned" ideas and work of others	☐ May take credit (directly or indirectly—by association) for the ideas, vision, or work product of others.
☐ Dress and grooming may be calibrated to project a desired professional image	☐ Prone to pay strong attention to appearances—may unfairly judge the appearance of others

CHANGE & RISK

☐ Bias for fact- and evidence-based decision making	☐ May be reticent to listen to individuals with good "gut" instinct
☐ Supports well-conceived change if it supports the agenda and the payoff will be high	☐ May be reticent to embrace change that threatens to undermine plans/objectives
☐ Willing to take risks when odds favorable or payoff will be high	

COMMUNICATION & COLLABORATION

☐ Relatively controlled, measured external demeanor	☐ May leave people unsure about where they stand
☐ Prone to be a highly reserved communicator—tends to share information on a "need to know" basis	☐ Prone to under communicate and leave people "in the dark"
☐ Prioritizes by assimilating high-level facts and data—prefers bulleted, clearly organized communication	☐ May be reticent to dive into explicit detail—may ignore key details that become important
☐ Prefers short, focused, concise interactions and communications	☐ Prone to become distracted and/or may tune out or glaze over in longer interactions
☐ Excels at steering dialog and collaboration in a productive direction to drive action/outcomes	☐ May consciously control discussions at the expense of others
	☐ May intentionally exclude persons viewed as detractors or distractors to keep things on track

RELATIONSHIPS

☐ Lower trust in relationships—cautious.	☐ Can be "difficult to read" or make others question where they "stand"
☐ Emphasis on networking and building strategic relationships with people who have power, authority, and influence	☐ May ignore or disregard individuals viewed as "unimportant"
☐ Prone to be bold and confident—sees opportunity and takes it.	☐ Potential for arrogance and audacity

☐ Recognizes the importance of, and excels at, strategic self-promotion	☐ May brag, inflate stories, or embellish details to bolster reputation
☐ Strategic relationship building skills fuel networking, alliances, partnerships, and deals	☐ May leverage relationships for personal gain
☐ General discomfort with emotion at work—though potential to use anger to underscore points occasionally	☐ May perceive emotion and passion in others as weakness
☐ Prone to believe that business should not be clouded by emotion or personal sentiment	☐ Behavior, communication, and decisions may hurt or damage others
☐ Steers clear of workplace drama and petty arguments—doesn't want to be associated	☐ May respond harshly or defensively if made the subject of gossip or insinuation
☐ Clearly differentiates between close, personal friendships and professional relationships (though this may not be transparent)	☐ Tendency to show favoritism to "key aligned people" (partners, peers, direct reports)

SCORING

Tally your positive (☑) and (☒) negative responses for both the pro and pitfall columns.

☑ Absolutely or _____ Mostly Like Me	☑ Absolutely or _____ Mostly Like Me
☒ Absolutely or _____ Mostly *Not* Like Me	☒ Absolutely or _____ Mostly *Not* Like Me
_____ No Answer	_____ No Answer

Note: A higher ratio of negative-to-positive responses in the "PRO" column may indicate this style is not your dominant style.

Calculate your total score by adding your positive ☑ responses in the pros and pitfall columns.

_____ **Total Score** *(out of 82 traits)*

CLIMBER FUNDAMENTALS

The Keeper & Driver of the Agenda

Climbers are best described as keepers and drivers of the agenda. They excel in helping organizations establish and reach desired objectives and scale to reach new heights. Climbers excel at prioritization and exhibit a methodical, laser-like focus in establishing and pursuing goals and objectives. Climbers demonstrate exceedingly strong drive and ambition to hit key milestones. Much like climbing a wall and leveraging hand and footholds to advance from one place to another, Climbers excel at leveraging people and situations to progress, moving an organization forward as they drive their own advancement and achievement.

Position Gravitation

You will find Climbers in any department or division, and at any rank, from the mailroom to the boardroom. However, wherever you find them, you can be sure of one thing: they will have ambitious plans for professional advancement. Climbers often gravitate to roles in business development, sales, product and account management, finance, investing, and public relations. They also make excellent attorneys, consultants, investors, and entrepreneurs. While the Climber is certainly not relegated to these kinds of environments, such roles use the Climber's analytical capabilities as well as their natural management, delegation, negotiation, sales, and persuasive abilities. Climbers naturally excel at assuming roles that involve overseeing, managing, and coordinating what may be programs, projects, products, people, teams, departments, divisions, and more.

Work & Identity

Climbers tend to view their jobs as stepping stones to something better. While there is almost always a strong delineation between the Climber's personal life and professional existence, work plays a significant role in the Climber's sense of self-worth and identity. Climbers are energized when they feel they are advancing and growing in experience, authority, influence, power, rank, and financial stability. When this is not the case,

Climbers may experience stress, anxiety, job dissatisfaction, compromised emotional well-being, and a lower sense of self-esteem.

Work & Purpose

Unless the job itself is directly tied to a mission or calling (e.g. a social-good business, non-profit, or religious organization) a Climber may not associate their job or work with a sense of "higher purpose" or "calling." However, the concept of "purpose" here may be slightly confusing. It is not uncommon for a Climber to feel a sense of destiny. In fact, many goal-oriented Climbers have exceptionally strong minds-eye visions or dreams that detail what their future professional achievement will look like. This may involve a rise to a level of stature, role, power, influence, authority, or even celebrity, and/or it may involve achieving very specific milestones. The Climber may associate the achievement of professional aspirations with a sense of purpose or "destiny fulfilled." However, this angle on purpose, which is mostly self-seeking, is markedly different from the association of one's work with a higher purpose, mission, or calling that seeks to *serve and benefit others*.

Employment Cycle

The career curve of a Climber looks less like path through the grass and more like a climbing wall dotted with countless hand and footholds. There might be twenty different paths to the summit, and how the Climber got where they are may well require some explanation. There may not be a direct relationship between the Climber's current position and their formal education or training. However, as you look deeper, it's usually possible to see how a Climber's career has evolved by looking for clues that indicate how positions have been leveraged, like hand and footholds, to move the Climber from one position to the next.

While Climbers may be prone to change jobs more frequently than Walkers, this isn't always the case. When a Climber finds a company in which they have the potential to advance quickly, the Climber may stay for a longer period of time, assuming various positions during their tenure. Because of their natural inclination to embrace the corporate agenda, speak the language of executive management, demonstrate respect for hierarchy and authority, and network very effectively, Climbers are often selected to lead, manage, oversee, and coordinate, and are often "fast-tracked" to managerial positions.

While Climbers conduct themselves with sensitivity to the roles and positions of higher-ups, they may feel comfortable subverting authority in the name of an ambitious power move. They can be adept at garnering political and emotional capital to gain favor, or build authority and power bases. Climbers often may make career leaps across organizations, when the opportunity for advancement seems evident. However, even when leaps occur, it is common to find that the Climber's new job maintains threads of continuity from past positions.

Where Walkers have a narrow and deep lane of subject matter expertise, Climbers are most known for their ability to work within and swing across business areas applying a unique combination of hard and soft skills. While their depth of expertise within any assigned area may vary, Climbers are eminently resourceful in adapting to a variety of roles in various areas of an organization, and often leverage the wisdom and insight of other employees to do this. In looking at the Climber's background, there may be specific training in a given area. However, with some exceptions, a Climber may not have a job that leverages that formal training. For example, Sheila has a master's in engineering. While she once used those skills in the power utilities market, she hasn't used her skills as an engineer for two decades. She worked instead for lobbying groups and today serves as an executive at a high-tech non-profit and, she excels in managing relationships, prioritizing, delegating, persuading, negotiating, networking, and coordinating aspects of member participation.

A Critical Driver

Climbers place an emphasis on goals, objectives, timelines, progress, and delivery. They will take measured risks if the risk/reward ratio is acceptable and biased in their favor. They will support change if the change is aligned to organizational objectives, well-conceived, and driven by people that are qualified. While positions may vary, Climbers (especially more senior Climbers) often excel at cutting to the chase to identify priorities. They are eminently practical and pragmatic in their approach to getting things done. They excel at delegating tasks, identifying and assigning responsibilities, establishing goals and objectives, removing obstacles, and seeing to it that key milestones are hit. Collectively, this means Climbers help drive an organization measurably forward to achieve meaningful outcomes.

Climbers prefer a level of autonomy in their positions as a general rule. This is true even early in their careers, when it's essential for accountability to be present. This can be challenging to manage, as some Climbers are naturally less communicative than others. Many Climber jobs require sensitivity to the politics of the organization, and necessitate work "behind the scenes." Climbers may find themselves very engaged in esoteric tasks—like vendor discussions, contract reviews, backdoor meetings, and time-consuming negotiations. They may be called away from the office and spend a great deal of time in meetings that may or may not involve other colleagues. As a result, there may be a certain amount of ambiguity around what a Climber does on a *daily* basis, and schedule demands, activities, and contributions may not be fully understood or appreciated by peers and direct reports.

A Dual Agenda

Climbers are, in general, unapologetically ambitious and are almost always driven by a "dual agenda." This two-sided agenda typically includes the goals, objectives, and the imperatives or priorities of an organization's leadership on one side—the attainment of which allows a Climber to advance professionally. On the other side are the Climber's personal, professionally-related goals, objectives, and priorities. While a dual agenda is almost never codified in writing, at a granular level, a Climbers agenda might resemble something like this for an executive in the aerospace defense industry.

A Dual Agenda Example

ORGANIZATIONAL AGENDA	PERSONAL AGENDA
• Q2 sales of $2M	• Earn provisional bonus
• Launch Project X Phase 1	• Present recap at launch with CEO • CEO, EVP drinks with Project X intro • CEO present client award (photo opp) • Personal mention in media release • Celebration in employee newsletter
• Q3 Sales of $2.5M	• Final Project X Payment—$350k and Prep Phase 2 scope at $1.5 M • Review scope at $1.8M and land Phase 2 • Conduct account reviews and billing with Grumman and Airbus
	• Discuss and secure promotion • Renegotiate salary/bonus • Jeff promotion (right hand) • Move Mary and Josh to my team • Delegate Mary as PM for Phase 2 • CEO briefing & drinks • Game/box Seats for Project X Leads
• Pursue key targets include Project X, Boeing, Northrop Grumman and Airbus	• Golf with Frank, Bob and Skip at Boeing • Formal Boeing capabilities pitch • Scope initial work phase (and use for promotion discussion) • Attend (speak) TNS and ICDMT (Biz Dev)
• Increase market share	• Analyst relations—secure top ranking
• Increase company public visibility	• Promote releases with PR Team • Secure permission to serve as spokesperson • Have Josh line up speaking for me (TNS) • Guest posts in company blog (1x per quarter) ghost-written by Lori for me

This is just an example that shows how organizational objectives align with a Climber's personal objectives. However, in reality, a Climber's agenda is unlikely to be formal like this and much more complicated.

The Climber's agenda fuels almost every move that is made, and is pursued with strong, competitive drive and ambition. Climbers, in fact, often have trouble paying attention to anything that might feel like a departure or distraction from the agenda. The pragmatic, laser-like focus that makes Climbers so effective at aligning and driving also makes it easy for them to tune out others or to make wrong assumptions about the compatibility of other agendas with their own. While the Climber's adamant focus and tenacity can be challenging, these qualities serve an important purpose in driving organizational focus, progress, and delivery.

While it may not be consciously asked, a Climber's first question (even subconsciously) when approached with an idea or request for help is likely to be: *"How does this get me closer to achieving my objectives?"* If there's no logical or obvious tie, it may be difficult to secure engagement and support. When misalignment to the agenda is present, Climbers are apt to boldly question priorities, especially if their own game plans, deliverables, or schedules are being challenged or threatened.

In a situation where new information is presented that suggests a course of change or switching horses midstream, a Climbers may have trouble adapting. In general, Climbers like to finish what they start without interruption or distraction, often because there are rewards attached for the completion of tasks. Typically, a course alteration will only be motivated by the presence of being given no choice or the presence of either great risk or great opportunity for a potentially huge (bigger) payoff.

For the Climber, the goal is to advance to the proverbial summit. However, the summit will be different for every individual. For the Climber, success isn't always about securing a top position in a department, division, or executive team. It may be a combination of things. Some Climbers are interested in growing skills, gaining experience, or expertise. Others are interested in general professional stature. Many are interested in expanding their base of experience to fuel the ability to take on a different type of leadership role. There may be a goal of advancement that involves a lateral move to a competitor, or a desire create an alliance between two companies, or something else. While the Climber is not likely to divulge their agenda or the ultimate destination of the course they have mapped to scale to the summit, developing understanding of the Climber's agenda can be key in establishing common ground for collaboration.

A Measured External Demeanor

Climbers pay great attention to image and external appearances in themselves and others. They often present with a reasonably well-manicured exterior. While Flyers may dress as *expression of self or creativity*, Climbers often dress to *project a desired image*. Depending on the industry and work culture, a Climber's image may vary. You might find a uniform, such as a Steve Jobs-like standard turtleneck and jeans, or a sales uniform, like a branded polo or button down and a pair of khakis. In large corporate environments, you'll likely find a tailored suit that projects authority, power, and upward mobility. The desire to project a desired image often extends to the person's accessories (shoes, rings, pens, jewelry), as well as to the automobile the individual drives.

Along with a buttoned-up appearance, Climbers tend to feel uncomfortable with emotional displays, such as joy, happiness, excitement, defeat, frustration, or sadness. Any outbursts you witness are likely to be intentional and/or strategically timed. For example, Climbers know how and when to project emotion in a sales pitch or how to leverage emotion to excite and motivate teams. They understand the power of a strategically timed angry outburst as a display of power and intimidation. Climbers understand that measured emotional releases can motivate action and can be very effective. Otherwise, however, Climbers keep a lid on their emotions and typically feel uncomfortable around those they perceive as being "too emotional" at work. The discomfort will generally extend to people they perceive as "emotionally unstable" (e.g. crying at work) but this can also be directed toward anyone that communicates with what feels like "excessive" passion or enthusiasm.

Needless to say, Climbers deplore workplace drama and interpersonal conflict. Even when they find themselves in a hot-seat (and they often do), Climbers may be more inclined to dismiss, deny, or downplay conflict than to fuel the fire of dissention. Climbers dislike being publicly accused, criticized, and/or having their authority challenged. They much prefer to ignore conflict or wait for things to blow over. When necessary, they will opt to resolve issues one-on-one with as little discussion and engagement as possible. They carry disdain for petty arguments, dislike being put in the middle or being asked to take sides. They are especially sensitive to any situation that may catch the eye or ear of executive leadership, as they don't wish to be associated with anything that may mar their reputations.

A "Closed-Kimono" Communicator

Climbers are, hands down, the most reserved communicators of all three operational styles. Climbers are naturally wired to communicate what they feel is a "sufficient level of information" for the situation or task at hand. This reserved approach to information sharing is driven by three things: first, there's a desire for control and efficiency; second, there's an inclination to maintain progress rather than waste time talking about things; and third, there's a competitive instinct at work. Climbers tend to regard knowledge as power. This can create a reticence to share anything that may be used or leveraged by others. While it's a stretch to say all Climbers go out of their way to hide information from others, many Climbers will admit to intentionally withholding information from others for confidentiality, competition, or control-related reasons. Unfortunately, this can sometimes result in unclear, cryptic, or confusing communications to others. At times, a Climber may not provide enough background, detail, and/or instruction, forcing people to read between the lines and seek clarification, which can become a point of frustration for others.

In general, Climbers prefer discussions that are quick and efficient. They like to have a clear understanding of the agenda and to start at the high-level. They like to feel in control of dialog, and seek to understand problems, challenges, potential solutions, key considerations, and fuel their decision making with facts and logic first, rather than gut or emotion. They may avoid delving into explicit detail unless there's a clear benefit for doing so. Climbers appreciate people who know how to deliver an "elevator pitch" and present information in clear, bite-sized pieces, such as bullets, or short, factual statements, as well as people who stay on topic.

When it comes to day-to-day interactions, Climbers generally prefer to keep discussions and meetings focused. As a result, they are often structured to include only the most essential, and often only the most supportive, individuals. Because they know how to run a meeting and get things done, Climbers may intentionally exclude participants they feel may cause distraction or impede them from achieving a desired outcome. This can cause frustration and hard feelings with colleagues who are excluded, and become a source of conflict. Climbers also tend to share thoughts in a plain-spoken and direct way, providing input that can be to the point. They can also demonstrate a lack of patience with others. For some, this can feel curt and dismissive.

Generally speaking, Climbers do not enjoy spinning around in "vision land" for long periods of time, especially if the exercise doesn't lead to concrete next steps or action items. Climbers can become overwhelmed by too much detail, and when this happens, they will often tune out or shut down, especially when the discussion does not align to current priorities or agenda. This is the polar opposite of Flyers, who are prone to brainstorm, ideate, over-communicate, and delve into issues in a way that can involve excruciating detail. When the Climber manages to survive a demanding, in-depth, overwhelming meeting, time may be required to recover and process the information shared. This may necessitate a later regrouping, which can frustrate people who hope to secure immediate feedback and solidify next steps.

Asking questions can be instrumental in drawing out sentiments and perspective from a Climber. Once, in a one-on-one meeting where a Climber had clearly tuned out, I stopped and allowed a short pause. Without any kind of tone or frustration, I gently said, "Hey, Ben. Time is precious, and we don't seem to be connecting. I'd love to gauge where you're at now, as I think we have the same priorities. Do you disagree with this direction? Does this conflict with your priorities in some way? If so, let's talk that through." This brought Ben back on track, and he ended up apologizing for becoming distracted and admitted he had a concern, which we discussed. Depending on the individual, a similar approach may be perceived as disrespectful, in a meeting with a larger group, so it's important to choose the right approach for the situation at hand when probing with a Climber.

For some Climbers, withholding information is also a measure of self-protection. The less information that is shared, the less risk or exposure there may be. This can be particularly useful for Climbers that within work environments that involve security, sensitive data, and/or confidential information. However, in some cases, (especially situations that involve competition or within which a Climber feels threatened), the lack of sharing can be overkill—especially if a Climber withholds information as a sort of power move.

All told, whether or not a Climber's communication becomes problematic depends on the individual. The tendency to under-communicate and/or to control interactions may be more pronounced in some individuals than others. Climbers with a higher level of emotional intelligence tend to communicate in ways that are more open, inclusive, and sensitive. When this particular Climber tendency combines with emotions like fear and insecurity, communication with a Climber can become problematic. Management, peers, and direct reports may feel "left in the dark," causing confusion and frustration. In sensitivity to this issue, it's essential for Climbers to develop strong communication skills, and to take time to proactively include and communicate to teams, peers, and direct reports. It's also important for managers of Climbers to help employees cultivate good communication and sharing in professional development.

Championship & Ownership

Climbers will rarely refuse an offer to run a high-profile project when they feel equipped to succeed. This is especially true for projects that are likely to increase their visibility within the organization, provide the opportunity to work with influential people, and/or result in professional advancement. Climbers remain on the lookout for opportunities, good ideas, and ways to expand their influence and power base. When Climbers embrace an idea, concept, design, or work product, and help to promote it, they can become a powerful ally. A strategically placed Climber's support can help an individual gain exposure, traction, resources, and support required to bring a concept to reality. A Climber will rarely champion an idea that does not align to his or her agenda, and/or the Climber's designs or ideas on the future.

The challenge remains that when an idea, concept, project, etc. is embraced, there's a natural inclination for Climbers to internalize ideas and assume a kind of co-ownership over them. On the positive side, when a Climber engages actively and assumes a sense of ownership, this indicates a commitment and strong intention to support, promote, champion, and to be an advocate for the idea, concept, or project. However, on the negative side, Climbers can sometimes assume *too much* ownership for the ideas and work product of others, outshining, overriding, or undermining the true owners in a way that can damage relationships.

Even with good intentions, Climbers have the propensity to confuse championship and advocacy with literal ownership. In extreme cases, a Climber may assume such a high level of ownership, it may be perceived by others that the Climber initiated the idea and/or that they are responsible. Some Climbers may also (purposefully or inadvertently) assume credit for the ideas and/or work of others in an effort to gain favor. This can become a problematic source of stress and conflict in the workplace. To avoid this, it's important for anyone working with a Climber to recognize the potential for this to happen and maintain clear boundaries. It's also keys for Climbers to manage this propensity, as they seek to advocate for the work or ideas of others.

RELATIONSHIPS

While Climbers can be personable and relational in the workplace, they typically demonstrate a strong delineation between personal and professional relationships and rarely confuse the two. There is seldom the level of transparency and openness displayed in a work relationship that might be found in a Climber's personal relationships. In work relationships, Climbers tend to maintain boundaries about what they share, who they share with, and insights they may give into their personal lives or future plans. One exception to this may be incidents where Climbers form work-related romantic entanglements, though these are not exclusive to Climbers, per se. However, when such relationships form, there is typically an attempt to conceal such relationships from coworkers and associates.

Climbers with a higher level of emotional intelligence usually establish strong, positive workplace relationships, and often stand out as dynamic, affable coworkers and people managers. Climbers are often described as having winning or charming personalities. While placement on the introversion/extroversion scale will vary, Climbers are often described as smooth operators with disarming and persuasive qualities. Many seasoned Climbers develop a keen ability to motivate, lead, and inspire people. When operating on all "pros," Climbers can make incredible leaders and managers, which often catches the attention of top brass.

While there is a reserved and competitive spirit in the ranks of the Climber, they usually partner well with people that have complementary or shared agendas. In general, Climbers tend to help each other out in the workplace. This comes naturally as Climbers tend to speak a common language that requires few words to communicate a motherlode, and selectively watch each other's backs. However as with all relationships, there tends to be a vacillation between collaboration and competition. Generally speaking, when Climbers work with other like-minded individuals, from shared goals and objectives, with clear roles and team members operating within their strengths, they can be highly effective in driving and supporting outstanding collaborations.

At times, Climbers often form strong and productive bonds with individuals that are so strong, certain individuals become right-hand resources for the longer term. Typically, these relationships are marked by a natural rapport and a mutual understanding that streamlines communication and fuels productivity. The "key people" in the Climber's inner circle understand the Climber's modus operandi and often become favored individuals upon which a Climber relies. Climbers and "key people" (who can be other Climbers, Walkers, or even Flyers) tend to anchor each other, much like someone handling the "belay" would on a climbing wall. As Climbers and key people belay each other on the wall of achievement, they help each other achieve and scale to new heights. These partnerships can be so strong and effective, it is common for Climbers to attempt to bring "key people" with them, from one position to another, as they advance from one job to the next.

The Light of Favor

When Climbers need something from someone, they have a unique ability to shine "a light of favor" that can make that almost anyone feel needed, useful, valuable, appreciated—even special and indispensable. These feelings often motivate people to provide generous, and even sacrificial support. This light of favor effect helps the Climber motivate, inspire, delegate, garner favor, and leverage people and situations to their own benefit. This can make Climbers super effective at delegation, rallying people to a cause. However, Climbers must be careful using this gift, as the "light of favor" also has a down side.

Climbers who don't have a high level of self-awareness or emotional intelligence must be cautious about having a "utilitarian" view of people. This is important because, when the Climber's focus shifts, the "light of favor" shifts, too. When this happens, people with whom the Climber has previously engaged may feel abandoned, disregarded, taken for granted, and/or used. They may also become jealous of the person on whom the light falls next. This usually happens inadvertently, as an outcome of the Climber's gift of laser-like focus that often involves the exclusion of all else! However, when the favor shifts and people suddenly feel ignored, it can negatively impact relationships, as well as the Climber's reputation. In such cases, you may hear people complain about a Climber being a person who uses or dumps on others.

I once had a Climber boss that did this so often, he prepared people for it up front. He described his management style with a speech like this: "Listen," he said. "When I need something, I will be up in your grill and it will feel invasive. When I am done, I will very likely go dark on you. When this happens, you may be inclined to think I am ignoring you, upset, or angry. I am not. I am merely busy and focused on other things. If you get stuck and need input, bust down my door. Otherwise, press forward without me. Don't assume there's a problem, unless I tell you there is one. If there is problem, I will let you know."

Master Networkers

Climbers are skilled at diplomacy, and as previously stated, they pay a lot of careful attention to social structures and networks, positional authority, connections, and politics in the work environment. They place substantial emphasis on building and strengthening strategic ties with influential individuals, including those in upper management, people in power, or in positions of influence. They will seize opportunities to meet and network with "the right" people. Climbers may also seek positions on boards and committees to bolster their influence. They are more prone to join professional and industry networking groups. They often exhibit a slick resourcefulness and leverage contacts to gain favor in places that matter. Climbers also tend to be confident about self-promotion. However, in presenting themselves to others, some may embellish the truth when it comes to past roles, responsibilities, and accomplishments.

Climbers leverage work-related social opportunities to make deals, form alliances, hatch plans or schemes, and solve problems. If there's a benefit to attending a work-related event, you'll typically find a Climber there, huddled over cocktails, taking time to schmooze with all the right people. Many make a concerted effort to engage in strategic recreational bonding with internal and external colleagues, too. This may be a meeting over drinks or a meal. You may also see a Climber shaking hands in a box seat at a sporting event, enjoying a round of golf with strategic contacts, playing racquet-ball with a department head, and more.

In the bonds of relationship, Climbers will often use political capital to pull strings, do favors, and connect people. In fact, gifts, notes, flattery, and personal or professional favors are important tools used to initiate, build, reward, or strengthen alliances. While Climbers often do nice things out of a genuine desire to help others, they remain consciously aware that acts of good will help bolster their relationships and set up the possibility of a quid pro quo down the road.

WORKING WITH & MANAGING CLIMBERS

Climbers tend to be guarded, and trust and mutual respect must be earned. The best way to earn a Climber's respect and trust is to maintain professionalism, map to his or her agenda, demonstrate strong boundaries, deliver well, and communicate succinctly. While chapter 12 contains specific insights and tips for managing inter-style dynamics, the following information may generally assist when working with or managing a Climber:

Resonating with the Agenda

A key component of working with and managing a Climber involves the ability to align to the Climber's agenda. This can be tricky because it's unlikely the Climber will show you that agenda. Instead, it's up to you to read clues, ask questions, and connect the dots. For colleagues, developing an understanding of Climber's role and function and working in a way that speaks to the Climber's agenda is critical to establish mutual understanding and common ground. When a Climber views you as instrumental in helping support their agenda, it opens the door for better communication and collaboration.

Managers of Climbers have the unique ability to help define one side of the agenda by helping establish role, authority, priorities, goals, objectives, and performance metrics. They may also be influential in helping the Climber determine the other side of the agenda, too, by supporting plans for individual growth and professional development. This is especially true for younger Climbers in earlier career phases. It's important to make sure to lay out priorities, goals, and objectives, as these will fuel the Climber's activities and behavior with sensitivity to pros and pitfalls. It's also important to set expectations related to conduct, communications, teamwork, and the rewards that will be tied to the achievement of goals, to keep the Climber motivated.

The Simple & Sensible Approach

You wouldn't approach an actual Climber, hanging off a mountainside from a rope, with a silver platter of tiny sandwiches and hot tea served in a delicate china teacup! Instead, you'd more likely, hand that Climber a Clif Bar along with a swig from a canteen. It's important to approach the Climbers in your workplace with the same resolve: Climbers are reticent to become tangled in too much detail. Help them process what you have to say by communicating your ideas in clear, digestible, and relevant pieces. Remember that Climbers demonstrate incredible tenacity in maintaining focus—like maintaining a grip. When it comes to changing ideas, game plans, or direction, remove threats to make it feel safe and sensible to alter the course. Remain firm and tenacious, matching strength with strength as you work with a Climber. Stay the course as you work to establish common ground and find mutual wins.

Dealing with Change

Climbers are much more likely to support change when it supports their agenda, or when the change-related initiative is clearly in an organization's best interest and/or does not impede or threaten the Climber's agenda. However, Climbers can also be skeptics when it comes to dealing with change inside an organization. There are a number of reasons for this. Like experienced Walkers, many seasoned Climbers have often seen more than their fair share of misguided attempts to change and improve the organization and remain skeptical about the potential for positive outcomes. In some instances, Climbers get too comfortable in their role or function and reject efforts to change things up because of the disruption, cost, and work it may entail. Change resistance can be particularly pronounced when a change-related initiative puts a Climber's goals and objectives at risk. In these cases, the Climbers can be more than skeptical—they can become obstacles.

When Climbers become threatened by change, they may exhibit resistance or denial. However, in worst cases, Climbers can become direct opponents of change, standing against it, or the agent(s) of change and even resisting or refusing to cooperate. The only way to deal with change resistance in a Climber is to meet it head-on. When the Climbers can see the benefits of cooperation, and understand how they will be measured through cooperation, they are likely to turn around. If they refuse, they are not likely to last with an organization long. Managers should confront resistance quickly, and make expectations clear. Peers in a position of driving change should do their best to demonstrate "what's in it" for the Climber. It may also be helpful to assist the Climber in sorting out the implications of the change initiative on specific goals and objectives, and help reset expectations as necessary.

Knocking Over Obstacles

Climbers are headstrong and determined to win. When obstacles exist, they typically study situations carefully and develop an approach to remove them. When the issues are political or leadership-driven, Climbers tend to be cautious in their approach, relying on private conversations to methodically break down barriers. Climbers are self-preservationists that may be generally reticent to create a political chasm by confronting leadership aggressively or ambitiously, unless a challenge is absolutely necessary to meet specific objectives. In resolving conflicts, they may demonstrate a quiet exterior, especially if they are busy working on issues outside of public view, leveraging situations and people to resolve problems methodically.

When issues or problems are not highly political, Climbers are not typically shy about taking decisive action or using aggressive tactics to remove competitors, stumbling blocks, or barriers to achievement. Climbers may publicly challenge or (depending on the individual) even denigrate people who get in the way, posing a threat or distraction from their agenda. They can, at times, behave in ways that are calculating, insensitive, and indifferent to the plight of others. This can get a Climber in trouble, as behavior can stray into grey areas of professional conduct and/or ethics.

For example, while many Climbers would never consider "throwing someone under the bus" for their own gain, there are plenty of Climbers that have no qualms about doing so. The same is true for crushing competition or taking out an enemy. Some Climbers will readily sacrifice a relationship or alliance if it meets a strategic aim. As a result, shrewd behavior and shifting loyalties can be common with Climbers. However, whether or not a Climber's behavior crosses ethical boundaries and to what degree this behavior occurs depends on the individual Climber, as guided by their own moral and ethical compass. In general, like all of us, Climbers need to exercise caution as they remove obstacles in ways that may take a human toll.

When roadblocks inside an organization become insurmountable, the investment necessary to turn the tide to a Climber's favor is disproportionately high, and/or opportunities for advancement seem limited, Climbers don't usually waste time in moving on. In response to overwhelming obstacles, they will often look for another hill to climb. This may involve an attempt to move laterally to another department, a new job search, or a leave of absence.

Managing a Climber

Climbers have a natural propensity to lead, but their ultimate success as a leader is dependent on their level of self-awareness, how effectively they manage their pitfalls, how well they've been trained, and their level of emotional intelligence. When managing a Climber, it's important to build in mechanisms to measure their success based on the quality of the journey and not just the arrival at the destination. Good Climber managers actively establish parameters that help Climbers learn to inspire, develop, and lead people, collaborate effectively, and ensure team success. Establishing performance metrics, key projects, and milestones along with goals for people management and communication can help any Climber successfully carve out a position that goes beyond entry to management to becoming a truly effective leader.

It's important for management to tune in to perceptions held about a Climber by other managers, peers, and subordinates. When operating from their strengths, Climbers are effective, motivational leaders that can drive exceptional business results and manage people well. When operating from pitfalls, Climbers can be very poor managers that may develop reputations that are less than positive. What a manager sees and experiences within the context of controlled meetings and interactions may not accurately represent the relational dynamics at play with a Climber direct report. This is in part due to the Climber's artful way of "managing up" with senior leadership. By tuning in to a Climber's pros and pitfalls, and obtaining feedback from others, Climber managers can help Climbers embrace strengths and potential, while they mitigate risks, learning to manage and delegate in a way that motivates and inspires others.

Cultivating a Climber's natural propensity to lead is an honorable task, and despite the potential an individual may show, it's important not to move too quickly. Climbers need time in the trenches doing the hard work to develop empathy and sensitivity to others. Fast-tracking a Climber too quickly can build ego too fast, and result in a headstrong managerial type that behaves more like a dictator than a leader. Good Climber managers help their Climbers understand how they are wired, where their natural pros and pitfalls lie, and help them tame ambition so they can grow to become inspiring and motivational leaders, who recognize that the journey we take people on is just as important as the destination.

Pitfalls & Coaching

While coaching needs vary with each individual, most Climbers need to work on emotional intelligence and carefully demonstrate respect for others in the workplace. While this isn't usually a problem for Climbers working with senior staffers, actively demonstrating respect with peers and direct reports may be entirely different. When Climbers fail to treat others with sensitivity and respect, their reputations suffer, and their delivery and leadership are compromised.

Climbers with many active pitfalls may be reputed as individuals who try to work around "the system" at the expense of others, as people who disregard rules, create additional work for others, or cause hassle and frustration for others. They may be accused of taking credit for the work and ideas of other people. They may be accused of dumping on people or using people. When things go bad, Climbers may seem unwilling to own their mistakes due to a natural self-preservation instinct and propensity to minimize their actions and pass the buck or blame on others. This is especially true when they feel threatened or fear retribution.

The most successful Climbers prioritize *care, communication,* and *credit* in their interactions with others. Without care, the Climber's demeanor may come across as self-seeking, short, rude, calculating, disrespectful, or dismissive. Without good communication, coworkers and direct reports may feel lost, disregarded, disrespected, and out of the loop, making it impossible to manage others well. Without giving others credit, a Climber may be accused of being usurious, or of being guilty of ethical violations, compromising trust and collaboration, and putting the organization at risk.

Upsetting a Climber

Climbers tend to mask their feelings rather well. However, there are an array of behaviors that are prone to upset a Climber that may result in backlash or retribution. These include:

- Being prevented from progressing against established goals and objectives
- Lack of career progression or advancement, despite hitting objectives
- Losing a fight or battle, especially in a publicly visible manner
- Having territory invaded or having staff commandeered, or reallocated
- Being forced to change course or switch horses midstream
- Being demoted, undermined, exposed, or professionally embarrassed
- Substantial delays that may compromise the accomplishment of key objectives
- Being drawn into conflict or drama or made the subject of gossip
- Being publicly criticized or challenged
- Subversive behavior—e.g. "going over my head"
- Behavior that indicates disrespect or disregard
- Lofty ideas or pontification, without action, real problem solving, or getting to clarity
- People who cannot focus, summarize, and present their ideas clearly
- Long, drawn out, questionably useful meetings
- Getting tangled in process at the expense of progress

Advancement & Rewards

Climbers often perform well with incentive-based pay structures that provide monetary reward and payouts tied to financial performance, deals, sales, and the achievement of key objectives. Climbers enjoy having the flexibility to work harder to improve their financial situation, and feel energized by rewards tied directly to accomplishment. Beyond pay structure, Climbers also care about compensation packages, including medical, dental and vision benefits; paid time off and leave policies; stock options;

stock purchase; profit-sharing plans; tuition reimbursement; 401(k) and pension plans; and other benefits.

At performance review time, Climbers typically provide excellent back-up material to illustrate how they have realized their objectives and goals for the year. When expectations are met, Climbers expect the company to fulfill obligations to reward good performance. Climbers can be bold in asking or demanding things they want, including pay raises and promotions, and often won't wait for a review to do so. During the review process, there may be a tendency for the Climber to fixate on goals and objectives that were met and/or exceeded. However, it's also important to examine *how* those goals and objectives were met and provide critical feedback, if needed, as a gateway for coaching.

Climbers are incredibly sensitive to criticism, and are hard-pressed to admit wrongdoing, so be prepared for defensiveness and to back up your feedback with concrete examples to make your case. In alignment with best practices, deliver feedback with positive body language, smiles, and positive gestures. Allow the Climber to thoughtfully respond and/or ask questions. Be sure to put the feedback in writing, to help codify and underscore the importance of it, and hold the Climber accountable and ensure improvement criteria are articulated in formal goal-setting.

Climbers are ambitious and often have high expectations regarding professional advancement. Sometimes those expectations may not be properly aligned, so it's important to level-set. As with anyone, when expectations misalign, rewards are withheld, and/or promises are not kept, the Climber may become disgruntled and dissatisfied. While big rewards, in a Climber's mind, often have to do with promotion and monetary gain, Climbers may also be motivated by the provision of additional resources, the chance to run a special project or high-profile initiative, to grow or build a team, to engage in networking opportunities, and other factors. If an organization is undergoing hardship, a Climber may be temporarily satiated by a bump in title in lieu of a raise. Other rewards that may be appreciated include comp days, conference attendance, networking opportunities, tickets to exclusive events, lunches with executive leaders, and other perks.

Climber Transitions

Climbers do their best to leave positions with relationships and reputation intact, and typically have no desire to leave on a bad note. However, this does happen. To protect your organization during a key transition, it may be helpful to consider the competitive nature of a Climber, as well as the strong level of ownership Climbers place on their work product and business contacts. It may be wise to have an iron-clad confidentiality, non-disclosure and non-compete as a part of the employment contract, as well as a clear definition of intellectual property. While it may be difficult to prevent a Climber from reaching out to business contacts upon departure, you can take measures to protect your organization. It may also make sense to have a provision that excludes the Climber from recruiting your firm's talent upon departure. Furthermore, when a Climber is terminated or resigns, it is also wise to make sure that any final paycheck or payout is contingent upon a full knowledge transfer and other company-determined criteria.

CHAPTER 7
FLYERS

FLYER
TRAITS & SELF-ASSESSMENT

Traits that are common in individuals with this operational style are listed below. Place a checkmark (☑) in the box next to each trait below that is "absolutely or mostly like me." Place an "x" mark (☒) in the box next to every trait that is "absolutely or mostly not like me." Leave anything you are not sure about blank. Answer objectively based on how you are in a *work-setting only* and *across your entire career*—not just your current job!

FLYER PROS	FLYER PITFALLS
VIEW OF JOB/WORK	
☐ Work is critically tied to personal identity	☐ Prone to anxiety and depression when work is not going well
☐ Work is integral to a sense of higher mission, purpose, and calling	☐ Takes work personally—can become invested to the point that it becomes unhealthy

EMPLOYMENT/CAREER PROGRESSION

☐ May have an "atypical" career back-story that links education, work history, and past positions to the present	☐ Career progression isn't always logical—might seem unfocused or "all over the place"
☐ May have entrepreneurial (self-employed/startup) or "intrapraneurial" (inside development) skills or aptitude	
☐ Multidisciplinary talent, ability, specialization, expertise, or knowledge—"swings wide and hits deep"	☐ Difficult to succinctly communicate and/or make people understand "what I do for a living"
☐ Motivated by freedom and latitude to explore and build	☐ May desire more freedom than a traditional organization may be willing to offer
☐ Doing stimulating, "cool," interesting work is more important than title, power, or authority	☐ May demonstrate insensitivity or disregard for the territory or authority of others, creating conflict—often inadvertent

FOCUS/PURPOSE

☐ "Future Builder"—establishes vision that drives the evolution of the organization	☐ Stimulus junkie with fear of the mundane
☐ Strategic visionary with broad, unique perspective—a true "out-of-the-box" thinker	☐ Vision and ideas are sometimes well "ahead of their time" and/or difficult to share in a way that motivates acceptance
☐ Develops strategies, roadmaps, new products, services, starting up ventures that position organization for the future	☐ Not "wired" for tasks such as ongoing maintenance, item processing, or overseeing repetitive or rote tasks
☐ Unique ability to both create actionable strategies and execute them	☐ Constant vacillation between big-picture vision and executional detail can "confuse and lose"

MANAGEMENT

☐ Tends to thrive in environments with less structure or hierarchy, and more flexibility	☐ Lack of structure and discipline may frustrate others
☐ Not bound by traditional way of doing things—leverages own, unique process for working and collaborating	☐ Unique process can feel foreign, uncomfortable, confusing, and/or hard to follow for others

MANAGEMENT *(continued)*

☐ Embraces "flow" in the completion of work or tasks—prefers to focus where the energy is found	☐ "Flow" may not align with deadlines and deliverable dates, causing delays or missed handoff (especially in early career)
☐ Broad, unique perspective challenges people to adopt bigger-picture view—explore, pioneer, and build	☐ May be prone to redirect people—preventing them from finishing other work that has been started.
☐ Works well autonomously without a lot of oversight	☐ May become "wrapped around the axle" when prioritizing or problem solving and require outside input
☐ When productively engaged and "in the zone," it can produce a caffeinated high that sustains engagement	☐ Prone to become "lost in work"—and may demonstrate insensitivity to the energy levels and engagement of others
☐ Dress/attire may be a form of self-expression or reflection of creativity	☐ May demonstrate resistance toward (or dislike for) traditional professional attire
☐ Typically works long days, intense hours	☐ Prone to take on too much—overwork and grapple with burnout
	☐ May have difficulty delegating or transitioning work in final stages to new owners

CHANGE & RISK

☐ Natural change agent, proponent of change and catalyst	☐ Propensity to "stir things up," making others feel uncomfortable or threatened and impacting relationships
☐ Unafraid to challenge the status quo, question, or probe into the way things are done, with an eye to improve	☐ Propensity to challenge, question, and probe may threaten individuals in "comfort zones"
☐ Transformation agent—helps organization embrace new ways of functioning	☐ Expectations or hopes for transformation may clash with an organization's inertia

CHANGE & RISK (continued)

☐ Higher proclivity to take managed risks	☐ May take risks that have negative downstream impacts
☐ Initiative taker—may prefer to ask for forgiveness rather than permission	☐ May proceed without clear mandate or authority, creating confusion, frustration, or trouble
	☐ Propensity to cross boundaries in ways that may concern, offend, worry, threaten, alarm others, and/or cause problems

COMMUNICATION & COLLABORATION

☐ Naturally open and inclusive communicator and collaborator	☐ Prone to overcommunicate, saturate, distract, and overwhelm people with ideas and information
☐ Typically willing to engage, help—desire to be useful and solve problems	☐ Prone to take on too much—may struggle to juggle competing priorities
☐ Energized by brainstorming, ideation, and intense engagement with others	☐ Intense engagement often exhausts others and can make them reticent to engage in the future
☐ Creative problem solver who generates prolific number of ideas—from practical to whimsical, tactical to strategic	☐ Produces more ideas than may be practical or actionable—ideas may outstrip organizational capabilities
	☐ Can become attached to own ideas or perceptions and inadvertently "steamroll" over others
☐ Demonstrates passion, enthusiasm, and excitement for work—may be a "whirlwind" of energy (especially early in career)	☐ Challenged to control energy levels—passion and excitement may overwhelm others and/or be perceived as immature
☐ Leverages diverse background, experience, and strong conceptual skills to help guide and facilitate teams and activities	☐ Prone to distraction that can interrupt focus—may pursue mental "rabbit trails" or topical tangents

COMMUNICATION & COLLABORATION *(continued)*

☐ Excels at assimilating information across an array of areas, stakeholders, disciplines, industries to inform approach	☐ May require reminders to ensure all necessary stakeholders are included (especially early in career)
☐ Naturally "maps" or under-stands the interconnections between people, process, flow, functional areas, etc.	☐ May become preoccupied exploring the many inter-connections between things
☐ Excels in ability to process and organize extensive, complex information across areas, specialization, or disciplines	☐ Devotes significant time to reviewing and processing information, making it difficult for others to keep up
☐ Places importance on adhering to the outcome that is visualized—wants to "get things right"	☐ Accused of perfectionism
☐ Ability to work cross-functionally to assume a variety of roles across any organization	☐ May have multiple jobs— prone to struggle with job "fit" / professional alignment

RELATIONSHIPS

☐ Prone to be open, transparent, trusting, and inclusive	☐ May be too open (frank, honest), trusting, and inclusive leading to offense or betrayal
☐ Bonds with others through collabora-tion, ideation, and building	☐ Intense engagement style may be "too much" for some individuals
☐ Establishes a "flock" of like-minded individuals from work, within trade and/or industry who become sounding boards	☐ May be difficult to find like minded, "people like me" job—resulting in "lone eagle" effect
☐ Significant number of personal friendships may be garnered from job, industry, or professional connections	
☐ Lack of separation between work life and personal life	☐ Work often invades personal time—causing backlash with loved ones

FLYER FUNDAMENTALS

The Future Builder

Flyers are visionary leaders that carry broad, unique perspective and fresh vision that drives the future development and evolution of an organization. Flyers have an almost prophetic ability to see and sense the future, and the ability to carve out paths to get there. Flyers see beyond traditional boundaries to reimagine work and business, thinking way outside the box with passion and excitement. They are inclusive catalysts who assimilate information to develop a "big picture" view of an organization's needs, working across stakeholder groups, departments, and divisions, and considering the needs of management, employees, customers, and prospects, as well as trends and market forces.

Position Gravitation

Flyers are not relegated to specific roles or functions and can operate at any rank within the organizational hierarchy. While they can be found anywhere, I have noted that Flyers often gravitate to positions involving strategy, creativity, and development. They may be active in supporting business, product, and channel development; starting new initiatives; or running leading edge areas of business expansion. They are often found working in areas like marketing, advertising, and creative services. They may leverage their skills as architects, developers, or technologists, or stand at the forefront of emerging technologies, business, and markets. Flyers may gravitate to "intrapreneurial" positions (e.g. incubators, new business development, spin offs) inside organizations. They may also be very active entrepreneurs (self-employment, startups). Flyers tend to thrive in positions that require multidisciplinary skills and can perform well in consultative roles.

Work & Identity

A Flyer's work plays a very strong, critical role in fueling a sense of personal identity. While a Flyer's identity may not *wholly* be defined by a job, the Flyer's work will have a very significant impact on the Flyer's sense of self-worth and well-being. Most of the time, Flyers find it hard to separate work from personal life. For the Flyer, this feels natural and comes with the territory. However, this is something that must be managed, if not to ensure a healthier work/life balance for the Flyer, but out of courtesy and respect to others who may not function the same way. The lack of work/life balance and boundaries, and propensity to become sucked in to work can often be challenging for those close to the Flyer, as work-related demands often invade personal time.

Work & Purpose

While a sense of purpose in work is not relegated to Flyers alone, Flyers are the most likely to associate their work with a sense of mission, purpose, and higher calling. As a result, Flyers devote an inordinate amount of time, passion, and dedication to work-related pursuits. Flyers tend to see the work they do as their contribution—to their organization, clients, industry, society, and even to the world at large. To do their best work, Flyers require a level of latitude and freedom and an organizational culture that welcomes their "wings." When work is going well, Flyers come alive with passion, demonstrating high engagement, energy, and productivity. Flyers fail to thrive, however, in workplaces within which their wings are clipped, they are put on a tight leash, or they find themselves feeling boxed in or suppressed. This creates an environment of stress under which a Flyer will have difficulty performing and can lead to frustration, disengagement, burnout, and/or depression.

Employment Curve

There's no equivalent of a jet trail that will help you follow a Flyer's career evolution. While a career history may contain threads of continuity, examining a Flyer's job progression may read a bit like an action novel—or even a comic book – depending on the individual. Whatever the case, Flyers usually have an interesting back story. They almost always have multiple lanes of specialization that tend to build over time, and with work experience. To some, a Flyer's a lack of "career focus" might seem undisciplined. However, in most cases, the Flyer's career history demonstrates the individual's ability to authentically "swing wide and hit deep" across many disciplines and areas of business.

In viewing a Flyer's resume, depending on length of time in the workforce, you may notice one or more career shifts. Flyers tend to have diverse interests and their job titles often map out the evolution of these interests and passions over time. This means Flyers typically move in fluid form across different industries and sectors, while obtaining experience with a variety of different companies. This fuels a multidisciplinary approach to work that can be highly beneficial to organizations.

In general, Flyers typically stay with companies for comparatively shorter periods of time when compared to Walkers. Typically, they will stay as long as they feel they are making a meaningful contribution. They will typically leave to pursue opportunity, challenge, stimulation, and do other "cool work." Flyers are natural pioneers and "builders." For this reason, a Flyer's work history may include period(s) of self-employment and will usually reflect intrapreneurial (new ventures, new products, etc.) and/or entrepreneurial (startups, self-employment, etc.) experience.

Broad Skills & Abilities

I once heard a woman describe the Flyer as a kind of human Swiss Army Knife. As she explained it, Flyers can be leveraged in many ways inside an organization and "come in handy" in various situations. Each blade of the knife is a different area of insight, specialization, or ability. In many ways, this is true. Flyers are multidisciplinary workers who excel at performing in a variety of roles. Many invent their own roles or job positions, and often maintain multiple roles within the same organization. This make it difficult for others to explain what a particular Flyer "does for a living." In fact, one of the telltale signs of a Flyer is the difficulty others have in explaining what they do, as very often, there's no short description!

Flyers almost always possess a diverse background and unique mix of hard and soft skills as well as the ability to think both conceptually and analytically. They are natural initiative takers, problem solvers, and builders who are knowledge-hungry and eager to learn things they don't know. They can be prone to distraction and may struggle with maintaining focus or juggling competing priorities. When they are focused intently, they are incredibly productive. Experienced Flyers are often known for being passionate and dedicated—often as being creative, though there are many Flyers who are more "left-brained."

Depending on maturity, discipline, and experience, however, the quality of execution may vary. In early career phases, Flyers are prone to testing waters in different areas of business, working in different areas and/or trades. This can make them behave in a way that seems non-committal or scattered in their focus. However, most are just trying to figure out what they like to do best, which can be difficult, because most Flyers like to do many things. With experience and time, these problems tend to resolve themselves, as Flyers lean in to the idea that they can be professionally happy doing many of the things they love, and find employers who appreciate the unique mix of skills and abilities they bring to the table.

Bold, Visionary Perspective

Flyers infuse an organization with fresh vision and open the door to new considerations and possibilities. Flyers excel at helping people adopt fresh perspective, think outside the box, press the envelope, and drive to the future with enthusiasm and bold confidence. They are natural risk takers who prefer to proactively address problems, without regard to ego or politics. They excel at truth-telling, problem-solving, and solutions development. Flyers point the way to the future by developing and executing strategies, creating roadmaps and development plans and products that fuel business development, organizational change, process improvement, and growth.

Flyers are rarely short on ideas. They produce many strong, practical, and well-informed suggestions ranging from the practical to the whimsical and even experimental ideas that often prove to be "years ahead" of their time. However, for management and coworkers, it may be difficult to *channel* the prolific ideas and vision of the Flyer, which can be overwhelming and challenging to manage. Further, Flyers don't always proceed with sensitivity to timing, organizational priorities, politics, and other concerns. As a result, they are often guilty of offending or making others feel threatened and of stepping on political landmines. For the "grounded" managers and colleagues that work with a Flyer, perhaps the biggest challenge of working with a Flyer involves processing the Flyer's many ideas to identify and selecting the ones that don't outstrip organizational capabilities, and are the most feasible, actionable, profitable, and beneficial to pursue. In fact, several of the Flyer CEOs I know wisely installed layers (of direct reports) between them and the rest of the organization, to absorbs ideas, so they do not constantly redirect people to new initiatives without finishing what has been started.

High-Level + Detail Focus

The Flyer's process for discovery, ideation, and collaboration can be simulating, fun, and engaging. It can also be completely overwhelming, frustrating, and exhausting to engage with a Flyer for Walkers and Climbers. Flyers can seem to be "all over the place" to outside observers. Flyers without maturity and experience often have a hard time "getting to the point" or reaching "actionable outcomes," which may frustrate others after intense periods of engagement. Seasoned Flyers typically manage this better.

From the Flyer's cockpit, an amazing vista of opportunity can be seen, with many different pathways to explore and interconnections to investigate.

Flyers are naturally curious and hungry to learn what they don't know. As a result, part of the Flyer's process involves probing and asking questions that may make people uncomfortable, seem questionably related to the topic at hand—and sometimes, feel invasive. It's very common for people to be thinking, "Why do you need to know this?" in discussions with a Flyer. However, it's important to remember that Flyers are connectors—of ideas, concepts, details, and data. When they are probing and seeking, they are really looking to inform their perspectives with as much information as possible. To the Flyer, there may not be a clear understanding of what data may be "extraneous."

For the Flyer, vision and ideas materialize like an emerging landmark from a great distance. They work hard to gather input and perspectives of diverse stakeholders to "break through the fog" of ambiguity. As information builds, so does the vision. What materializes can be a slew of ideas and a clear picture of an organization's "landscape of opportunity," including challenges, risks, or areas of potential weaknesses and opportunities. This can fuel plans and recommendations for the future that merit further discussion and evaluation, as well as entirely new undertakings and initiatives.

Flyers excel at assimilating information across disparate parts of an organization, and mix in an understanding with knowledge of operations, industry, markets, trends, and other information. Visioning work for the Flyer is typically challenging, primarily because they work with individuals from different areas of an organization that operate from "different elevations" or vantage points—who often have very different perspectives. At times, these individuals also have competing priorities, which can complicate collaboration and the problem-solving process. This can make it hard for Flyer catalysts to establish a central-point of reference or starting point that has everyone "on the same page." As Flyers assimilate information from different stakeholders, they begin to develop a clear picture of the forces at play, or the "30,000-foot view." The challenge remains that it is often very hard for the Flyer to describe what they see without overwhelming or losing people.

In truth, a Flyer's process can feel like a bit of a "wild ride"—like jumping in a small aircraft to explore a landscape, mixed with some disorienting aerial maneuvers. When participating in discussion, ideation, brainstorming, or collaboration, it may be difficult to deal with what may be described as a Flyer's "rapid rack focus." At one minute, you may find yourself talking about things at a very high picture level. Suddenly, and often without warning, the Flyer may "tuck the wings" and dive down to explore something in great detail—often for reasons that are not clear to others. Minutes later, the Flyer may shoot into the clouds again, and resume discussions at a high level—or move on to examine another part of the territory they see in depth. This process can be very hard to follow for others, who can become frustrated, overwhelmed, and lost. Flyers often forget that in collaboration and discussion—unlike a real plane ride—collaborative participants are not riding *alongside* in the Flyer's cockpit. Therefore, it is up to the Flyer to bring the audience along on the journey with good communication and facilitation skills to make them feel more comfortable and safe. Depending on the Flyer, as well as the individual's level of experience and the audience, results may vary. Less experienced Flyers may struggle to communicate and facilitate well. More seasoned Flyers typically learn in time. Others bring in backup facilitators to help.

Challenge & Change

Flyers are stimulus junkies who love a challenge and who are often proponents of change. They are most interested in doing work that involves planning and building for the future, moving the organization into a new way of doing things. They tend to have a fear of the mundane and are typically uninterested in maintaining anything for any extended period of time. When given a choice, a Flyer will prefer a job or role that involves critical thinking, agility, variety, spontaneity, and challenge. They may not prefer jobs that feel restrictive, involve rote assignment, collation, processing, repetitive tasks, or a great deal of regimentation.

While Walkers and Climbers can also be knowledge hungry workers, Flyers in particular enjoy learning new things and often teach themselves new skills "for fun." Many of these skills become handy and useful at work, becoming "additional blades" on the "Swiss ability knife." Also, because Flyers enjoy interacting and learning, they especially benefit from the knowledge and insight of subject-matter experts like Walkers. Flyers have a knack for discovering gaps, pain points, and potential problems that may disrupt productivity or compromise outcomes. However, while they do this with earnest intentions of making improvements, this can feel a bit threatening to other people. As such, Flyers can gain a reputation for stirring up trouble!

Just like eagles stir up the air with their wings, Flyers stir up the winds of change inside the companies they serve. Flyers naturally challenge the status quo, willingly and intentionally crossing boundaries. The ideas and perspective Flyers offer will almost always rock the world of people who work within a comfort zone. Further, while the Flyer's maneuvers are often well-intentioned, they can (especially in earlier career phases), be ill-informed and problematic—especially if the Flyer has not been given a mandate to change things! When Flyers begin to challenge, criticize (directly or indirectly), or question the way things are, people often feel slighted or threatened, and backlash can ensue. Flyers can come across as "know-it-alls" that invade people's spaces, and must carefully manage how they engage with others, and manage the perceptions of others. Collectively, a Flyer's ability to serve as a positive change agent depends on the individual's maturity, ability to engage with others effectively, communicate well, and become well-informed by successfully engaging the right people, the right way.

It's important to recognize that Flyer behavior is almost always motivated by a sincere passion and desire to usher in mutually beneficial improvements. Flyers don't mean to step on toes, and they tend to be equal opportunity "toe steppers!" Part of the Flyer's gift is an almost naïve willingness to question the way things are done, to upset hierarchy, test authority, contest the rules, cross boundaries, experiment, and challenge the status-quo. While this is part of the Flyer's gift, at times the Flyer naivety can work against them, as they assume other people will be as open to change and challenge as they themselves are! While Flyers can present great ideas and recommendations for future innovation and improvement, the invasive questioning or probing can raise some hackles. This is especially true for Flyers that don't have the right positional alignment, authority, or executive support. To avoid painful clashes and costly setbacks, Flyers must use caution to avoid stepping on landmines or upsetting the wrong people, working with mandate and authority with a strong sensitivity to others.

Structure & Balance

Flyers tend to thrive in environments marked by ambiguity and a lack of structure. In fact, Flyers tend to be rather unstructured, themselves—especially earlier in their careers—and like to progress with a degree of freedom to embrace a kind of energetic "flow" in their work. Flyers tend to have their own, non-traditional approach to getting things done. They don't typically require a lot of supervision, although many do like to touch base periodically (and usually with intensity) to validate they are on the right track with management and peers.

Flyers are resourceful individuals who can easily carve out their own role or function, if one has not been clearly established for them already. They are highly adaptable and tend to figure out quickly where they can make themselves most useful. This can make Flyers ideal for startup companies or departments that tend to be under-resourced. Flyers are happiest when purposefully engaged and often wear multiple hats or fill multiple roles. The most effective Flyers establish their own kind of structure to optimize their own productivity, and appreciate (and take seriously) delivery dates and milestones. They seek assistance when they get stuck, and often take pride in *overdelivering.*

It is important for Flyer managers to keep tabs on the Flyer's progress to help ensure Flyers adhere to expectations regarding activities, outputs, and deliverables. Some Flyers—especially those who are less experienced—struggle with focus, and may have difficulty articulating when they can complete an assigned work task, simply due to the many variables they see as being attached to them. Variables can cause a Flyer to become "wrapped around the axel" when problem-solving, causing them to become stuck, distracted, and causing delays in productivity. While this is typically managed better by seasoned Flyers, it may be especially problematic for more junior Flyers.

Flyers are generally flexible when it comes to work schedule, although individuals with families may have to "reign in" their natural propensity to work intense hours and long days. When engaged in an area of passion, Flyers will often lose track of time, and it's not unusual to find them working crazy hours in the throes of development. Flyers will often bring work home at night and on weekends, if they don't come in to the office. They may also work non-traditional hours. When purposefully engaged, the Flyer's hard work tends to have an energizing or "caffeinating" effect. Flyers appreciate jobs that offer flexibility to work when the inspiration and productivity are high, and to rest when required. They also appreciate managers who provide them with the support to work in ways that work best for them. Good managers will recognize and remain sensitive to the "caffeinated highs" produced by intense productivity, as well as the times when a Flyer needs time to rest and recharge.

RELATIONSHIPS

There isn't an association between introversion/extroversion and operational style. That said, introverted, extroverted, or "ambiverted," Flyers tend to be more outgoing within the comfort zone of work. When they are working within their "strike zone," Flyers often demonstrate passion and a genuine love for what they do. This can have an energizing effect that fuels passion and enthusiasm in others, in a way that can be positive and contagious. Flyers tend to be inclusive, relational workers and typically require human interaction to fuel ideation, fill gaps in knowledge, explore problems, troubleshoot, and conduct reality checks. However, in earlier career phases, Flyers need to be reminded and encouraged and coached on how to work inclusively and with sensitivity to co-workers and politics, so they don't just "plough through" to get things done at the expense of others, producing backlash.

For the Flyer, work is missional and therefore tends to be very personal. It follows that Flyers often form bonds with people who have shared interests, passions, do similar work, and carry a sense of mission, calling, or purpose. Flyers bond through shared experiences—through brainstorming and ideation, as well as building things. Individuals who enjoy participating in this process—especially those with an eye for quality—often become friends. Due to the Flyer's lack of boundaries between work and personal life, the strongest bonds formed with co-workers can extend into close, personal friendships that often transcend jobs and employers. Other Flyers, compatible Walkers, and Climbers can become sounding boards, confidants, co-conspirators, and future collaborators. In fact, it is very common to find that a Flyer's social circle is filled with friendships that have been garnered through work-related pursuits.

Generally speaking, Flyers don't do well in isolation, though they do go through periods of intense work where they prefer to shut out distraction. However, there are some exceptions to this. There are many introverted Flyers who may seem less relational or engaged. In reality, they are just wired differently, preferring to manage interaction and ideation in other ways. Introverted Flyers often require less deep engagement with groups of colleagues, preferring instead to engage on a one-on-one basis. Such individuals may work in roles that are suited to a greater level of isolation, such as research, analysis, programming, or product development. I have also known actors and artists that fit a similar profile.

For example, years ago I worked with a Flyer developer named Will, a MENSA-level genius and a remarkably talented programmer who was incredibly left-brained, analytical, and introverted. Will was socially quirky, odd, and a consummate nerd. In a diva-like manner, Will would engage with our team only when necessary. In fact, he mostly seemed to tolerate us, as reflected in his singular way of making us all feel like mental midgets. Will exceled in his ability to take a roughly communicated concept and turn it into code at lightning speed—and he did so with the deft strokes of an artist. A quick study, he would collect the information he needed, assimilate what needed to be done with incredible speed and, poof! He would vanish, working behind the scenes to get things done. While I originally assumed he worked in isolation, I learned in time that Will had his *own secret network* of code monkeys, par excellence with whom he communicated on-the-job, by phone and online. These relationships helped fuel his ability to form feats of greatness. While we never knew *when* Will would produce something magic, he almost always did, resurfacing with a proof-of-concept or a prototype that almost always blew our doors off. I was surprised to learn that Will wasn't less relational than I was—he was just more introverted and preferred to interact with his own posse of fellow brainiacs who spoke his "language!"

In like manner, I have a friend who is a professional comedian who has had parts in several major motion pictures. On stage, he is the most insane, extroverted, confident ball of energy you have ever seen—presenting humorous insights with the energy of a thousand suns. In person, he is a surprisingly introverted, quiet, philosophical type. I was surprised to find him very shy, quiet, and humble. Most of the time, he is not clowning around, unless surrounded by a tribe of trusted fellow comedians, which tends to fuel his funny bone. Off stage, he is contemplative, somber, and introverted. It's quite the contrast! From what I've been told, this is not unusual for many entertainers.

The mix of Flyer relationships in any workplace may depend on the style mix present within the organization. While Flyers are prone to flock and enjoy playing "brain hockey" together, they will also form close connections with Walkers and compatible Climbers. In organizations where a style imbalance is present, Flyers can feel like "lone eagles" that work in a kind of style isolation. They will attempt to bond with Walkers and Climbers, which can have a positive, grounding effect on a Flyer. They will also reach out to their existing network of Flying friends outside of the organization for support, as feasible.

More than a fair share of Flyers has, at one time or another, considered themselves "misfits." As a Flyer myself, I have *always* identified as a corporate misfit. Early in my career, I was legitimately concerned there was something wrong with me. Later in my career, I began to wear the misfit title as a badge of honor. I often joke about my own "pretend island" of professional misfit friends, with whom I "mind meld" on a regular basis. While the misfit title is, in one part, a joke, many Flyers do legitimately struggle with finding the right professional "fit." This applies to job fit, as well as the ability to mesh well within the organizations they serve. On one hand, Flyers don't particularly care about "fitting in" as much as they care about building something that matters and doing great work. However, Flyers frequently struggle with feeling isolated, misunderstood, and misapplied at work. That's why it's critical for Flyers to establish bridges of understanding with people, as solid professional relationships play an instrumental role in fueling Flyer ability to optimally perform well. Walkers and Climbers help Flyers "land," become more grounded, assist with focus and prioritization, and help them do their best work.

In chapter 12, Working Adaptively, you'll find a description of the natural compatibilities and tensions between operational styles. In general, the passion and energy of the Flyer, combined with the Flyer's alignment as a change agent, may impact relationships at work. Operational styles are meant to complement each other, and Walkers and Climbers can be instrumental in helping temper a Flyer's approach, so they don't overwhelm or offend people with ideas and passion, vision, and communication. In exchange, Flyers can provide remarkable vision, ideas, and solutions that help solve problems, open doors to new opportunities, drive an organization forward, and support the attainment of goals for colleagues and managers.

WORKING WITH & MANAGING FLYERS

Perhaps the toughest career challenge faced by a Flyer, beyond dealing with loneliness, is finding the right professional fit. This extends from finding an organizational culture where "wings are welcome," to finding a good management relationship where a Flyer feels understood, properly mentored, and coached. It's also important for the Flyer to have "safe places" to share, process, and ideate—and to find trusted sounding boards for validation.

Many, if not the majority of, Flyers have been through a professional wringer on some level. Flyers have often been in jobs where they've been misaligned and misunderstood, and many have endured more than a fair share of professional anguish. Many have never experienced a job where they felt free to be themselves. While chapter 13 recommends relational ways to approach and build common ground with Flyers, the following high-level admonishments can help as you manage and work better with Flyers.

Latitude & Flexibility

Flyers require a certain amount of professional latitude and flexibility to engage inside an organization, gather and process large amounts of information, and piece together a comprehensive picture of the "landscape of opportunity" for the future. This is a complicated process, and having the freedom to work is a necessity, not a luxury. Allowing a Flyer to work this way requires a certain amount of trust for all involved.

Some Flyers attain the freedom and latitude they require by going out on their own and working independently. Others, like my friend Valerie and my friend John, have found companies that can provide the paycheck stability, benefits, and security they need, as well as a sufficient "tether" that allows them to fly, soar, and do good work.

John, for example, is a futurist for a very established high-tech firm and (shockingly) one of the only Flyers in his entire division. While he often feels like a "lone lunatic at large," he enjoys having the freedom of being paid to do work at the leading edge of technology advancement, and stands as a well-known subject-matter expert. In many ways, it has been his dream job. That's why I was surprised to get a call from John eight months ago, anxious and talking about resigning.

John's company had undergone a reorganization, and John's boss asked him to begin to collaborate with a rather clueless group of people from another department who were not forward thinking. Worse yet, John was asked to hand off several of his pet projects to the group, who proceeded to mishandle them in ways that felt misguided. Two months before, he had spelled out a vision for a new initiative to his boss that he was excited about, but was left hanging for two months about how to go forward. He proceeded with the project anyway, passionate about the opportunity and not wanting to lose it. However, in the absence of follow up and being instructed to hand off his other work, he suspected something was up at work—like perhaps he was being set up for layoff. As I listened to him describe things, he seemed worried he was being reeled in, roped down, and about to have his wings clipped or feathers plucked. "I'd rather leave on my own accord than have them bring me down," he said.

I told John to immediately get some face time with his boss. Having heard all about his new initiative months before, I became totally overwhelmed. So, I suspected he had totally overwhelmed the boss, too. After two months, it was time for an update and clarity. "Get on his calendar immediately," I said. "He knows he can trust you to use your time wisely, so call him, give him an update, and prove it." John's boss was a Climber, so I encouraged John to lay out the project once more, in bullets, very simply, and highlight three critical opportunities associated with it. At the end of the call, I instructed him to specifically ask whether his boss supported the effort or not, and whether he could continue with his blessing. "Get your answer," I said. "Then you can decide whether you stay or go. You're not quitting out of fear."

A month later, John called back and thanked me. His boss had become so excited by the project and John's progress, he took it to the higher ups, who swooned. John was given carte blanche to pursue that initiative. The other projects, in light of his new mandate, were no longer worth his time. John had feared his firm was reeling him in to clip his wings, yet they ended up giving him more latitude to soar!

Ground Control

Flyers play a critical role in bringing fresh vision and insight, helping an organization remain agile to meet the challenges and demands of the future in a boundary-less way. Yet because of the unconventional way Flyers work, they are often hard pressed to fit in or find organizational cultures that are hospitable and open to their way of working. Flyers that come in at Mach 10 with hair on fire may have good intentions, but may be misguided by a lack of experience, a desire to prove themselves, or poor self-awareness. Furthermore, emotional triggers like insecurity or impatience can exacerbate Flyer pitfalls and can lead to "crash and burn." When this happens, Flyers can fail to drive momentum and progress, lose credibility, create defensive posturing in others, and face an uphill battle in gaining traction with management and colleagues.

In truth, Flyers need to soar, but every bird needs to land sometime! To be most effective, Flyers need to feel grounded, and that means they need people to gently encourage them to land, and/or to pull their feet down to earth from time to time. In some cases, the manager's role is to provide enough tether to provide a feeling of freedom, and to periodically reel in a Flyer to agree on focus, priorities, objectives, and next steps. Here are some ways to positively ground a Flyer:

- Establish structure and boundaries for interactions (e.g. agenda, time limits)
- Ask a Flyer to slow down when you sense people are getting confused
- Request complicated concepts be better explained, to ensure people understand
- Encourage the Flyer to deliver messages in digestible pieces and "bullets"
- Help keep discussions and conversations on track and focused
- Teach Flyers how to establish common ground with others
- Provide reality checks and feedbacks to the Flyer privately
- Help the Flyer become more aware of situational politics and agendas
- Encourage Flyers to slow down, rest, pause, and "land"
- Develop facilitative, consultative, and self-awareness skills

I have been the Flyer going Mach 10 with hair on fire before. I've had managers signal me in meetings to change my approach—and I have always appreciated it. Sometimes simply saying something like this can help: "Hey, I am lost here. Can you go back and re-explain this to me like I'm a rookie?" Suggesting groups take breaks to reset, and helping the Flyer "read the room" can also help. Helping a Flyer control the energy, slow the roll, and speak with greater clarity can result in better group engagement and more productive outcomes. This is especially needed for Flyers with less work experience.

For specific recommendations for working adaptively with Flyers, please reference chapter 13.

Ideality, Reality & Simplicity

Flyers are often accused of perfectionism, partially because they pay such careful attention to meeting the needs of the many stakeholders they serve. However, for the Flyer there really is no such thing as perfection. Flyers do, however, recognize the battle that rages between ideality vs. reality. Differentiating between what is realistic and proper to include in a discussion—or a product in development—against what may be ideal involves complex consideration. It can be time consuming to prioritize features and functionality in a way that ensures there's a proper value equation and return on investment. Choices often involve compromises and trade-offs. Flyers can become preoccupied when weighing such considerations, especially Flyers who do not have a lot of experience or maturity.

One of the biggest struggles for a Flyer is to make things simple, and/ or to present things in a very easy-to-understand manner. This is primarily because the process of creating something simple is actually a rather involved, complex, and hairy activity. For example, I once had to simplify the user experience of a 20,000-page, static HTML website, which had fifteen different user interfaces and about twenty different transactional capabilities. It took *eight months* to comprehensively restructure the site's content and develop the wireframes for the new website, which consisted of 8,000 pages and one single, robust user interface. It was quite an exercise!

As previously described, it is very easy for a Flyer to get wrapped around the axel on detail and struggle to properly process and organize information so that when it is communicated, people can easily understand and absorb it. This is true for a product like a website, and true when telling a story or communicating a vision in a logical, ordered, and digestible manner. This can be hard for anyone—but remains especially hard for Flyers because they see everything as "related." Having input from outside parties, especially people who excel in prioritization and simplification are essential and underscore the reasons why different operational styles need each other.

For example, I have a two brilliant Flyer friends who have had consistent trouble getting their startups off the ground. Both have highly complicated business models and products with rich features and functionality. Both have products designed to disrupt an existing market—creating a totally new paradigm. However, it's painful to watch them pitch and describe what they are setting out to do. Neither can articulate their ideas in a simple way that resonates with investors (who very often turn out to be Climbers).

When my friends present pretty, lofty, overly complicated pitches that aren't grounded or targeted to their audience, they are often shut down. If both of these individuals would establish common ground with a few Climbers, listen actively, and internalize some coaching, I feel they would have a very different outcome. We are not meant to work in isolation!

Periods of High Engagement

Managing the overwhelming energy of a Flyer is not for the faint of heart. Flyers will vacillate from needing very little contact to requiring intense periods of engagement for validation and reality checks. They can be self-sustaining for long periods of time and suddenly emerge to demand attention or information. While Flyers with higher level of experience and greater situational awareness tend to manage this tendency better than others, less experienced Flyers can seem "high maintenance."

Flyers really need "safe zones" for intense engagement. This may involve using associates or understanding managers as sounding boards. This can help prevent the Flyer from becoming burdensome to other colleagues, by giving the Flyer the opportunity to pre-process and prepare for more focused discussion.

When it comes to requests and demands, Flyers tend to save up their ammo and machine gun people with questions and/or requests for support from management and colleagues. They can often carry a sense of urgency that can be overblown and undermine the priorities and demands that weigh other people down. Flyers can start mentally spinning and make requests or state things in ways that are inadvertently insensitive or which may feel self-important or demanding to others. Because they operate from passion, they can sometimes become indignant, frustrated, or offended when they feel shut down, challenged, or refused.

To avoid escalation, try to be patient and maintain positive assumptions. Find out what's driving both the sense of urgency and the litany of requests. Asking a Flyer to explain the urgency may help. If you don't have time to help, explain yourself. Perhaps there's an easier solution. You may not be able to fill a request 100 percent, but opening up dialogue and mutually understanding needs, intentions, and expectations will help.

During engagement it's important to realize that when Flyers begin communicating an idea, they have an innate need to be heard—to see that idea through to the end—as a form of thought completion. Interrupting, asking them to switch mid-stream, or to leave something unfinished can be unsettling and frustrating—especially if they feel they are on the brink of a realization or breakthrough. The same tends to be generally true for work in progress. Flyers like to take their work to a proper level of completion before handing off or moving on. However, the level of "proper completion" may not be well-defined, and may require assistance from management to determine.

Flyers may often grapple with what I call the "Chicken Little" effect: They often can see or sense a storm or problem looming but struggle to have people take them seriously. Sometimes the problem ends up being "no big deal," and other times problems that are underestimated and not well understood can be significant. When a Flyer tells you there's a problem, it's important to make sure proper research has been done, and take time to look at it. While your Flyer may be correct about the problem, the true scope, urgency, and impact of the problem may require the involvement or input from a larger team.

Management Relationships

Most Flyers are grateful to find a good manager, and prove to be loyal, valuable resources in exchange for genuine investment of care and interest. Managers who steward Flyer direct-reports assume the role of a gardener, cultivating the potential of the individual, helping build management skills, and serving as an Encourager, sounding board, advocate, and champion. Good managers also help weed out problematic behaviors, protecting Flyers from "invasive species" and toxic people that seek to subvert, shut down, or compromise the Flyer. Patience is required, as well as the ability to firmly direct, coach, and support a Flyer. However, with proper management, a Flyer can produce a rich harvest.

Flyer managers should be sensitive to the Flyer's propensity to overwhelm people; Flyers that are overly attached to their ideas or perceptions can unknowingly steamroll over others. They can also become very fixated on their own ideas without being grounded in larger realities—especially early in their careers. Flyer managers are often tasked with conducting resets, providing wake up calls, and helping Flyers slow down and engage thoughtfully, while acknowledging the good intentions of the Flyer. Working to develop a Flyer's ability to read people, listen, and communicate well will be a gift that keeps on giving. Good leadership and coaching that help Flyers manage and lead well by example and influence can be instrumental in their future success.

Good Flyer managers know how to resonate against a Flyer's sense of mission and purpose and desire to build something that matters, and providing the opportunity to do this is a reward of its own. Managers who have had adequate training and coaching understand how to give Flyers the latitude to solve problems and create improvements, while providing proper oversight and support. They also apply focus and discipline to help the Flyer produce reliably and consistently in the present while thinking ahead about the future evolution of the business. They know how to field the Flyer's stream of information and ideas—many that concern the larger organization and which fall outside of their own purview or comfort zone. They understand how to keep Flyers motivated and engaged. They also recognize when it's time to transition projects to new owners and move a Flyer on to the next challenge—managing those transitions in a way that makes Flyers feel recognized, appreciated, and rewarded for their contributions.

An organization without Flyers is like a pond without a stream to feed it. Without that influx of fresh, oxygenated water, stagnation can occur. To avoid this, organizations need Flyers to infuse the fresh ideas that help balance the ecosystem and encourage vitality and new life. To help create balance, managers must focus and direct the Flyer's constructive and often disruptive energy, flow, and passion, recognizing it as a much-needed ingredient to success.

Upsetting a Flyer

While Flyers aren't typically easily upset, there are an array of behaviors that are prone to create stress, upset the Flyer, and/or result in a negative response. These include:

- Being shut down without being able to finish train of thought, statement, or idea
- Attempts to suppress, cage, or clip the Flyer's wings
- Dismissive behavior, being disregarded, and/or ignored
- Passive aggression, silent treatment, or ignoring the Flyer, which signals disrespect
- Exclusion from meetings and discussions that pertain to a Flyer's domain
- Having other people claim credit for the Flyer's intellectual property
- Watching others promoted on the heels of Flyer contributions, without being rewarded
- Being prevented from providing insight or sharing convictions when it matters
- Irrational, defensive posturing and territorialism
- Abject laziness and incompetence/people who do the minimum or "phone it in"
- Being misapplied or misunderstood at work
- Being forced into rote or maintenance-driven work for extended time periods
- Extended isolation and uncertainty
- Inability to get feedback and validation, or being "left hanging" by others
- Broken promises and significant breaches of trust

Advancement & Rewards

Flyers place incredible value on finding a professional home within which they can do their "best work." This serves as a primary motivator. Flyers want to find work that leverages their skills, abilities, and talent, and that resonates against their own sense of mission or purpose. They want to build things and make contributions that matter. They love to be stretched, to learn, and grow, and to gain the opportunity to do work that is leading edge, "cool," and/or pioneering. To do this, they need the right management, team, resources, and tools. They work best with management and colleagues who are accepting, appreciative, and understanding, and long for managers that are willing to provide an appropriate level of oversight, along with the freedom to soar, ideate, and build. They appreciate working with great minds and inspiring people, to gain solid mentorship and coaching, and to advance professionally with recognition and appreciation for their accomplishments.

Equal or secondary to this consideration, Flyers care about compensation, benefits, time off, and leave policies; stock options; stock purchase plans; profit sharing; educational benefits; and retirement benefits. Typically, they are not obsessed with rank or position. In fact, a Flyer will rarely obsess over a job title, unless a certain title may be instrumental in helping them gain access, traction, or drive results in their work. However, having an appropriate level of authority—and the ability to move the needle, make decisions, and drive results—tends to be critically associated to a Flyer's ability to drive great results.

Beyond the traditional raises and advancement, rewarding a Flyer with the opportunity to grow, learn, and build "cool stuff that matters" will go far in keeping an individual engaged, motivated, and inspired. In fact, to a Flyer, this feels like a huge prize. Another way to keep a Flyer engaged and motivated is to recognize when it's time to move projects off a Flyer's plate and into "maintenance mode" with someone else. While letting go of responsibilities may feel awkward, a Flyer will be motivated to do so if he or she understands it's an effort to "clear the plate" to pursue opportunities. Periodic public recognition for a job well done, notes and gifts of thanks or gratitude, and opportunities to present, inspire and motivate; additional comp time for hard work are other ways to reward and motivate a Flyer. In addition, permission to go to landmark professional events or conferences may be supplemental rewards that may express your gratitude for a job well done, and give the Flyer a chance to "flock" with other like-minded individuals.

Flyer Transitions

Flyers move on to new opportunities for a variety of reasons. Some leave because they feel the "season" of doing compelling work has ended, and move with a desire for greener pastures. Some are dismissed due to a lack of proper job fit. Others may be recruited for their talents. Many leave due to burnout or feeling misapplied, ineffective, or frustrated. The cost of attrition depends on role and function, as well as how reliant the organization is on the individual. Because many Flyers tend to fill multiple roles and work cross-functionally, they may possess a depth of insight that is not easy to relay to a replacement within a knowledge transfer session. Very often, it can also be difficult to find a replacement.

Depending on the role the Flyer held, they may leave a significant gap that impacts multiple areas. It may also be difficult to find a comparable replacement with the same unusual mix of skills the departing Flyer had. This may force an organization to change job descriptions and shift their approach, parsing work out to others or replacing a single Flyer with multiple resources. This can be time consuming and costly, so be sure to weigh the cost when you're at risk of losing a valued Flyer and consider countermeasures that may motivate the Flyer to stay. Make sure the Flyer conducts a detailed knowledge transfer prior to final payout and that your organization is covered by sufficient non-compete, non-disclosure terms within employment contracts.

CHAPTER 8
DRIFTERS: THE FOURTH STYLE?

While the focus of this book is on Walkers, Climbers, and Flyers, through-out the years, I have encountered a fourth style that's worth mentioning, which I call "The Drifter." While many readers may recognize a Drifter from their own past or present, these individuals are *unlikely* to play a significant role in the modern workplace. As a result, we won't delve deeply into operational style dynamics between Walkers, Climbers, Flyers, and Drifters in this book. However, because you may encounter one, I wanted to lay out a brief description of the key traits of the Drifter.

BUCKING CONVENTION

In short, Drifters are individuals who dance to the beat of their own drums. They come from all walks of life, and all backgrounds. They are often intelligent, educated, and curious. Many have colorful pasts and surprising experiences to share. Drifters are often dreamers or lay philosophers. They almost unilaterally value freedom, flexibility, and individuality over other pursuits. They typically live by their own unique credo or values system that bucks tradition. Very often, Drifters may demonstrate a lack of regard for rules or convention and may not feel that legal rules or social mores apply to them personally—though there may be an expectation that they do apply to others.

Drifters may be surprising on many levels. In getting to know these unique individuals, they often to prove to be sources of unexpected insight, information, knowledge, or experience. Looking back at a Drifter's professional past, it's not unusual to find professional accomplishment that may be surprising in light of their current state. Unfortunately, upon scrutiny, the accomplishments of a Drifter's past may not be making a material difference in the individual's present.

WORK IS A CONSTANT BATTLE

On the whole, Drifters will seek employment primarily in the name of practical survival. You will almost unilaterally find the Drifter disinterested and/or somewhat resistant to traditional employment. A Drifter may take a day job when led to believe the reward for the work will be disproportionately high. However, where possible, a nine-to-five job will be avoided with an array of claims and excuses. Drifters are often drawn to temporary or part-time employment, as well as contract work, and they are prone to change jobs frequently. As an alternative to traditional employment, some Drifters choose to start their own businesses.

The same reasons that make traditional employment problematic for the Drifter make it difficult to produce sustainable independent income. Drifters can successfully complete tasks—at times performing very well and even exceeding expectations. However, they typically struggle to perform *consistently over time*. They can be challenged to complete tasks, finish on deadline, and frequently exhibit problems with focus. Drifters are often prone to distraction or to have difficulty maintaining concentration. Conversely, Drifters often may demonstrate a pattern of selective focus or hyper focus, which may result in the individual becoming heavily engrossed in tasks, even if they do not exactly align with priorities, needs, or managerial direction. Focus issues make it difficult for the Drifter to use time productively. Further, when problems are called to their attention, they may fail to fully appreciate the magnitude of the problem. The need to keep the Drifter focused often results in a greater need for direction and oversight from management.

A TROUBLED PROFESSIONAL HISTORY

As a result of these challenges, Drifters typically have a troubled employment history marked by frequent job changes, employment gaps, and a history of layoffs or terminations. In processing the past, Drifters may have difficulty describing events that transpired clearly or rationally. In some cases, they have trouble separating their own perceptions from reality and/or accepting their responsibility in past problematic employment situations. Some Drifters may express resentment toward authority or feel frustrated and misunderstood. As a result of their problematic work history, it's not uncommon to find Drifters who live in debt; rely on assistance from family, friends, or colleagues; and/or who receive regular public assistance.

Many Drifters feel discouraged, frustrated, and unmotivated to try. When asked about their feelings about work, they may express a sense of hopelessness related to the task of getting ahead in life via traditional skilled or unskilled employment. They may also complain about the futility of the corporate "rat race," "working for the man," or express an existential crisis related to the modern work world. While it would be natural for any person to carry such frustrations, the Drifter is most likely to leverage these arguments as justification for not engaging in the professional world.

Drifters often grapple with fear, resentment, and/or disrespect for "authority," hierarchy, and modern power structures. However, some respond in a manner that is overly respectful to authority—even to a point of allowing themselves to be abused and pushed around unfairly by authority figures. Others carry an undercurrent of resentment and distrust that never manifests in any outward aggression. In some more extreme cases, Drifters may exhibit active rebellion and hostility toward authority, institutions, corporations, government, and the law. This may manifest in merely a cavalier attitude or (especially if provoked) an outright demonstrative disrespect for authority, which may include protests, activism, and law breaking.

A pattern of denial is common with the Drifter. For some, denial gives way to delusional thinking. Many Drifters carry incredibly high opinions of themselves and the values they extol. Most of the time, a Drifter's delusions are subtle—but when combined with mental illness or psychological disorders, such delusions can become grandiose. They may demonstrate a high ego or build themselves up to be "legends in their own minds." They may also carry a very strong sense of entitlement. As mentioned, a Drifter may believe that the rules and social mores that apply to the rest of society do not apply to them individually. Going further, they may accept the belief they are "special" and entitled to unique privileges, support, or assistance.

THE DRIFTER'S PLIGHT

The Drifter presents a conundrum for people who have an easier time finding their way. However, it's important to understand that a Drifter's behavior is not a reflection of intention, intelligence, IQ, capability, or skill. I've met a number of Drifters that are perfectly kind, sincere, relatively high-functioning people with what are likely to be relatively-high IQs. In many cases, I have sensed the Drifter's plight is something beyond the individual's control, potentially exacerbated by learning and cognitive disabilities, emotional trauma, psychological disorders, and/or substance abuse problems. Every individual is unique, and it's important to consider all angles when working with a Drifter.

Steve's Story

An extreme example of a delusional drifter is Steve, who was married to Melissa. Steve was raised in an affluent family. His father was a physician. His mother was a stay-at-home mom and member of the PTA. On the weekends, they socialized at the country club, playing tennis and golf. Steve received an excellent, private education and was active in debate, athletics, and other activities at school. An average student, he was a socially outgoing college frat boy and a partier who, from a relatively young age, enjoyed active, recreational experimentation with drugs. He never completed his degree, because he didn't show up for the tough classes. Eventually, he was expelled.

After college, Steve held a string of jobs he never really talks about. His longest stint was with a startup company, where he achieved some success as a self-taught database developer. When he was in his early thirties, the company he worked for was acquired. The new parent company offered Steve a full-time employment package, which he declined. Instead, he accepted a modest severance package and took a nice vacation. Eventually he moved back in with his parents, and couch surfed with friends in the pursuit of fun and adventure.

While Steve made overtures toward getting a job and starting his own business, his "all talk, no action" ambition eventually became the subject of teasing from his friends, who had gone on to establish successful professional lives. Steve dabbled here and there, picking up contract jobs to fund his lifestyle, and shuttled up and down the west coast, visiting buddies and attending concerts and events whenever possible. His primary quest was having fun, and he had a lot of it. To support his travels and partying, he artfully shuffled debt back and forth on credit cards and often relied on the good graces of friends and his parents, who bailed him out on several occasions and prayed he'd grow out of his dependency.

A consummate nerd, Steve was charming and somewhat popular with the ladies. However, his lack of employment and drive, combined with his drug use proved to be a deterrent to securing a life partner. He had met Melissa a decade earlier, when they both worked at the same company. In 2008, they became reacquainted through mutual friends and, while planning a trip to her city, he asked if he could stay with her for a few days. Steve crashed on her couch and turned on the charm, explaining he had "cashed out" of a successful startup he worked for and was trying to "figure out what was next." It wasn't exactly the truth, but the two established a strong intellectual connection and began a romantic entanglement immediately. She knew very little about his past.

Melissa was a very successful CEO and owner of her own multimillion-dollar company. She worked long hours in a high-pressure environment and made a great living. Her professional success was overshadowed by a near total lack of personal life and, approaching her late thirties, she grappled with nagging reality that she didn't yet have the family she had always dreamed of. When Steve arrived with no other obligations, he turned his complete focus on Melissa, making her feel special. He expressed dreams and plans for the future. She enjoyed their connection and the time and attention he offered her. Steve enjoyed the lifestyle she afforded, and became a permanent fixture at her place. Only four months later, Melissa became pregnant. While slightly concerned about Steve's lack of progress toward securing employment, she was excited about Steve and the baby. They married just prior to the birth of their son.

Melissa had mistakenly assumed Steve's lack of employment was a "phase." However, before the baby arrived, it became clear that even though Steve was intelligent, educated, and capable, he had *no intention* of securing traditional employment *or* helping at home. After making many excuses for the lack of a job search, and a lot of pressure from Steve (and despite the protests and warning of friends), Melissa allowed him to help with her own business. Unfortunately, the grandiose claims he made regarding his abilities failed to line up with reality, and his involvement with Melissa's company proved to be disastrous.

Steve was often a no-show, failed to deliver on time, and was completely unaccountable for the work he promised to do. When the team pushed back at Steve, he would storm around and throw things, yelling "How dare you! I am the owner of this company!" On the side, he was abusing drugs, bringing himself up on ADHD and smart drugs he procured from "friends," then bringing himself down with alcohol and marijuana. To avoid marital stress, Melissa gradually pushed him out, keeping him on as a staff member in name only. He showed up periodically to mark his territory and delivered almost nothing. Her friends and work family were deeply concerned. Melissa acknowledged that she was in hot water with Steve, but had just become pregnant with her second child, a little girl, and didn't know what to do.

Steve had agreed to take care of the children during the day, and they had agreed that he could start his own business on the side. Melissa fronted him a lot of cash, and Steve went out and hired a nanny. Much to Melissa's frustration, he never produced a business plan, burned through a ton of cash, buying toys and "investing" in expensive computer equipment that often went missing. He stayed up all night and slept until noon. He disappeared conveniently to avoid family responsibilities at critical times—including the birth of his baby girl—and even vanished for hours on family vacations. He hid a growing daily drug habit and masked his activities by disappearing for weeks at a time—going to visit friends and his parents, skiing, and attending concerts, including Coachella and Burning Man, where he blew through even more money on credit cards.

Steve suffered from depression and deep insecurity, and lapsed into rages when he felt challenged, undermined, or disrespected—which was much of the time. For Melissa, their relationship was a constant source of pain and frustration. She tried everything to be supportive, get him working, to find him a counselor, and to care for her family while managing her business and more. Steve could be disarming, engaging, charming, and fun—about 20 percent of the time. While he didn't spend much time with the children and never managed daily routines like a normal adult parent, he seemed to love his kids and was good at sporadically being "fun Dad." Melissa didn't want the children to suffer through a divorce and remained torn about leaving Steve.

Steve was a total consumer who outright refused to work. He expressed delusions about his own abilities and contributions while he chided Melissa, sabotaging his business and his reputation with her company. He was also patently dishonest—blowing through cash at an alarming rate—and running up an insane amount of secret debt on credit cards. He also carried on affairs (including a multi-year tryst with the nanny), which were not completely revealed until after Melissa filed for divorce. Regardless, in true form, Steve sued for full spousal support, claiming that it was Melissa's duty to keep him in the lifestyle to which he had become accustomed.

Without question, Steve's story is a rather extreme example of a Drifter and a prime example of how a Drifter with mental illness and a substance abuse problem may present. However, everyone is a bit different. So, for context, here are a few other Drifters I have met, with names and stories slightly altered.

Jane, Age 30

Jane is an affable thirty-year-old woman with an associate degree in communications. When Jane's administrative temp job ended, she decided to start a small "business" making simple beaded jewelry. Her ink-jet-printed business cards read "artist, designer, stylist, interior designer." When she lost her job, she couldn't afford rent and moved in with her well-intentioned sister in what was to be a temporary arrangement. Jane became hyper focused on pursuing her "jewelry business" and was convinced she could give it a good run to make a living. She spent everything she had on supplies and cluttered the house with projects, going on public assistance to buy herself groceries and promising to pay her sister back for bills and utilities from the proceeds of her first jewelry show. After two months of preparation, she managed to sell ten pairs of earrings for $24 each at a craft fair with an entry fee of $50. While the economics would suggest otherwise, to Jane, this was a hopeful sign. To her sister, it was a signal that she should find a new job! To appease her sister, Jane applied for a new position but continued to pursue her craft. However, without employment, Jane simply ran out of money. She borrowed on credit cards, and later asked family for support. Having overextended her welcome at her sister's, Jane finally landed a job with a temp agency and started a thirty-hour per week position. Today, while Jane actively laments about the toll it has taken on her business, she has remained in the position for six weeks. Relieved over her progress, Jane's sister hopes Jane will soon be able to move out on her own.

Mark, Age 26

Mark is a twenty-six-year old husband and father of two who has overcome many difficulties in life. He graduated from high school despite some learning disabilities and cognitive challenges. He joined the Army after high school and was medically discharged in four years due to a back injury. Married at the age of twenty-one and a father at twenty-two, Mark has always felt the burden of being a provider and has done his best to provide consistently. He has worked as a handyman, janitor, and security guard, and has had difficulty performing consistently to retain work. His family has subsisted on food stamps and public assistance from time to time. Mark's plight is complicated. On one front, he struggles with back pain and no longer qualifies for disability. On another front, Mark performs inconsistently and makes a lot of excuses for his mistakes. Mark has been laid off, downsized, or let go four times over six years. He also quit two jobs voluntarily. Mark tries really hard and he's a good guy, but he lacks attention to detail. As a janitor, his work was inconsistent, and he was fired for leaving the property unlocked, resulting in a costly theft. As a security guard, he was reprimanded for taking extensive breaks and failing to follow sign-in protocols. While he is very well liked, his management struggles with Mark's reliability, judgment, frequent absences, lack of attention to detail, and need for perpetual oversight and support. He's a nice guy, so instead of letting him go, they moved him to the night shift. Mark now works a six-hour evening shift five nights a week, and hopes to secure more hours. However, he has built up resentment toward management over what he believes has been unfair treatment. Two weeks ago, a friend offered him a good paying job at the parts counter at his shop. It was a local job, forty hours per week, with great benefits. As a car aficionado, his friend thought it would be a perfect for Mark. However, it was a traditional eight-hour day standing behind a counter on a concrete floor. Mark rationalized that this would hurt his back, and that taking the job might damage his friendship, so he declined. Mark's wife loves him dearly and has gone back to work as a nurse to bridge the gap financially for the family, but wonders whether Mark's professional plight will ever improve.

Candy, Age 40

Candy is a forty-year-old creative, educated, and passionate world traveler who hails from a middle-class background. Candy knows exactly what she wants in life: freedom, flexibility, and to travel the world! She has no desire for a career and lives a simple, modest life with few possessions. Her daily rituals involve long walks, juicing, yoga, and reading. She loves books. She lives with multiple roommates in a rented house decorated with found objects and thrift store finds. She is happy, bright, and resourceful, and volunteers three times a week with a local food pantry that distributes food to the poor. Due to her low income, she obtains her groceries from the pantry as well, and survives financially by taking odd jobs. She scours online ads and local job boards to secure positions cleaning houses, doing seasonal gardening and yard work, dog sitting, and babysitting. While she doesn't make much, she covers her bills and manages to squirrel away money to support her great passion: travel. When she can afford it, she embarks on low-budget extended backpacking trips, making friends and staying in hostels and camping out as she journeys. She has been to Latin America,

Thailand, Indonesia, and India so far. Candy doesn't have benefits, a trust fund, retirement savings, or even a resume. These are not artifacts of her world. She lives a simple, adventurous life and carries few concerns or plans for the future. She is prone to move or change course without notice. This can frustrate and worry those close to her, who care about her well-being. These are just a few examples that create color around how a Drifter may present. It's important to understand that while this operational style may not be something to which many people can relate, the plight of the Drifter is typically complex. J.R.R. Tolkien once wrote "Not all those who wander are lost," and in Candy's case, this may be partly true, as she enjoys the freedom and simplicity that many people crave.

Regardless, there's little use trying to change a Drifter, as most of the time, they are fully attached to their perceptions and delusions. Some, like Steve, have a plight that is compounded by narcissism, substance abuse, and depression. Others, like Candy, live in a Peter-Pan-like, happy alternative reality. Many live in a place of struggle, oppression, discontentment, and excuses. This can make the Drifter very frustrating to work and live with, damaging relationships and even ending marriages. Those whose lives have been impacted by a Drifter can also attest to the need for very strong, clear boundaries. This is also why in the workplace, Drifters are not typically around for the long-haul.

It's important to note that, in the past, I have encountered a few individuals that I mistook for Drifters. I later discovered that the individuals in question were actually people with other dominant operational styles who were completely burned out, suffering from abuse or trauma, trapped in a style identity crisis, sick, or damaged. These individuals all demonstrated shared characteristics: they weren't satisfied with where they were, they were tired of making excuses, and they were genuinely interested in finding a better way proceed. It's important to know that we will not always recognize someone's style accurately. Sometimes people who seem to be drifting are just stuck in life. Recognizing the truth requires an established relationship, time, thoughtful inquiry, objective observation, patience, and understanding.

CHAPTER 9
EMBRACING YOUR DESIGN

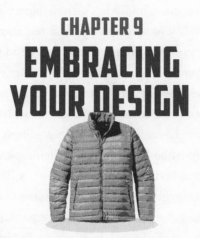

Embracing my design was a gradual process for me, and it may be for you, too. There was a discovery process within which I had to come to terms with my pitfalls—many of which I didn't particularly want to own. However, I found that my denial didn't work so well toward making my weaknesses vanish. Instead, as I began to recognize truth and embrace my style, my weaknesses became much easier to manage and no longer served to define me.

Take a minute to go back to the self-assessment, and spend a few minutes reviewing answers. If you've narrowed down to a style, examine the traits and chapter materials for your style. If you haven't honed in on your style, review the styles to which you are most likely to be associated. Ask yourself some key questions.

- What responses can you adjust, now that you have read the chapter materials?

- What traits are your strongest and weakest?

- What traits are dormant or non-applicable? Are you sure they don't apply?

- What traits make you the most uncomfortable?

- Have any traits surfaced as strengths or weakness in performance reviews?

Embracing what's great and what's challenging about ourselves is important—and a bit like looking in a physical 360-degree mirror! Where we should see beauty, we are often overwhelmed by flaws that seem hyper-evident. You don't have to love your flaws and weaknesses. However, when you embrace and acknowledge truth, your flaws can be easier to manage, as you learn to "work" your strengths.

My neighbor's son, Logan, is nine years old, almost five-foot-two, and wears a men's size nine shoe. While he's not built for speed, Logan can knock anything down that stands in his way, and often does, inadvertently. He is a charming, polite, clumsy giant. He has recently taken to fashion and spends regular time grooming. He likes to dress up, frequently wearing ill-fitting men's suits with bowties to school, just for fun. During "back to school" shopping, Logan's mom bought him an expensive pair of brand-name turquoise-and-red athletic trainers. He pulled them on and immediately "sprinted" down the driveway like a lumbering mini-giant. Rambling back to his mom, breathless, he exclaimed, "Mom! These shoes are the bomb! They make me so much faster! I have the reflexes of a cheetah!"

Logan believed this, wholeheartedly. In fact, it is clear that with very little exception, Logan believes he can do anything. Logan's mother acknowledges the great kid she has, and remains dedicated to raise him right. I have seen in Logan some Climber potential. Simply play a game of monopoly with this kid, and you'll see his operational style come out in true form: this kid has an agenda, he is competitive, he is calculating, he cares a lot about winning, and he knows how to negotiate to get what he wants. His mother has lamented his unwavering attachment to his own ideas, agenda, and opinions. She has expressed frustration over Logan's insistence on negotiating everything to his own benefit—refusing take "no" for an answer. His intelligence and overconfidence makes it hard for him to be teachable and sensitive to others. She remains obsessed with finding ways to instill empathy and sensitivity in Logan. She's doing a great job, and she has time. I am touched by her sensitivity and dedication to helping

Logan understand areas where he needs to improve without having him be defined by his weakness.

While, like all children, Logan has insecurities, he is largely unflappable and admirably unapologetic about who he is! Logan has fully embraced his design as only a child can—in a world full of possibility. However, doing the same for grownups can be a challenge. We often become distracted by our insecurities, have a grass-is-greener mentality, idealize the plight of others, or lament what we perceive to be deficiencies in ourselves. We yearn to be different and yearn to have what other people have. However, when we come to a place of acceptance—of our own design, our pros, and pitfalls—it can be incredibly liberating. Further, when we align ourselves more thoughtfully to our design, we can create a more peaceable existence with this thing called work.

STYLE CONFUSION AND IDENTITY CRISIS

Embracing your own design sounds simple enough, but many people have a hard time letting go of what they *wish they were*. Some people may assume their style is somehow insufficient to take them where they need to be in life. Because they don't truly understand the opportunities that exist, or the truth of their operational style, they may resist attachment to their own dominant style, harboring a desire to be someone or something else.

Carrie is a Flyer friend who tried to switch styles in response to a rough professional journey. Carrie was, and is, a quintessential Flyer who possessed the innate pros and pitfalls of her operational style. True to form, because of her abilities to see so many issues simultaneously, Carrie could be overwhelming to work with. She was frank in her communication and often right. She felt comfortable crossing boundaries. As a result, she often made people feel threatened and exposed. For example, in a thirty-minute review of a proposal, Carrie could easily identify errors and problems that could have sweeping impacts. Calling out her concerns was great for thwarting downstream business problems, but to the author of that document, Carrie's unsolicited input could feel embarrassing, or like an attack. I believe that earlier in her career, Carrie wasn't as aware of how her way of working made other people feel, and her inability to manage things like this compounded her struggle. As background, Carrie had been chewed up and spit out by several companies so badly that she began to believe the only way to survive would be to alter her style. Her bosses didn't always know how to manage her. She felt unrewarded for her hard work. She was burned out and craved more balance in her life. Once, in the middle of a job change, Carrie called me with an announcement.

"I've decided I'm not going to be a Flyer anymore," she proclaimed. "I'm going to shift and become a Walker."

She continued, "I've decided I'm just not going to care anymore. I'm going to take a job and just walk through my day!"

While I certainly understood the emotion and frustration behind it, Carrie's assumptions were way off base. The thing was, Carrie could no more become a Walker than a leopard could change its spots! I sucked in my breath and issued a gentle rebuke.

"You know," I said, "insinuating that Walkers don't care about their jobs is insulting and wrong!" I explained that everyone longs for a job with meaning and reward, and that drives a sense of satisfaction and gratification. I reminded her that Walkers care just as deeply about the quality of their work as Flyers do.

I asked Carrie what she thought a Walker possessed that a Flyer couldn't have. Carrie confessed that what she really craved was the acceptance and fit that Walkers enjoyed. She also wanted to attain some of the work/life balance that seemed to come easier to a Walker. This made sense to me, as I had been there myself: I struggled with finding a good fit for myself before. I could acknowledge some of my own past jealousy of Walkers I'd known, who seemed to have an easier time of establishing boundaries between their work and their personal lives, while I struggled. However, having come through the other side of that frustration, I rejected the notion that attaining a fit and work/life balance were unattainable to Carrie *as a Flyer*.

For years, Carrie had tried to retrofit herself to positions and companies that were entirely wrong for her. In attempting to "switch styles" she was trying to pretend she was something she was not in order find a better fit for herself. Her inclination not to care anymore wasn't a shot at Walkers, as much as a reflection of being exhausted from working the wrong way for so many years. I walked through the logic of that with her and explained that when we try to cram ourselves into a mold we're not designed for, it rarely produces a positive, long-term result.

"Carrie," I said, "Flyers can establish work/life balance too. It may not look exactly the same, because we are simply wired differently than Walkers, but you can find a fit and balance, too."

Carrie responded by confessing her fear that there was something deeply wrong with her because of her struggles. I reminded her that while we are all human and imperfect, my belief is that we are all designed with a purpose, and that as a Flyer, there wasn't anything wrong with her design, though perhaps some better ways to work. We talked through pros and pitfalls and discussed her needs. She needed to be in an environment that appreciated her wings—that let her soar, build, and develop. She needed to work for people who rewarded truth tellers and taking initiative. She needed management that "got" her. She also needed rest. To help her find a more hospitable environment for her Flyer wings, we mapped out a list of questions for her to ask in her interviews that looked something like this:

- Describe your workplace culture.

- What are the best things about this place?

- What are the top challenges of working here?

- Can you describe a day in this workplace or in this job?

- How do you see the person in this role interfacing with others?

- Describe the team—what are they like?

- How does your organization respond to individuals who stir things up—who like ideation, fixing problems, and challenging the status quo?

- In your mind, how will the ideal candidate for this role, and what will they accomplish?

- How would you want to see me approach this position, job, or task?

- In your mind, what does success look like for this position in one year?

Questions like this helped improve Carrie's ability to discern whether she was gravitating toward the right environment or not. Her next job proved to be a slightly better situation, if only because it was a less demanding environment. They didn't quite know what to do with the powerhouse they'd hired, and it wasn't an optimal fit, but the slack allowed her to slow down and heal. It also helped her draw some much-needed boundaries between her work and personal life.

When Carrie became ready to fully stretch her wings again, she went out and secured her dream job in an organization that celebrates her wings and gives her latitude to soar. That's when Carrie really began to really come into her own as a Flyer! Today, with wings spread, she has come through the other side of denial and a style identity crisis. Carrie has moved from barely surviving to a thriving position. As a senior executive in the entertainment industry, she is far more gratified in her work than ever before.

Style Confusion can be a natural part of the process of aligning yourself with a level of comfort to a dominant operational style. During this process, I often encounter people who identify with—or want to identify with—a style other than their own. Many of these individuals, like Carrie, have been through some professional turmoil, wherein they find themselves confused and frustrated. These individuals can take Style Confusion to a new level, persisting in a kind of style identity crisis that may frequently be associated with burnout. Over the years, I have noted that Style Confusion or an identity crisis is compounded by one or more of the following issues:

Lack of Understanding of Operational Styles

While there may be a high-level exposure to operational styles, an individual's true understanding of operational styles is typically insufficient, immature, and/or off-base. They may make assumptions or associations that are not accurate, mistaking the traits and qualities of operational styles. They may misunderstand how traits align and manifest in different individuals. They may have failed to properly internalize (or may not have read) the book material on each operational style. In these cases, Style Confusion is usually easy to correct by reading the dedicated chapters in this book that describe operational styles and style dynamics.

Idealization of Another Style

People who idealize a certain operational style often do so at the expense of others. This can make it hard to identify with any other style. For years, I devalued being a Flyer, lamenting my design and wishing I were different. Depending on the situation, I wished I had the qualities of a Walker or Climber. However, my "grass is greener" view of the operational styles pasture was unproductive, distracting me from objectively embracing my own strengths and addressing areas of weakness. While this kind of "style envy" is somewhat natural, it's unproductive. There is no style that is superior to another, and trying to be something that you are not requires a lot more energy than simply aligning with your design and actively managing your areas of weakness.

Low Self-Awareness

At times, an individual's self-perception may not fully align with reality or the observations and perceptions of others. Low self-awareness occurs when a person doesn't see themselves accurately, carrying misperceptions, misunderstandings, or even delusions. This can be hard to overcome. For example, there are many people who would consider themselves strategic, and there are all kinds of ways to strategize. Some individuals pride themselves, however, in being much more strategic than they actually are—claiming the ability to see the future that may not exist. In other cases, people may be completely unaware of their pitfalls in action. To raise a person's level of self-awareness, it can be helpful to secure outside feedback. This can be done through the provision of constructive feedback from management. When someone is recalcitrant, collecting 360-degree, anonymized feedback from peers and presenting that feedback can serve as an important wake-up call. Individuals with low self-awareness may further benefit from professional coaching or counseling.

Bad Coaching

Management, mentors, and coaches can have a great deal of influence over your self-perception and/or the way you value certain traits or behaviors. Sometimes the counsel people receive is good. Sometimes, it's misguided, and may direct a person in a way that doesn't best fit with their design or heart's desires. For example, instead of being coached to manage weakness and perceptions, an individual might be coached to suppress their own natural traits and adopt others that don't come as naturally. This can warp an individual's self-perception, disrupt their ability to embrace their true design, and cause them to undervalue the qualities that may make them special and unique.

Unfortunately, bad coaching and mentoring are common in the Workplace Wilderness today. According to a 2018 study by West Monroe partners, 59 percent of managers supervising one to two employees and 41 percent supervising three to five employees have had no training whatsoever. Further, the study reported that 42 percent of managers admit they developed their style by observing and mimicking a previous manager rather than through any type of formal training. While these are just US figures, they serve to underscore how likely it is for you to be aligned with an inexperienced manager. In short, it's very likely, over the course of your career, to become the recipient of advice from people who may not be qualified to give it! That's why it's important to be cautious about the advice you internalize.

Having really positive experiences with a manager can be transforming. My first job out of college, for example, was working as ecommerce manager for 1-800-FLOWERS. I was hired directly by CEO Jim McCann after being recruited by a rising executive there, just after college graduation. For a short season, I reported directly to Jim, a savvy and successful entrepreneur, risk taker, and a smart marketer who understood supply chain economics. He'd built an empire and had revolutionized his industry. He was approachable, engaged, and open to ideas. He led by example and knew how to take measured risks. He rolled up his sleeves, worked alongside his people in busy seasons, and expected other executives and managers to do the same. Jim appreciated my wings and put me to work without prejudice for my age and inexperience. It couldn't have been a better place for me to thrive.

During my tenure at 1-800-FLOWERS, the company endured exponential growth. This opened doors for me to work with Jim, his brother Chris, and his sister Julie (both terrific in their own rights) on multiple initiatives spanning branding, retail expansion, training, catalog, marketing communications, and ecommerce. Within months, I made the choice to co-found the company's ecommerce team, under Chris, helping the company become an early pioneer in that field. Together, we built sixteen digital stores in under two years across every imaginable digital channel.

In that operational culture, nobody forced me into a mold. I was able to define my own position and leverage my smarts, talents, and abilities to create a position for myself that was a great fit. While I often pulled all-nighters and worked weekends, I mostly did so out of a love and passion for my work. As a result, I was engaged, energized, and rarely felt burnout. I also enjoyed a good relationship and a shared sense of mission with my direct manager and team, and we were all energized and proud of our accomplishments.

It was a blessing to have experienced solid leadership and a culture that embraced me so early in my career. If I hadn't, some of my earlier career setbacks might have wrecked me. Many of my professional experiences were not this positive. In subsequent years, I enjoyed some exceptional reporting relationships. However, my experiences with managers have been a mixed bag. I'd estimate that I probably had three bad managers for every decent one. There were the absentee, unapproachable managers. There were the dictators. There were the dreaded micromanagers, and the individuals that mistook coaching for self-cloning. In the latter case, rather than helping me forge my own path in alignment with my talent, vision, skills, and abilities, these managers just wanted to create a "Mini Me." As a result, they would push me to follow the path similar to that which they themselves had forged, even if that path wasn't right for me. It's likely they didn't know any better.

Bad coaching can often compound an identity crisis in an employee. That's why it's important to use caution when you give, ask for, or receive advice. For Heaven's sake—don't take everything at face value! The best mentors will never force cookie cutter approaches on you, but will seek to understand you, speak to you as an individual, and provide insight and feedback that helps you cultivate your unique strengths and abilities. They'll also speak to you with candor about your flaws and weaknesses, and help you find ways to minimize them as you develop your skills, your niche, and forge your own path. To avoid going off course, be sure to weigh the advice you receive against your own convictions and understanding of your design, operational style, needs, desires, and what feels right for you. It's okay to get advice—just don't replace common sense, lest you be pulled off-course.

Years after my time at 1-800-FLOWERS, and before I met my Flyer friend, Carrie, I found myself smack the middle of my *own* identity crisis. I had been recruited to a company from my prior employer. I had previously enjoyed my past experience working with entrepreneurial companies that rewarded risk-taking people who took initiative, and who challenged the status quo. I stepped into the new position motivated and ready to lead. However, without knowing it, I walked into a new culture that was the polar opposite of what I'd experienced before, and wasn't sure how to find my way. After about four weeks of trying to acclimate, I sought advice from the VP who hired me.

I had come in and assessed how things were being done in my area of responsibility and found a lot of room for improvement. I had composed a set of recommendations to streamline operations and reduce costs by 100 percent, while driving up sales and profit margin. I thought this was what they wanted. However, when I produced my recommendations, management responded by shutting me down. I didn't understand why, then, except that perhaps I'd been too critical or gone too far. I'd not only highlighted some big inefficiencies under their purview, but I sensed that I had perhaps tread on some sacred ground, putting myself at odds with an agency they worked with. I desperately wanted to exceed expectations, so I asked my boss what I could do to improve. She thought for a minute and suddenly, like an epiphany came, she exclaimed, "You know what? You need to just watch Michelle and do *everything* she does."

Michelle was a top-tier analyst with an Ivy League education. She was incredibly composed, data-driven, analytical, and enviably organized. She spoke the language of executive leadership fluently and had a computational ability to produce facts, as well as data-driven reports packed with impressive graphs and charts. She was great at following orders and dutifully delivered on every front. To add insult to injury, she was breathtakingly pretty. A petite 5'5", she pieced together clever outfits from designer sample sales and always looked sharp. I wanted to hate her, but the truth is, everyone, including me, loved her. She was low ego and funny, which made her endearing.

Michelle was like a magical, sparkly, corporate unicorn. I was so far away from being anything like Michelle, it was painful.

First there was the physical intimidation. Michelle entered the room like a swan, gliding in to her place with a confidence, ease, and grace that commanded attention. I was a jock that had been voted class clown in high school. Standing at 5'10" in heels, I was a klutz with a developing weight problem and suits that were too snug. No matter how composed or polished I tried to be, I always felt like a clumsy, honking goose next to Michelle.

Next, there was her political and cultural astuteness. Michelle had been with the firm for three years and was steeped in the organization's culture. She understood the pecking order and hierarchy, and how to navigate the spoken and unspoken rules. She knew where the sacred cows were and wasn't foolish enough to recommend slaying one. In contrast, I'd cut my teeth at companies with little hierarchy, rules, or red-tape. I had been encouraged to break rules, take risks, speak my mind, and slay the status quo. Further, I wasn't one for politics, having delved rather deeply into them in college, and determined it was not my interest or calling.

Finally, our roles, skills, and work approaches were totally different. I did have an undergraduate degree from an Ivy League contender. However, I was no numbers cruncher. I had gone to film school, pioneered in ecommerce before it was a "thing," and had become an industry-recognized leader. I was a conceptual thinker with design abilities and an unusual combination of skills including ecommerce, UX, media production, retail, operations, and supply chain. I even knew two programming languages and how to use a number of proprietary tools.

There was just very little comparison between the two of us.

At the pinnacle of my frustration, I told Michelle about our executive's advice. She laughed out loud—aghast and baffled by the suggestion. She reminded me of why they recruited me to the company. She admitted that she couldn't do the things I could do. She didn't have the extensive background or experience I had. She wasn't media or tech savvy and giggled when she admitted she didn't have a creative bone in her body. We both thought it was crazy.

I knew my problems had nothing to do with needing to emulate Michelle, though I probably needed some of her polish. The real issue was the clear divide between my management's expectations and my understanding of the job itself. They paid high-priced agencies to give them advice. They didn't really want my opinion, even if it was backed by facts and an unprecedented level of experience. They maintained a culture of people who toed the line, snapped to attention, and did what they were told. It was clear that, in kind, leadership wanted me to do the same. They also wanted me to back up and validate some very bad choices and decisions—rather than to challenge or point out potentially better options.

I couldn't escape the fact that this company had recruited me for my brain and extensive experience but didn't want me to use it. I managed to do some excellent work there before I left, exponentially increasing revenue, introducing new efficiencies, and reducing costs. However, it was an uphill climb, and I stepped on more than a few landmines in the process, in a culture where my wings were definitely not welcome. When I left the organization, I breathed a very deep sigh of relief, cheered on by a handful of other suppressed colleagues who had watched things go down. For a long time, I carried the weight of failing to win everyone over as I had successfully done in past jobs. However, I took comfort in the fact that, even if I had gotten really good at faking it, I wasn't cut out for that place.

Further, I had experienced such highly positive employment experiences in the past, I *knew* there were companies that would welcome and embrace someone like me. I felt grateful to have that understanding as a base of reference, because many people do not. While this was one of the tougher professional experiences of my career, I learned a great deal from it! It played a critical role in awakening me to the cultural realities that exist in many companies and the importance of choosing my employment wisely. It also alerted me to areas of strength and weakness that I would later recognize as the pros and pitfalls of my operational style.

GETTING OUT OF THE WEEDS

If you struggle with your design and your flaws, you are not alone. Just as Carrie and I killed our style envy and crushed our own identity crises, you can, too. As you embrace your operational style, you'll become wiser about how to find the right fit for yourself and to better align your work to your design. As you learn to work adaptively with others and recognize styles at work, you can maximize your potential and minimize weakness. As you begin to see results, you can also course-correct with more confidence—making changes like Carrie and I did—to secure positions that honor you, as you do honor to your employer.

Circumventing Style Confusion or an identity crisis requires time, patience, introspection, and most importantly, developing a better appreciation for who you are and standing confident in it. Having an identity crisis is a lot like getting lost in the weeds. Be patient with yourself as you back out of the tangle. Give yourself time to find your way out and back on a good path. Leveraging the exercises in this book can help you reconnect with suppressed hopes, dreams, desires, priorities, and help you realize what motivates and energizes you. This can also help you develop a better idea of the kinds of work culture and reporting relationships that are best for you as you course-correct for the future.

CHAPTER 10
RECOGNIZING THE STYLES OF OTHERS

Developing the ability to successfully navigate interpersonal relationships and establish common ground is a critical skill for anyone in the Workplace Wilderness. In this chapter, I'll talk through my process for style recognition, talk about some of the challenges of style recognition, and provide some insight that can help you recognize the styles of people in your workplace.

The 2018 CPP Global Human Capital Report surveyed full-time employees in nine countries. The report states that 85 percent of global workers deal regularly with conflict, and cites the primary causes of workplace conflict as personality clashes and warring egos (49 percent), followed by stress (34 percent), and heavy workloads (33 percent). The report further states that the average employee spends 2.1 hours per week dealing with conflict. In the USA alone, this translates to 385 million working days spent as a result of conflict at work!

Understanding the classic tensions and compatibilities between operational styles, as well the as the traits of each style, can help you work more effectively with others. This will not only reduce interpersonal conflict, but will also reduce stress, improve collaboration, and help you share the workload in a manner that leverages communal strength. With time and practice, leveraging the information in this book, you should be able to identify the operational styles of the individuals in your workplace with a decent level of accuracy about 70–75 percent of the time. The remaining 25–30 percent should become evident with time and a little additional study.

ASKING, OBSERVING & INVESTIGATING

Again, while style recognition can sometimes occur quickly, it's more often a process of discovery. The discovery process is a good thing, as getting to know others in your workplace is critical to *more* than just style recognition. Teddy Roosevelt once said, "Nobody cares how much you know until they know how much you care." When we reach out to better understand and adapt to work well with others, we signal that we care. This helps open others up in return, opening a channel of communication and building bridges of understanding that lead to common ground. Common ground creates the platform for good communication, collaboration, and mutually beneficial outcomes.

After fifteen years, I've become pretty good at recognizing the operational styles of others. In general, the more you know about someone, the easier it is to do. My approach is relatively straightforward, and involves observing, asking, and investigating.

Observing

The most powerful way to identify someone's operational style is to observe others in action. This includes watching people's behavior and actively listening to the things they say. As you study individuals, look for strengths and weaknesses to identify style traits. Pay attention to an individual's preferences for getting things done, their schedule, and appreciation for process and protocol. Observe social behavior and see if you notice active networking, "grapevine" connections, circles of trust, and other associations. Pay attention to areas of specialization. Tune in to priorities, goals, and objectives. Examine how people respond under pressure, threats, or duress, or when people with authority and power are present. Pay attention to how people share and communicate. Leverage the Tips for Style recognition (highlighted below) to collect as much data as you can, and compare what you observe to the chapters on Walkers, Climbers, and Flyers. This will help you align the people you know to a dominant operational style.

Asking

It sounds obvious, but we often fail to ask basic questions that help us understand an individual's role, function, priorities, objectives, and relationship within the organization. When you don't know someone well, but have mutual associates, you can also ask questions of others to fill in your understanding about someone. Asking questions of others can be very helpful in building dialogue and understanding, too. There's no magical list of questions to ask—just apply common sense and don't get too personal, probe too hard, or ask questions that are out of context. Tailor your questions to the individual and situation. Choose questions that are contextually relevant and common-sense, and demonstrate your genuine interest and desire to get to know a person and work collaboratively.

For example, it's always good to ask practical questions. "What's your schedule like—is there anything I need to be sensitive to?" In addition, it's never a bad idea to ask a person how he or she would prefer to work with you moving forward. For example, "How would you like to review this together—is there a format you'd prefer?" It is also totally acceptable to ask, at the outset of a meeting or project, what a person's top priorities, concerns, or questions are, so that you can better address them.

It's also possible to ask questions that are style-related. For example, as a Flyer, knowing that people don't process things the way I do, I will always ask how much time a person or group has to interact. I will also ask whether people are energized or exhausted by brainstorming and ideation, so I can actively respond and tailor my approach for my audience. In a worst-case scenario, the answers people give in response to your ask will be pragmatically useful. In a best-case scenario, the answers will provide clues to a person's operational style.

Investigating

When it becomes challenging to determine an individual's operational style, it can be helpful to conduct a little stealth research to obtain some extra information and context. When this becomes necessary, social media channels like Google, Linked In, Twitter, Facebook, Instagram, or even regional social media sites like Badoo (UK/EU), Viber (South America), and others can be incredibly useful in helping you learn more about an individual. On several occasions, when conducting some stealth research, I stumbled on a blog, You Tube Channel, and/or podcast. Obtaining some first-person narrative can be incredibly useful when you don't know someone well—and having insight into the topics they chose to write or talk about can also prove interesting. While your research shouldn't replace building an in-person relationship with someone, it can provide some additional context to fill in gaps related to an individual's professional history, career path, interests, and activities. It can also give you ideas for ice-breakers.

As you investigate—use discretion! *There's a fine line between simple, professional research and being creepy!* Most people would feel awkward and violated to discover you've been doing stealth research on them in social channels. Most strangers don't want you to follow them on Facebook. For example, when using LinkedIn, remember that unless you have a Premium account, individuals are likely to receive notice that you've perused their profiles while logged in. Apply caution! Don't violate someone's boundaries when observing, asking, and researching. As a rule of thumb, if the probing *feels* invasive, it probably is! Don't make your actions or interest too obvious. Further, be careful about divulging what you learn, lest you come across like a stalker!

SOME EASY, SOME TOUGH

The operational styles of some people are easier to identify than others and the more information you have to work with, the better. Hands down, it's easiest to identify the operational style of a person with whom you have some professional exposure. Furthermore, it is often easier to identify an individual's operational style when they have a lot of active pitfalls. As I mentioned, this may be true in part because it's human nature to be more critical. However, the presence of many active pitfalls can also make a person into a kind of "negative stereotype" of the style. Here's a decent example of this:

A client I'll call Samantha, a successful VP, called me disturbed about a new VP who was hired as her peer. He had come in to the organization from a large competitor, full of ego and ambition. While he boasted about his experience and capabilities, he spoke to people in ways that felt condescending and rude. In just a few weeks, had alienated several people with his comments and behavior.

The week he arrived, he announced to one of his direct reports: "Within a year, I'll be in a corner office at Corporate HQ." He proceeded to ask probing questions about the ages of senior executives in an attempt to identify their anticipated retirement timeframes. As if this audacity weren't enough, at one point, he began looking into Samantha's boss, an SVP who'd been with the firm twenty years. After hearing about her, he pronounced, "Well, she'll be retiring soon. I could easily do her job."

The new VP had rattled Samantha's cage more than once. In their first meeting, he made an overt move to have some of her staff transition to report to him! When she raised an eyebrow over the comment, he looked her in the eye and said, "Oh, don't worry, Sam. I'll take you, too." Management asked Samantha to give him an orientation related to her organization, structure, mandates, and activities, as she was responsible for three, very big operational areas that impacted him. She blocked off a half day to work with him and sent an invite, which he accepted. She then scheduled meet and greets with her staff and prepped to brief him.

The day of the meeting, the new VP showed up thirty minutes late with no warning or apology. He then sprawled out in her office chair and talked about himself for twenty minutes. Samantha tried to segue into her planned agenda but as she got started, he rose, saying he had to go. Perplexed, Samantha reminded him that she'd cleared her schedule to meet with him. He shrugged, and said, "Yeah, well, I have some more important things to take care of. I will have to circle back with you later." When he returned to his office, he complained to Mary, a direct report who had worked with Samantha for fifteen years, claiming Samantha was ill-prepared for the meeting and it was a waste of his time. Fortunately, Mary had Sam's back and tipped her off to the new VP's behavior. Samantha was stymied, threatened, and angry. She called me to ask what she should do.

Based on the guy's overt posturing, positioning, and self-declared intentions to rise to power, I suspected that he was Climber operating on boatload of pitfalls. He had no poker face at all, which was unusual; it seemed to be overridden by an insane amount of ambition, pride, ego, and insecurity. I guessed that he had also had some misperceptions related the firm's structure, strategy, and plans, as well as Samantha's role and mandate. While it was relatively easy to figure out his operational style, to manage him, Samantha needed a plan.

We went through the traits of a typical Climber and discussed the factors that may be driving his behavior. This helped to depersonalize his behavior for Samantha. However, she remained concerned about his "land grab" with her direct reports, as well as the way he threw her under the bus with Mary. Samantha said, "Leigh, I am a Walker. I cannot, in any way, relate to this guy." I responded, "Samantha, you don't have to relate to him. You just have to understand him and what he's capable of, and figure out how you're going to respond."

In allowing herself to become shaken and upset, Samantha was giving the guy more power than he'd earned. To help give her back some of her power, we reviewed the facts, starting by looking at his LinkedIn profile. The guy was younger than she was, had held down three jobs in his lifetime. His claims to greatness were overwrought. He was recklessly ambitious, full of ego and pride, eager to prove himself, and deeply insecure. He had a big mouth that had already gotten him in trouble. He had a little experience yet seemed to consider himself an expert on all things.

I then reminded Samantha of who *she* was: She had earned her position. She had a spotless, stellar reputation and a fifteen-year history with her firm. The new VP was one stakeholder out of *many* that she was tasked with serving. He wasn't special. He did not have any authority over her. He was not in a position to take her down. She had a clear mandate and the resources to fulfill them. He had only *delusional* claims to her people.

I explained to Samantha that the only way to work with this new VP was to own her power and position, and match strength with strength! I encouraged her to set firm boundaries and reinforce them. We then laid out a very specific plan for her to do just that, working strategically to set the record straight and nip the bad behavior in the bud, and put it into place. He wasn't a fan of her newfound confidence, but the plan worked well. At the end of the day, this guy's pitfalls made his operational style hyper-evident, and it empowered Samantha to respond in a way that neutralized him. Today, he remains squirrely, but he's in check!

STYLE MASTERS

On the opposite side of pitfall-driven caricatures, you'll find individuals I call "Style Masters." Style Masters have such a high level of emotional intelligence and adaptability, it can be very hard to discern their operational styles. Most often, however, this won't matter. Style Masters can easily to work with almost anyone, handling themselves and others so artfully in the workplace, there's little friction with others. They are generally well-liked, effective, and even pleasurable to work with. They also tend to manage people exceptionally well. If you find a Style Master in your workplace, watch and learn! They usually have strong emotional intelligence and often make terrific mentors.

One my favorite managers is a guy I'll call Matt, a Style Master I worked under for almost a year. Matt is a Climber and (in contrast to the nightmare VP Samantha dealt with) one of the best managers I've ever had the pleasure of working with. He seems to operate on every strength and demonstrated few weaknesses. For this reason, it took me about three months to figure out what Matt's operational style was, and figuring him out almost drove me nuts. In my lifetime, I have met few individuals that could better manage themselves in the workplace. Matt had a terrific ability to arrest his own pitfalls and magnify nearly every strength in a kind of Jedi-like style.

Perhaps a big part of Matt's leadership success can be attributed to his huge heart and high emotional intelligence. Matt is a lover of people. He is low ego and understands how to lead and manage people based on their individual needs. He is great at reading others and knows how to inspire and motivate people. Matt excels in creating common ground and establishing the "win angle" for everyone. He also knows how to ask for what he needs and almost always gets what he wants, in part due to the fact that he's a nice guy who is a lot of fun—and in part because he has an inherent ability to make others feel innately special.

The "light of favor" effect works well for Matt, whose leadership style motivates people to move mountains for him. An artful delegator, Matt has a way of orchestrating things effectively to hit key milestones. One of the executive administrative assistance once summed up Matt's motivational and delegation prowess well when she said: "Oh, that Matt...every time he comes to my desk, I know that when he walks away, I will have ten times more work on my plate than I do now. But for the oddest reason, I like him *better* for it!"

As a senior executive and a Climber, Matt drives against a focused agenda. He consistently delivers. He hits deadlines while he remains ambitious with his eyes on the prize. At the same time, he remains one of the most flexible, sympathetic, and empathetic managers I have ever known. I have never seen him posture in a manner that feels fearful, threatened, territorial, or selfish in his pursuits. While he typically has the authority and power to plough through obstacles, he uses that power in a disciplined way that gives and garners respect. As a result, people are motivated to work with him, and obstacles often dissolve in front of him.

While it took some time for me to figure out Matt's operational style— the Climber in Matt later became more evident. However, what I admire most is how evenly tempered his style is by a high amount of emotional intelligence. Matt demonstrates a strong level of ownership of his thoughts, emotions, attitudes, and behaviors. He is determined to treat others with respect and demonstrates a real passion for bringing out the best in people, as well as having fun.

At this point, I've given Climber-based examples that help describe the two extremes of style recognition: the stereotype (super easy) and the style master (super hard). It's important to note, however, that most people will fall somewhere in between those two extremes. The styles of some individuals will be easier to recognize—while others will just be tougher. It's like this in life, too: Some people are harder to get to know. They may be more antisocial, closed off, or more inclined to be clandestine about how they conduct their affairs at work.

Style recognition can be especially difficult when you haven't worked directly with someone. A lack of firsthand knowledge or exposure to someone can be tough when you are thrust together and told to work together. My advice in these situations is to take the time to get to know people. Make time to grab lunch or coffee. Be patient with the tougher characters—and continue to ask, observe, and do your research. In time, operational styles eventually reveal themselves. Remember that you will never lose by authentically getting to know other people—or by responding to what you learn by adjusting your approach.

TIPS FOR STYLE RECOGNITION

To help you recognize operational styles, the information in chapters 4, 5, and 6 are a rich resource. Chapters 12 and 13 provide information on Style Dynamics and specific tips for working adaptively that will be helpful too! The trait lists for each operational styles traits may also serve as helpful cheat sheets. However, keep in mind that the traits expressed on that checklist are high-level statements that can leave things up to interpretation. It's fine to use them, but try to absorb the information in the chapters to supplement the checklists. With observation and research, you will collect clues that can help you align individuals to a dominant operational style. As you seek to identify the styles of others, here some that may prove to be helpful:

Body Language

It's easy to tell what a person likes and doesn't like, or whether they are telling the truth or withholding information, with an understanding of body language. Can you tell if someone is being honest, or deceptive? Do they seem distracted or tuned out? Are they irritated or conveying hostility? Understanding body language can help you read body signals to better understand people. For example, Climbers tend to care about the professional stature they project and will often power posture and "dress the part" to project authority, power, and even affluence. In contrast, you may find a conceptual Flyer to be more prone to use a lot of hand gestures to describe ideas. Flyers may also have a more casual stature and/or dress to reflect their individuality or creativity. To learn more about body language, I recommend Jo-Ellan Dimitruius and Mark Mazzarella's book *Reading People: How to Understand People and Predict their Behavior, Any Time Any Place*.

There are also some good tutorials for reading body language online that can help you read people more accurately.

Relationships

It can be very useful to pay attention to the relationships people form at work—how people socialize, work together, and leverage others to get things done. Pay attention to who people associate with. Try to pick up on friendships, alliances, and competitions. Look for people who are great networkers. Sniff out the delegators and the people with "grapevine" connections. Pay attention to the classic tensions and compatibilities between styles! All these things can provide clues to an individual's operational style.

Power, Authority, Hierarchy

It can be insightful to note how much attention other people pay to titles, rank, power, or authority. The way a person introduces themselves can also be insightful. You can also learn a lot about someone by observing how they treat people at various ranks in an organization, from executive "brass" to lower-level staff. Generally speaking, with Climbers, rank, influence, power, and authority really matter. In contrast, Flyers are far less preoccupied with these things, putting more attention on the work and the mission, crossing boundaries in a way that turns heads in a positive *and* a negative manner. Walkers tend to take the middle road, respecting authority while working within the chain of command very well. What's interesting about Walkers is how they leverage individual and collective power behind the scenes to turn tides in their own favor!

Focus & Priorities

It's not only practical but incredibly useful to develop a clear picture of an individual's focus, priorities, or agenda. As previously described, Climbers always have an agenda and remain keenly focused on it, making it hard to entertain ideas and requests that are unrelated. Walkers tend to stay focused within their assigned areas of responsibility, managing a very neatly stacked proverbial "apple cart" of assigned tasks and responsibilities. They like to be able to anticipate what's coming and keep things manageable, and dislike having their order upset. Flyers tend to vacillate from laser-like detailed focus to very broad, high-level strategic focus, in a way that can be hard to follow. Again, all these patterns serve as helpful operational style clues!

Communication Style

Watch how people communicate for clues into their operational style. Flyers tend to treat topical discussions like ever branching explorations— rather than focused paths. They find it hard to summarize and are prone to overcommunicate and often overwhelm people with information and conceptual ideas. Again, Walkers tend to share information in a manner that is very relevant to the discussion at hand and have a deep well of focused knowledge and expertise that can be highly insightful—if they don't withhold information due to competitive instinct, feeling threatened, or a trust imbalance. Climbers have a natural inclination to keep information closer-to-chest and remain guarded when it comes to information sharing. They prefer to discuss things at a higher level first—and engage best when a topic or discussion aligns to their agenda or interest.

Employment History

While there's no clear giveaway here for a Flyer or Climber, a Walker can often be identified by the telltale "*clear path through the career grass*" effect. Again, the Walker's lane of expertise is focused and clear, and job progression from one position to another tends to be logical to follow, forming a proverbial path. For Flyers and Climbers, specialization and career progression may not be as easy to trace. As outlined previously, Flyers leave no "jet trail" to follow. They often have several "lanes" of specialization with expertise that may be totally disparate or overlapping, as well as multidisciplinary skill and cross functional ability—this will make the Flyer's specialization(s) hard to describe. Further, Flyers may engage in professional maneuvers or have a work history that looks like several careers rolled into one. In a similar manner, Climbers, leave few traces as they "scale the career wall." However, each job represents a point-of-leverage to jump to the next position, and you can often see, looking at a resume or professional profile, this leverage at work.

STYLE RECOGNITION EXAMPLES

Here are a few style recognition examples, provided to give you some context as you attempt to identify the styles of people in your workplace.

Corrin, Age 32

Corrin received a BS in accounting at Virginia Tech. Her first job was as a Senior Accountant for Ernst and Young. She later became an accounting manager for a dot-com startup, where she worked for five years before moving on to a senior accountant position with a large accounting firm. Today, she is the controller for a government organization. She is organized, process-driven, and runs a pretty tight ship. Over the years, she has gained numerous certifications pertaining to her work. You can clearly see her "career path through the grass" when looking at her LinkedIn profile. She keeps a pretty regular schedule, working a typical nine-to-five day. She has a lot on her plate and manages a staff of seven, who help ensure that financial statements, general ledger, accounting, payroll, receivables, budgets, taxes, and financial analyses are managed properly. She remains close with her team, who keep her in the loop on office buzz and gossip, though she isn't one to gossip herself. Corrin helps organize the company's United Way campaign each year. On the side, she is active in the local PTA and coaches girl's softball.

Clues: Specialized focus. Deep knowledge, training, and certification. Keeps things running. Critical, core, operational function. Process oriented. Keeps a predictable schedule. Grapevine connection. Relational. Seems to have more work/life balance and "compartments" of life that extend outside of work.

Operational Style: Walker

Bob, Age 56

Bob has a degree in engineering from Georgia Tech. He served in the Army Corps of Engineers for fifteen years. After the Army, he landed a job with a government services firm, moving quickly into a program management position that oversaw the work of other engineers. He moved from a relatively junior position to management rapidly, advancing from associate to vice president. After twelve years at his firm, his advancement slowed. Bob then took a leap to assume a president and CEO role for a startup company. He led the company into an initial public offering and laid the groundwork for it to be acquired by another firm. After this, he assumed a sequence of C-level positions, working between commercial and government services organizations in a CEO role. While the companies were each very different, Bob's responsibilities always focused on the same thing: managing mergers and acquisitions. Bob is always in a suit and readily postures at the head of the room. He makes sure people start with a clear agenda and stick to it and will readily shut down anyone he feels is "off topic." He wants the bullets, the facts, and the elevator pitch. In response, he is a tough read, keeping knowledge close-to-chest, and sharing reservedly. He is an authoritative, tough boss who can, at times, be dictator-like in driving to his desired outcomes. He is a phenomenal negotiator and deal maker, and a master of delegation. He is conservative with his words, leaving some of his direct reports frustrated by undercommunication. Bob knows how to run a company, mobilize and manage teams, and drive to key milestones with an emphasis on measurable outcomes and fiscal responsibility.

Clues: Jobs as leverage. Emphasis on authority and delegation. Personal "power" grooming and posturing. Authoritative self-carriage. Dictator, closed communicator. Relatively rapid rise to executive position. Focus on goals, objectives, milestones, and prioritization (agenda). Delegation and negotiation skills. Focus on power and authority. Disparity between formal training (engineer) and work discipline (mergers and acquisitions).

Style: Climber

Kory, Age 45

Kory has a bachelor's degree in communications from USC. On his LinkedIn profile, there are seventeen different positions listed since the late '90s. He has been a marketing manager, technology consultant, executive producer, editor-in-chief, director of creative services, and president of a software company (I am summarizing). He served as the president for a media studio, as professor at a film school, and instructor for an art and design school. He serves on the boards of Eco Fashion Week, an arts committee, and on the Board of Advisors for TED and SXSW. He is an award-winning tech photographer, a mentor, and founded his own apparel company that benefits eco-friendly causes. He is missionally-minded, and he selects clients and jobs based on their social conscience. He is a respected visionary and a creative, conceptual thinker who has worked in many positions involving strategy and building things. While people who know him can describe the work they've been exposed to (e.g. his photography), if asked to categorize or describe what Kory does for a living, most would be hard pressed to figure out what to call him. The term "Renaissance man" might come to mind for some. His appearance can be misleading. He is a scruffy guy, who wears tie-dye and cargo pants, and looks like a Hippie. He drives a VW Bus and lives off the grid when he's not moving in tech influencer scenes. While he's socially outgoing, "in his element" he is also a classic introvert. However, when people engage with him, they almost always find him overwhelmingly insightful, wise, and thought provoking, with an uncanny professional instinct and the ability to forecast the future. While he is a tech influencer who hangs out with a who's who list of luminaries, he's largely unimpressed by power, authority, and titles, preferring to hang out with smart, missionally minded people building cool things.

Clues: Work aligns to mission/purpose. Visionary. Strategist. Builder. Multiple lanes of expertise. Multidisciplinary. Strategic executor. Different "careers" in his lifetime. Hard to describe his occupation. Dress as expression of self. Wild back story. Lack of regard for power, position, authority.

Style: Flyer

While these examples are more corporate/white collar professional jobs, you can find the same pattern in any kind of employment situation—whether a person is in retail, shipping, manufacturing, healthcare, government services, entertainment, startups, a service industry, or another sector.

EXERCISE 8
STYLE RECOGNITION

With time and practice, you will learn to pick up clues that will help you identify and adapt to the operational styles of others. As you plot your course forward, let's start by identifying the operational styles of some of the individuals you work with. You can begin by taking a general look at some of the people you work with each day, examining the traits they share in common.

A. EASY PEOPLE	
List the names of three-to-five "easy" people, with whom you work well and enjoy good rapport. List the traits that make each person comfortable to work with. Circle any traits that repeat themselves from one person to another.	
NAMES	**TRAITS & CHARACTERISTICS**

B. PROBLEM PEOPLE

List the names of three-to-five of the most problematic people you work with. List traits that either make it difficult to work with each person, or which bother you about your problem people. Circle any traits that repeat themselves from one person to the next.

NAMES	TRAITS & CHARACTERISTICS

C. HOW YOUR PROBLEM PEOPLE VIEW YOU

With time and practice, you will learn to pick up clues that will help you identify and adapt to the operational styles of others. As you plot your course forward, let's start by identifying the operational styles of some of the people you work with. You can begin by taking a general look at some of the people you work with each day, examining the traits they have in common.

THEIR NAMES	YOUR TRAITS & CHARACTERISTICS

D. STYLE IDENTIFICATION

Now, go back and select one easy person and two problem people. Take some time to do an internet search and check out their Linked In and social media footprints. Take down notes. Try to identify each person's operational style. If you are stumped, take some additional time to observe, ask and investigate!

NAMES	TRAITS/NOTES/CLUES	STYLE?
Example: *Paul*	• *Driven by plan and objectives* • *Fast tracking to leadership* • *Ambitious, driven, competitive (crush competition)* • *Good manager—delegates/motivates* • *Charming—wins people over easily* • *Closed information sharing—can be frustrating* • *Dictatorial at times—alienates others* • *Networker—great at relationship / partnership* • *Self-promoter—sometimes at expense of others* • *Territorial and protective of contacts and projects* • *Tension with Eva (a Flyer?) and Randy (Walker?)* • *Seems strategic? (Flyer trait)*	*CLIMBER*

D. STYLE IDENTIFICATION *(continued)*		
NAMES	TRAITS/NOTES/CLUES	STYLE?

PART THREE

NEGOTIATING CHALLENGING TERRITORY

CHAPTER 11
MITIGATING WEAKNESS

PITFALLS AND TRIGGERS

After reading the chapter materials on Walkers, Climbers, and Flyers, you should have a general understanding of the operational style to which you most likely align, and a better understanding of how the traits of your style tend to manifest in you, personally. Again, our pitfalls are style traits that, when active, can prove to be distracting, negative, destructive, career limiting, and/or problematic stumbling blocks. While it's unlikely that all the pitfall traits listed for your dominant operational style will apply to you personally, it's a good idea to have an awareness of the pitfalls that are typically associated with your dominant operational style so you can proactively manage areas of potential weakness, lest they be activated. Essentially, there are two types of triggers that can activate pitfalls:

Situational triggers are external factors beyond your control that may impact you and/or your ability to do your job well. For example, perhaps you're in an environment where you have been given responsibility to do a job, but your boss won't give you the *authority* to make critical decisions. You might find yourself in a position where there's not enough budget to do what you need to do. Alternatively, perhaps you are dealing with a boss or coworker who is behaving badly. Other examples of situational triggers include a company undergoing a downsizing event, a hiring frenzy, or a reorganization. Situational triggers impact you and others and can set off chain reactions by triggering emotional responses and reactions.

For example, a poorly handled team reorganization or layoff (situational trigger) may *trigger* buzz and gossip (pitfall) in a Walker that might spread through the grapevine. On another front, putting a Climber in a situation with shifting priorities and a poorly defined role (situational trigger) may motivate a Climber to behave shrewdly in defending their "turf." (pitfall)

Emotional triggers are exactly as they sound: emotions you feel, which have the potential to impact others. While we can't always control our emotions, we can control our responses to our emotions and which ones we choose to entertain. When we allow negative thoughts, motivations, and assumptions to lead us, they can naturally activate and/or exacerbate our pitfalls, pushing us into negative frames of mind or "headspaces" that can potentially disrupt interpersonal and team dynamics and undermine us in doing our best work.

For example, Climbers tend to be reserved communicators. Combine this trait with fear and insecurity (emotional triggers), and the Climber may intentionally under-communicate or leave people in the dark (pitfall). A Flyer who is insecure (trigger) may have the tendency to try to communicate too much, overwhelming and confusing others (pitfall).

Pitfall Triggers

EMOTIONAL TRIGGERS SUCH AS...			
• Arrogance	• Critical Spirit	• Greed	• Laziness
• Anger	• Disrespect	• Ignorance	• Negativity
• Bitterness	• Ego/Pride	• Indifference	• Resentment
• Blame	• Envy/Jealousy	• Impatience	• Selfishness
• Confusion	• Fear	• Insecurity	• Unforgiveness
• Contentiousness			

OFTEN LEAD TO...			
• Aggression	• Exclusion	• Passive Behavior	• Retribution
• Argument	• Fights	• Lack of	• Territorialism
• Apathy	• Gossip	Cooperation	• Tuning Out
• Controlling	• Miscommunication	• Poor Listening	• Withholding
• Dishonesty/Lies	• Negative	• Reactive	•...and more
• Denial	Assumption	Behavior	

Earlier in my professional career, I was a newly hired executive in a startup company. The CEO was a Flyer with a high degree of emotional intelligence. We got along famously and enjoyed regular rounds of intense, frank, open ideation we jokingly called "brain hockey." He asked me to provide input on a product redesign the team had started before I joined. They had come pretty far along on things already, so I conducted an exhaustive review of the progress-to-date. Afterward, I met with the CEO to download some concerns about the planned changes. The CEO found my feedback insightful and asked me to attend a meeting with the development team to discuss these considerations.

The meeting got off to a great start. When the CEO asked me to speak, I began by sharing how excited I was to be there, issuing kudos to the team, acknowledgement of the mission, and some positive words about the product and the direction of the company. However, when I transitioned to a discussion of the team's product redesign, things went south rather quickly. Emboldened by my senior position and executive support, and eager to prove myself, I delivered my input the same way I had to the CEO: "Hockey-style," with a bold candor and frankness. I began to highlight the things I thought were wrong with the new product version, pulling no punches in making some very salient points. I was clear, direct, and open. However, I became so caught up in my own head, I wasn't paying attention to the responses of the people around me. I didn't ask a lot of questions and the team didn't offer a lot of input. When I was done, there was a lot of silence.

After the meeting, the CEO pulled me aside and asked me how I thought the meeting went. Perplexed, I said I wasn't sure. The team seemed open at first, and then became very quiet. He side-eyed me. "Leigh, did you pay any attention to how the people responded to you in that room?" he asked. "In the beginning, you had everybody eating out of the palm of your hand. They were all leaning forward at the table, looking right at you. They were fully engaged and eager to hear what you had to say." He continued, "But then halfway in, you decided to list everything they had done wrong. I watched as every single person in that room leaned back in their chairs, pushed back from the table, and crossed their arms in front of themselves. Leigh. You lost them all. They totally shut down on you."

I grimaced as my heart rate shot into the stratosphere. He continued, "You know, they've worked for months on redesigning this product. You just told them what they did was wrong. It was like going up to a proud new mom and saying, 'BOY! Your baby is ugly!'" I was speechless and ashamed. He paused for a moment, and, sensing my horror and distress, he came over and patted me on the shoulder. "Know what I think about you?" he said with a wide grin, "I think you were *right* about everything you said. In fact, I think you are probably right a lot of the time—and that may be your biggest career handicap." He continued, "I hired you because you are smart. The thing you need to learn is that being smart is useless if you can't use truth to motivate and inspire people. That discussion shouldn't have been a diatribe about what was broken—it should have been a dialogue about what comes *next*." He then left me with marching orders to mend those damaged relationships. I was determined to do so, and eventually, I did.

On a *situational* level, I was brand new to that team. I didn't have enough background information to inform my understanding of the thinking that went into the redesign, or strong relationships that could withstand the force of my opinions. To make things worse, I made the mistake of not asking enough questions up front—engaging people in a dialogue, instead of going on a diatribe. On an *emotional* level, I was pretty full of myself as I expressed my thoughts. Looking back, I can see how this may have been driven by a certain amount of insecurity as I attempted to prove myself and my worth in that new position. Without question, I was remarkably selfish and insensitive in my approach and it was a recipe for disaster.

I'll never forget that day, how embarrassed and humiliated I was, or how bad I felt. I will also never forget my CEO's incredibly wise, insightful, and empathetic counsel. It took months to fully recoup from that gaffe and build trust-based relationships with the development team. However, I did manage to do it. Together we went on to do some really innovative work we were proud of. I am so thankful for that experience. It served as a humbling foray into leadership and a foundational lesson on the importance of attuning to others.

CHOOSING OUR EMOTIONAL WAVES

"Feelings are much like waves. We can't stop them from coming, but we can choose which ones to surf."

—JONATAN MARTENSSON

Controlling our emotional triggers can be a challenge. For example, at the present, I have a client who is undergoing a significant reorganization that has resulted in layoffs and a lot of internal upheaval. I don't know that I've ever seen morale so bad at this company, and my heart goes out to the team. Our calls are short and depressing. Energy levels are low. People obviously feel deflated and disengaged. While they are probably warranted in their feelings, as they continue to struggle with them, the negativity seems to spread, resulting in lost productivity and increased stress.

In like manner, I watched our son riding a negative emotional wave once, and it brought out a keen insight. The background is this: Lego pieces are the bane of my existence. Our son is the only grandson and only nephew and is summarily spoiled by grandparents, aunties, and uncles. As the result, he has a shamefully prolific Lego collection that spills out of every nook and cranny of our lives. If you visited my home today, you would find Lego in the living room, on the dining room table, on the hearth, on the floor, in the couch cushions, in the guest bedroom, and quite possibly in the bathroom, garage, and both cars. There are also several in my purse right now, and I just found a few on my desk. If I had a dollar for every Lego I have stepped or sat on or every time I said, "Pick up the Lego, NOW!" I'd be rolling in cash.

Our son is regularly in hot water for leaving Lego pieces everywhere. Once, at age eight, our little engineer left a brand new, partially assembled Lego set, complete with box and Lego kit wrappers dead in the middle of the hallway. My husband got up in the middle of the night to get some water, and, impaling his feet on a series of Lego piles, slipped on the wrappers and ended up kicking the box, audibly swearing, into a wall. He then angrily collected those Lego pieces, put them in a plastic garbage bag, and took them to the garage.

Upon rising the next morning, our indignant engineer flung open our bedroom door and demanded to know where his Lego set went. My husband informed him that he could earn them back one at a time by doing chores. Needless to say, our son was really upset about the loss of his new Lego set and a tearful protest ensued. He did *not* like this punishment much. We were, on the other hand, disproportionately pleased with this idea, especially as he proceeded to be unapologetic about leaving everything in a busy walkway. We were so tired of stepping on Lego! The kid had to learn some way!

My son began stomping and sulking around the house, head down, lower lip extended. This continued for most of the morning, until I gently intervened. "Dude," I said, "how many times have we warned you about the Lego mess? How many times did we tell you to pick up that set last night?" He scowled at me in return. "Look, bud, you did this to yourself—but you can earn them back. Fortunately, Dad didn't throw them away. It will just take a few days!"

Our young engineer side eyed me with a quivering, pouting lip and crocodile tears in his eyes. "I know that, Mom," he said. "I just want to be mad right now. *I feel good feeling bad.*"

Sometimes, it *does* feel good to feel bad, especially when we're stuck in an environment that is stressful, or we're working with people who drive us nuts! It's especially true if we have been wronged and are justified in our outrage, anger, or hatred or disdain or judgments about people and situations. The thing is, when we decide to indulge negative emotions, they can take over, forcing us to lose objectivity and a balanced perspective, leading us into unproductive behavior and the activation of pitfalls.

Without question, it's perfectly valid and okay to feel angry, rotten, insecure, threatened, or just perturbed. We just have to decide how far we're going to ride those emotional waves, and remain conscious of where they can potentially lead us! We become weakened when we let emotional triggers cloud our judgment or drive our responses—and more than it hurts others, this undermines our own success. To overcome our negative dialogue, we have to manage our emotions and take them captive.

MANAGING YOUR HEADSPACE

To manage our pitfalls, tuning in to the internal dialogue that tends to run at a subconscious level in our headspace is key. When we do this, it becomes easier to arrest negative chatter that plays in our minds. I often envision my internal dialogue as being driven by a chubby "head-space hamster" who runs slowly on a steadily squeaking hamster wheel. He is a greedy little creature of habit who, having feasted on my past experiences, is always hungry and ready to devour negative emotion, fear, and doubt. He feels it is his job to keep that wheel going 24/7, spinning off negative thoughts and judgments at lightning speed in an effort to get me into a primal, defensive posture.

Every single one of us have a Headspace Hamster—though some of them are more active than others. Many of us have become so used to the squeaking sound, we don't even hear it anymore. As a result, we allow that negative dialogue to play in the background. However, just because we aren't aware of it, doesn't mean those feelings don't trigger negative conscious thoughts and behaviors. Hence, the key to mitigating our weaknesses lies first in tuning into that internal dialogue and putting the hamster on a diet!

I found a great way to do this under the mentorship of a high-powered female executive in Washington, who had an impressive list of accomplishments that extended to working with the White House. She was a Climber who worked in the civic and political scene. As an African American woman, she understood the struggles of female executives and minorities. I met her as a young executive at a women's meeting, during a time when I had very few female leaders to whom I could go for counsel. During this season, I was facing some very real challenges related to having my ideas heard. I found myself battling with incredibly negative thoughts about myself, my situation, and others. One night, as we discussed things, my mentor pulled out a legal pad and challenged me with an exercise.

She drew two vertical lines on the page of the pad, dividing it into three columns. Over the top left column, she wrote "Thoughts." In the middle column, she wrote "Reality," and in the third column she wrote "Corrective Statement." She then handed it to me, smiling. "I want you to carry this with you for a week." She said, "If you need more pages—and you will—you have a whole pad to use here." She instructed me to tune in to my internal dialogue and write down my thoughts—good and bad—as they came to me during the day. These could be thoughts about myself, situations I found myself in, and others. As the day transpired, each time a thought or feeling came to mind, I was to record it under the "Thoughts" column. She instructed me to do this after every interaction and every meeting, as I sat alone working, throughout my day. Then, when I got home at night, she instructed me to critically evaluate the validity of each thought or emotion in the "Reality" column, and to write a "Corrective Statement" in the third column.

Now, this particular mentor was also a God-fearing woman who was very strong and outspoken in her Christian faith. She suggested if I needed help in coming up with a corrective statement and/or correcting my "stinking thinking" with truth, that I consult my Bible. She sent me away with my marching orders on a Tuesday night and told me to come back Friday with my notes.

I was relatively certain this would prove to be a silly exercise. However, I wanted to honor my mentor's investment of time in me and decided to do my best. About four hours into the first day, I was surprised to find I had a full page of notes already. The first night, I sat down, completely humbled and stunned to see the number of times I expressed insecurity, unworthiness, lack of trust, fear, self-loathing, a victim's mentality, and more. I was also shocked to see how I projected my own insecurities on others, with statements like "He doesn't respect me" and all kinds of other negative judgments. I began to see how my thoughts were creating a defensive posture in me and how that influenced others to steer clear—even tune me out. As I began to issue corrective statements and speak the truth over my situations, I began to feel things shift. In just a matter of days, I began to feel very differently. This was proving to be a powerful exercise!

On Friday, after reviewing my results, she instructed me, from that point on, to actively confront my internal dialogue, speaking truth over my life and my relationships as I went through my day—using the journal to help me if needed. She reminded me that taking our thoughts captive is a violent act that requires us to address them, arrest them, jail them, and guard them, lest they try to escape. The goal was to effectively end the negative "spinning" and thought patterns *as they emerged*.

Her advice was powerful. Slowly but surely, the squeaking wheel of my Headspace Hamster ceased. As I began to tune into my headspace and actively correct negative self-talk, negative assumptions about myself and others and defeatist, pessimistic attitudes were replaced by a clarity that neutralized the negative. I began to feel more positive and empowered, as I marveled at how often my perspectives were tainted by my insecurities. As I began to confront my internal dialogue with truth, everything shifted. As I consciously corrected as I went through my day, I found myself working with a lot more positivity and freedom. While my situation remained the same, people seemed to become more receptive to me. I still use this technique today. For this reason, I strongly recommend that you try this exercise yourself.

EXERCISE 9
HEADSPACE JOURNAL

Keeping a thought diary for three days can help you better tune in to your internal dialogue and make conscious changes in the way you choose to think about yourself, the situations you face, and the people in your workplace. It can also make you aware of the impact of your emotions in triggering your pitfalls, and help you deactivate them, as you arm yourself with objectivity and truth instead of allowing yourself to be driven by emotional responses.

Grab a notebook or legal pad, or download a worksheet from www.walk-climborfly.com, because the pages in this book probably won't be sufficient for this exercise. Divide your pages into three columns and record your thoughts as you go through your work day, including notes that can help you remember context. When you have lunch or go home at night, take the time to challenge every negative thought or assertion with facts and truth, and issue your own corrective statements. Confront your thinking using insights you find in books like this one, from the wise counsel from a trusted person, or your favorite religious or philosophical text. One of my clients really loves Yogi Berra quotes. Another finds wisdom from Oprah, Maya Angelou, and Annie Lamott. A thought diary will help you sneak up on negative thoughts and wrestle them to the ground. It can also help you clearly identify the emotional triggers that are driving you, so you can begin to take every thought captive to truth.

Headspace Journal Example

THOUGHTS	REALITY	CORRECTIVE STATEMENT
James is an utter jerk. I hate him.	James is difficult and rubs me the wrong way. He is probably insecure and compensates by acting overconfident. He may wish to provoke me, which isn't worth my time.	I may not like him but he is probably doing his best. I can respond with courtesy, keeping my eyes on the prize and maintaining my dignity.
Eva doesn't respect me.	Eva did brush me off, but she didn't have time to talk and she told me that twice. I wasn't being very sensitive to the demands on her time, even if she was a bit rude to me.	I need to set time with Eva when it works for her and reset things with a quick apology.
I am a failure.	The truth is, I don't suck nearly as badly as my insecurity tells me. Failure happens but I am not a failure. Look at my past successes!	"A person who never made a mistake never tried anything new." —Albert Einstein
		Time to move on!

While we can attempt to resolve the situational triggers around us, we can't assume responsibility for things beyond our control. However, we can be responsible for ourselves. While we've been given our instincts for a reason and we need to pay attention to them, unlike animals, we don't need to be *ruled* by gut reactions and instincts. The truth is, if we are not careful, our instincts can very well lead us in the wrong direction.

For example, if I'm out hiking and spot a mountain lion fifty feet away, my instinct might be to turn and run. However, that fear-based instinct to run is very likely to trigger the cat's predatorial instinct to chase prey. In like manner, if I crouch down, I make myself look submissive, like prey. Experts say that when you encounter a mountain lion you must stay calm, hold your ground, stand up confidently, face the lion, and do all you can to look intimidating—making noise, waving your arms in big motions, using a deep, powerful voice. This is not something your instinct is going to tell you to do—yet it could save your life.

Just like you may encounter a predator in the woods, the work world is full of jerks. Certain people, environments, and situations will simply trigger visceral responses that are accurate and justified. However, again, you must choose the waves you'll ride. You can arrest a critical spirit, irritation, and judgment. You can look past external behaviors and find truth and grace. You can refuse to allow others to undermine your own self confidence. Leveraging OST can help. As you begin to recognize operational styles, and notice pros and pitfalls at work, you will more naturally understand how people are "wired to function" and the things that may be triggering them. This insight can have the effect of depersonalizing bad behavior, making it easier not to react. This is especially true as you realize that the behavior of others often says more about them than it does about you. When we take the high road and approach people from a more objective, fair-minded, and calm place, we not only conserve our energy, we can also become powerful forces in shifting relational and workplace dynamics.

CHAPTER 12
WORKING ADAPTIVELY

Styles fuel the fire of collaboration. If you've ever been on a sports team, or if you've ever witnessed a truly remarkable sports play—the kind you'd like to replay in slow motion several times—working in an environment with good style dynamics feels just about as good. Striking the right balance on a team can lead to a transformative game where everyone picks up the slack and remarkable plays happen. When styles are appropriately balanced and people are operating on all cylinders—working adaptively, arresting pitfalls, staying aligned to the right tasks—a natural flow and rhythm can exist that naturally encourages people to do what they do best. This inspires good communication and beautiful collaborations that are greater than the sum of their parts. When styles mesh, this is how style interaction should feel:

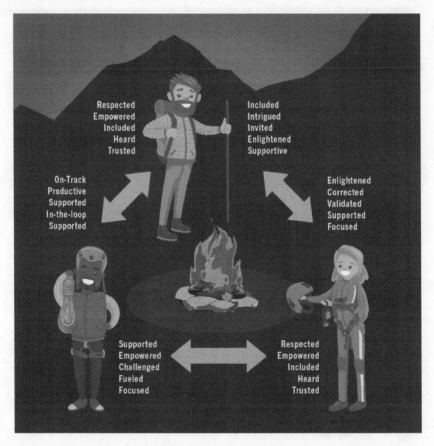

However, when styles *clash*, the opposite becomes true. As people with differing styles deal with interpersonal conflict, negative assumption, and rampant situational and emotional triggers, the fire of collaboration is extinguished. When conflict spreads to teams or between departments, it undermines collaboration, efficiency, and productivity. When problems go unchecked and unresolved, it also undermines morale and increases employee disengagement and can have a cascading effect.

This is how it feels when styles collide:

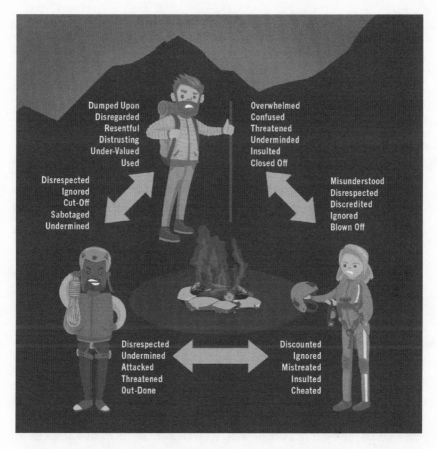

When you really understand and can readily identify the operational styles of others, it becomes easier to build bridges of understanding with others and avoid style clashes. Using what you learn here, you can tailor your approach to work with others effectively and establish common ground for collaboration and mutually beneficial outcomes. This is the crux of working adaptively. Individuals who excel at working adaptively not only work hard to mitigate their own weakness, they also excel in developing an understanding of others in light of the situations they face.

KEYS TO WORKING ADAPTIVELY

While some of this involves review or the underscoring of previous points, the following recommendations will help you become a better adaptive worker:

Understand Others

Most of what you need to know about each operational style, style dynamics, and how to recognize operational styles is presented in the chapters of this book. By developing a firm grasp of the three operational styles, you can quickly assess people, appreciate their strengths, anticipate and take measures to avoid conflict, and establish common ground for collaboration. The primary goal here is not to build some kind of "style cult" or fixation on operational styles. Instead, the primary goal of working this way is to train people's brains to look beyond themselves to consider the plight of others. As people practice OST, my hope is that style recognition will become a gateway to greater human understanding, as we leverage that understanding to work more flexibly and with greater empathy with others. I believe that working this way, we can collectively build a healthier, more functional, and habitable workplace.

Embrace Empathy

Empathy can be described as the ability to recognize emotions in others, or to be able to "put yourself in someone else's shoes," to grasp another person's perspective or reality. Operational Styles Theory was developed to help people more quickly attune to others and empathetically adapt in the mutual interests of both parties. As your gaze shifts from self-focus to a stronger emphasis on others, you may find yourself with a greater appreciation for what people bring to the table, as well as a more sympathetic awareness of the demands and pressures they face. As understanding and empathy grow, it becomes easier to depersonalize the behaviors of others, and respond with a level of care, concern, and sensitivity that is often missing in the workplace today.

Empathy does not come easily to everyone. However, there are things you can do to develop greater empathy:

- Check your attitude—abandon self-superiority
- Imagine yourself in the other person's position
- Listen and look for clues and insights into context, style, emotion, and triggers

- Take a personal interest in the human side of the story

- Ask leading questions

Empathy is one component of Emotional Intelligence or "EQ." According to *Psychology Today*, EQ is "the ability to identify and manage your own emotions and the emotions of others." EQ involves having an *awareness of emotions*, being able to *harness emotion and put it to work,* and being able to *regulate emotion*. I highly recommend working hard to build a greater level of emotional intelligence at work. Two older, but still highly relevant "staple" books on this topic include: *Working with Emotional Intelligence* by Daniel Goleman and *Emotional Intelligence 2.0* by Travis Bradberry.

Establish Common Ground

While I've alluded to this several times, common ground is a "neutral territory" where individual priorities, goals, objectives, and ways of doing things become balanced against the priorities, needs, goals, and objectives of two or more people. When bridges of understanding are created between Walkers, Climbers, and Flyers, they naturally lead to the establishment of common ground.

When common ground is established, it becomes much easier to communicate, collaborate, and produce. As we identify shared goals and objectives of the parties involved in any exchange, and seek to ensure those needs and objectives are addressed in that exchange, an alignment and a shared sense of mission and purpose in teams blossoms. This alignment is often the missing ingredient in the modern workplace, where teams are prone to work in silos or factions with misaligned goals and interests. OST seeks to open up communication, build bridges of understanding between people of differing styles, and help people establish common ground that motivates and inspires collaboration and productivity.

Find the Win Angle

Once common ground is established, the icing on the collaborative cake is making sure there are mutually beneficial outcomes for all involved. I call this finding the "win angle." The win angle answers the question: "What will make this collaboration (discussion, collaboration, meeting, project, initiative, etc.) a success for all involved?" The win angle seeks to find a benefit for all parties in an exchange or collaboration—even if the win for one party is something that is minor, delayed, or delivered later on. This idea of establishing mutual wins helps foster an environment where co-workers have each other's backs, and are motivated to sustain participation and positive contribution that benefits the whole.

An example of a "win" may include ensuring someone hits a deadline or sales objective. It may involve getting something (e.g. budget approval) for something that's materially needed, resolving a problem, or putting an open issue to rest. For some individuals, a win may involve gaining a place at the table, attaining recognition, or trading a favor for another favor. When a task or collaboration concludes, people paying attention to the win angle will liberally express gratitude, share credit, and celebrate, promoting goodwill for the future. There will be occasions where the benefit to some in the exchange exceeds the benefits to others—and that's okay. In these instances, it's important to remember that sometimes, the best way to create a win angle is simply to express heartfelt thanks, return a kindness, or keep a promise!

Listen Actively

Active listening involves concentrating on what another person is saying, being able to understand what is being communicated, thoughtfully responding—and also *remembering* what was said. Unfortunately, in conversation, many of us become too busy planning what we will say next, rather than focusing on really hearing others out. Active listening requires you to silence your internal dialogue and tune in to others. Here are some tips for active listening:

- Concentrate on becoming a better listener through diligent practice and habit
- Check yourself during conversation to ensure you are hearing what is being said
- Shut down your internal dialogue with a determination to listen to others

- Remove distraction; put down your mobile device and turn off the smartwatch
- Don't plan what you'll say next—listen, pause, and then respond
- Don't be afraid to refocus or ask people to repeat something if you missed it
- Make eye contact and combine it with other "positive signals" that you are listening
- Posture (nod, smile, face the person, lean in, don't "block" others with arms crossed)
- Make verbal acknowledgements ("yes," "uh-huh," "hmmm,") to indicate attention

My husband is a great listener. He is patient most of the time, he thinks before he responds, and he reads people well. He is an introvert and a man of comparably few words, so when he speaks, it usually matters. I am an extrovert who runs heavy on words. I struggle to listen and am prone to interrupt. I tend to be impatient and naturally inclined to multitask. My mind tends to run away on me and go off on mental "rabbit trails" that often feel beyond my control. I regularly fight the urge to assume that I already know what someone is going to say before they have said it.

In short, we are quite a match!

Once, in a moment of vulnerability, my husband told me that in conversation with me, he felt like a guy with a rubber-band gun going against a woman with a machine gun. This was a powerful analogy that resurfaces when I find myself going on a *diatribe* instead of focusing on *dialogue*! Being married to an introvert has forced me to exercise more patience, to ask leading questions, and wait for the answers. He has helped me become a more engaged partner, though I remain challenged to take a breath, pause, think about things, and listen. I admit that I have to work consciously at this, and fail often. However, I also understand that making sure other people feel heard is one of the best gifts we can give—and the wisdom they offer us can be enriching and even life-changing!

Tailor Your Communications

In addition to listening during conversations, it's critical to be mindful of and adapt to other people's communication preferences. Start with a high-level appreciation for the preferences of each style, and try to attune to people's *individual* preferences for communication and processing information, too. For example, Climbers prefer the "elevator pitch" approach: starting with the high level, focusing on facts, bullets, graphs, and charts. They also like to know how things relate to their agendas. Flyers are more conceptual, prone to overcommunicate and get down into the weeds, and may take over a white board until they run out of space. Walkers tend to prefer focused engagement, leading with an understanding of how things relate to their areas of responsibility or knowledge.

It's just smart business to develop an understanding of how the people you work with prefer to give and receive information. Are you dealing with someone who is inundated and likely to skip through or miss emails? Does the person you're talking to need more methodical explanation and details? Have you aligned yourself to the priorities, objectives, and concerns of the person you are speaking to? Get out of your own head and take the time to *package and tailor* your delivery, choosing your timing and method of communication wisely! It can make all the difference in people's receptivity your approach and the time this planning takes up front, can save a lot of time later!

Embrace Humility

Humility is not a popular word in our modern work culture. Perhaps it's because people associate the word with "humiliation"—or the embarrassment of a weak and powerless state. However, there's a big difference between being humiliated at the hands of someone else and choosing to be a humble person. The definition of humility involves "having a modest view of one's own importance." There is great power in humility, primarily because a humble person is innately aware of their place within a larger ecosystem. Rather than being weak and powerless, a person with humility is able to effectively own and use his or her power *without* feeling the need to impose and assert that power unnecessarily on others. In fact, a humble person is more likely to *serve* others. Humble leaders tend to be more persuasive, honest, and have the ability to set aside personal gain for a greater good. They also respond with grace when attacked. With humility, work becomes less about the individual's own experience and more about the plight of us all.

People who demonstrate strength with humility tend to garner more support and respect from others. They feel more approachable. They walk away from interactions with a clearer conscience. Humility contributes to an even greater ability to speak to shared motivations, goals, and mission. Humble leaders do not fixate on weakness, but carry a healthy respect for the humanizing force of weakness in us all. They also tend to demonstrate a level of gratitude for the lessons they've learned, which they are more willing to share with others. A humble leader recognizes the need to own mistakes and to make apologies if necessary. This goes completely against the grain for many leaders today. In particular, this level of openness can be especially hard for some Climbers, who are more inclined to project a strong, composed, "no mistakes," "never let them see you sweat" demeanor. Ultimately, the gift of humility is the ability to own and wield your power, within the empathetic constraints of your human connection with others.

Manage Well

Regardless of what position you hold, every single one of us—regardless of rank, title, or experience, is in some sense, a manager. As each one of us juggles the demands of life, work, family, personal affairs, and more. In life and in work, we *already* manage in several directions:

- **Managing up** involves being accountable to the people who have authority over us, including our bosses and their bosses.

- **Managing across** involves managing our interactions and behavior with peers as well as other professionals we may encounter outside of our workplace, who have a level of authority that is similar to our own.

- **Managing down** involves working successfully with people who have less authority or experience than we have. In some cases, they may be direct reports for whom we are responsible. In other cases, they may be colleagues or coworkers.

Adopting the stance of a manager—whether you wait tables, stand on an assembly room floor, or shuffle mail and answer calls—is an empowering mindset that can help you approach work with the professionalism and grace required to work with others well and professionally advance. Here are ten attributes demonstrated by a good manager:

1. A high level of ownership in creating success or failure
2. Competence and dedication to your responsibilities
3. Accountability for personal and professional conduct
4. A positive attitude that focuses what's possible
5. The ability to prioritize and focus
6. Respect for people and culture
7. The ability to lead from both the head and heart
8. Strong decision-making ability
9. A desire to empower and ignite others
10. Genuine empathy and human warmth

CHAPTER 13
STYLE DYNAMICS

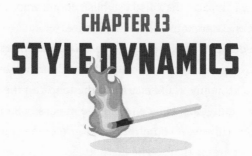

This chapter provides a helpful overview of the natural tensions and compatibilities between operational styles, inspired by my client work. I am constantly asked questions like: "I am a Climber—what do I need to do to work better with a Flyer like you?" So, I thought it would be good not only to provide an overview of style dynamics, but to include specific inter-style dynamic tips that can help you work better with others. Some of this material and recommendations may be a review, but is included here for ease-of-reference.

WALKER/WALKER DYNAMICS

Often, a large part of the Walker's social network is composed of other Walkers, though there may be select Climbers and Flyers that make it into the Walker's circle of trust. Walkers generally work well together due to a natural alignment in the way they go about doing things. Walkers appreciate order, process, and having systems in place that create efficiency. They also tend to be more relational and social in the workplace, which can extend to things like planning company picnics, celebrations, parties, volunteering, and other activities.

Because Walkers leverage relationships to work more efficiently, they're not only well connected, they're also socially active inside the organization.

Walkers are often the individuals who place reminders in the kitchen about washing the coffee mugs and "clean out the refrigerator" days. Walkers don't just establish frameworks for productivity, creating a kind of grounded stability in the workplace; they also establish community and friendships that can, at times, extend outside the workplace.

As mentioned, the Walker network serves as the backbone for the "grapevine" at work. The grapevine is typically filled with stories, buzz, news, and gossip. As a result, many Walkers are "in the loop" on the latest hearsay. However, it's an individual choice to engage in gossip. Some Walkers do, and some don't. However, sometimes, the grapevine can contribute to internal rumor or drama that can be disruptive.

On the down side, when a Walker upsets the balance of another Walker—especially in a repeated manner—it can result in conflict. Furthermore, because Walkers tend to demonstrate a high level of ownership of their areas, conflicts can arise and a sense of competition can develop between Walkers working together. When this happens, there may be noticeable friction, a reticence to share information, collaborate, or be transparent about each other's activities. It isn't uncommon to find Walker groups or "cliques" that compete with or have borderline adversarial relationships with other groups.

FLYER/FLYER DYNAMICS

Birds of a feather stick together, and in the Flyer's case, this is also true. Flyers enjoy collaborations with other Flyers and soaring around in vision land, engaging in mental acrobatics and diving down into detailed areas of concern together. Flyers are stimulated by ideation, brainstorming, experimentation, and testing, and they feed off each other's energy and passion. Flyers also love to build—whether conceptual ideas, pitches, prototypes, proofs-of-concept, new products, services, high-level strategies, or roadmaps. In collaboration they tend to become so involved with work, they often lose track of time, working long hours in periods of heavy engagement. Flyers often vacillate between periods of intense interpersonal collaboration and independent periods of intense focus that may spill into evenings and extend over weekends.

While Flyers might not intentionally "network," they often encounter "kindred Flyers" at work, within third-party agencies or partners, through industry connections, and through extracurricular pursuits. They love to connect and play "brain hockey" (unlike tennis, it's a full contact sport). Collectively, Flyer/Flyer relationships often morph into deep friendships that transcend jobs and employers.

There are challenges present in Flyer/Flyer relationships but they may not be what they seem. The obvious challenge of Flyer/Flyer relationships is that they can create a frenzied energy marked by shifting priorities, ideas, and focus. This can make it hard to maintain productivity in a Flyer-dominant environment. At the same time, finding an environment abundant with Flyers is uncommon. One of the biggest challenges the Flyer faces is finding fellow Flyers with whom to flock. Depending on the organization, Flyers can be "rare birds," making it hard find other Flyers with whom to bond ideate, explore, and validate ideas.

Flyer collaborations can be very productive. The deep bonds, mutual respect, and understanding founded by Flyers help them weather storms of disagreement, where battles are fought over differences in perspective or opinion, and discussions can become very intense. While there's not always a battle, there may be a struggle to define solutions, or to determine what "good enough" is, as it involves separating ideality from reality, in pains-taking fashion—that considers many business needs, angles, stakeholders, and other considerations.

While Flyers typically have a deep regard for one another, they can also experience feelings of jealousy for each other. This is especially true when one perceives the work of another to be cooler, more stimulating, more advanced, better supported (with budget, scope, people, tools, and tech) or more "fun." Because Flyer freedoms and privileges may vary, Flyers may also be jealous of Flyers that seem to enjoy more latitude to "soar and fly."

CLIMBER/CLIMBER DYNAMICS

While Climbers often compete against one another for advancement, they also help "belay" each other on the wall of professional achievement when mutual goals are present. This collectively creates an environment of "coopetition." As previously described, Climbers tend to cluster together, forming alliances and congregating recreationally over business lunches, a game of golf, or a sporting event to discuss mutual goals and objectives. Climbers often bond over deals, new initiatives, taking down the competition, dominating over another team, and other activities. They may support each other's projects or initiatives, engage in covert operations (teaming up), and/or connect each other to useful and/or powerful contacts. They frequently have each other's backs, as extending favors tends to pay off in the future in the form of returned favors. Climbers will also make a concerted effort to garner favor with strategically useful Climbers—especially at higher or influential levels of any organization—and may go out of the way to form and strengthen such bonds.

While strong relationships are often established, it's important to remember that typically, "business is business" to the Climber. In the bonds of all professional relationships, most Climbers remain more guarded, sharing information on a need-to-know basis. They will often compartmentalize what they share with others, providing incomplete or misinformation or concealing key details to make it harder for people to take over, or take credit for ideas or work. They also do an exceptional job of forming alliances and counter-alliances—especially with other Climbers. When it's time to make decisions, and/or when individuals get in the way (including other Climbers), a pragmatic Climber may adopt a kind of "every man for himself" attitude. The extent to which this occurs depends on the individual. However, as a result of these dynamics, it is not unusual for Climber loyalties to shift, along with the balance of power inside an organization. At times, there can be "all-out war" between competing Climbers, which may or may not be evident to others.

WALKER/FLYER DYNAMICS

Walkers and Flyers often form close relationships, especially when they are in a position to support each other in doing great work. I once worked with a Walker named Lorraine who was an ace developer with a real talent in ecommerce-related programming. Our relationship worked exceptionally well, though I often overwhelmed her with ideas, forcing her to sit me down to prioritize. I oversaw multiple areas in our business, relying on others for daily operations and development work. Lorraine managed retail merchandising and ecommerce development. She had great ideas, understood the power of contextual merchandising, and she was great at prototyping. She was a dynamo and a right-hand resource for me—someone that was not only streamlining and optimizing the purchasing experience but developing revolutionary ecommerce functionality, the first of its kind, at the time. We made a great team.

A good Walker/Flyer relationship is marked with a measure of self-understanding, self-control, a willingness to meet halfway, patience, and a sense of humor! In the most compatible relationships, a Walker will appreciate a Flyer's infusion of energy, new ideas, and perspective, and the Flyers demonstrate deep regard and respect for the Walker, combined with demonstrating advocacy for the individual. There can be great symbiosis between Walkers and Climbers, and the order Walkers create can serve as a direct benefit to Flyers.

At the same time, the energy, focus, and interests of a Flyer can also prove to be distracting, disruptive, overwhelming, and exhausting for a Walker, creating tension in relationships. Flyers that demonstrate insensitivity, violate boundaries, and/or upset the Walker's order and balance will encounter problems. In turn, confident Flyers may make assumptions or develop attitudes about Flyers who are reticent to engage, referring to such individuals as closed, non-strategic, evasive, passive-aggressive, and even questionably intelligent.

Tips for Walkers Working with Flyers

Walkers that bond with Flyers demonstrate patience, good boundaries, and communication skills. A sense of humor is a plus. Some tips for working with a Flyer include the following:

- **Be clear**—Articulating your needs, limitations, boundaries, and goals helps a Flyer work more seamlessly with you and makes interfacing easier.
  - *Boundaries*—Articulate and reinforce necessary information about your boundaries or limits and process as it relates to the Flyer.

- *Roles*—Ensure roles, responsibilities, tasks, deliverables, and timing are clear.

- *Schedule*—Highlight your schedule demands and constraints. Make it clear how much time you have for interactions.

- *Agendas*—Clarify agendas for meetings, set goals and expectations for discussions and collaborations—and stick with them!

- *Understanding*—If you are lost or confused, or don't have time to process something "right now"—say so! Make your thoughts and hesitations known.

- **Be helpful**—It's easy for a Flyer to get off course, especially when "shiny things" (ideas, new information, related topics, things to discuss) are present.

  - *Encourage the Flyer to "land"*—Sometimes reminders can be helpful in getting a Flyer to slow down and speak more clearly. Simple requests like, "Hey, you're going too fast and losing me! Can you slow down?" or "Wait! I'm lost. Can you explain that more simply?" can help.

  - *Stay on track*—Be patient with a level of deviation from a Flyer, as it often serves a purpose. However, when needed, provide gentle admonitions such as, "How did we get here?" or "How is this relevant to our discussion?" or "This is slightly off focus. Can we table this and get back on track?"

  - *Correct when needed*—When a Flyer is off base, make it known. Help the Flyer understand what you know, debunk wrong assumptions, and fill knowledge gaps. Speak up! Your insight will be put to good use!

  - *Relax defenses*—Most likely, when a Flyer enters your "territory," there's no intention to undermine or threaten you. They are wired to cross boundaries. While this may make you feel uncomfortable, providing good information with the right boundaries can help establish common ground and make the Flyer an ally in your cause.

- **Be patient**—Understand that, to become a good ally, Flyers may require quality time to understand your process, area, and priorities. Their process and headspace are complicated, as they are wired to understand the connections between things, sometimes at a detailed level, which may require periods of intense engagement.

  - *Set boundaries to protect your energy*—While longer periods of engagement may be needed, small spurts are generally more efficient than drawn-out interactions and can protect your time and energy.

  - *Abandon your comfort zone*—Give in to the Flyer's process and participate in ideation and brainstorming *where you can be useful*. However, don't underestimate how you can be helpful! When a Flyer includes you, there is usually a good reason. Engaging can stimulate new ideas and creativity that can have other positive, energizing effects on everyone.

  - *Endure the "processing"*—The Flyer's process may feel uncomfortable, laborious, unnecessary, or questionably useful to you. Many Flyers need to verbally download their understanding of things before they can even listen to someone else. This processing is critical to building understanding, solving problems, and working through issues. Try to stay engaged!

  - *Have a sense of humor*—When you feel the tension or irritation rise, choose humor over the humanity of the situation. Crack a joke—or poke fun at yourself, or if you've got a good relationship, the Flyer, to break the tension.

Tips for Flyers Working with Walkers

Flyers who bond well with Walkers take a genuine interest in the Walker's role, function, and process. They also do a good job of building trust, approaching them right, and staying focused, which helps maintain the relationship and preserve the energy of the Walker. Beyond demonstrating an understanding of how a Walker works, here are some tips for Flyers that may assist in building good relational dynamics with Walkers:

- **Build trust**—If you dive in, wings tucked, going Mach 10, invading a Walker's territory or probing and demanding answers, you will alienate a Walker and have a harder time securing engagement.

  - *Approach with sensitivity*—Manage your energy so as not to overwhelm! Always seek to remove threats, disarm, and make it clear you "come in peace."

  - *Honor the schedule*—Be attentive to a Walker's schedule, demands, and bandwidth. They can't always engage exactly when *you* need input.

  - *Ask, don't demand*—Be gentle and sensitive when making requests. Applying too much pressure may create backlash. Ask for insight, favors, and handoffs with sensitivity and kindness.

  - *Listen actively*—Your need to "process" can "steam roll" over a Walker who wants to give input. Let the Walker speak! Don't interrupt or a Walker may shut down and be reticent to engage further.

  - *Explain your mandate*—If you've been brought in to solve a problem that impacts a Walker, lead a project, or something else, explain this! Express your desire to proceed in a way that respects, honors, and protects their position and interests.

  - *Establish common goals*—Identify mutually shared goals aligned to individual responsibilities to create common ground.

  - *Respect boundaries*—Stay attuned and respectful of the Walker's energy level, demands, boundaries, protocols, structure, and process. This will help you work in a way that honors the Walker and motivates his or her desire to collaborate.

- **Come in for a landing**—"Wing flapping" behavior can be overwhelming and threatening to others, and it's not necessary all the time. Tuck your wings in, get grounded with an understanding of your audience, so you can ravel at the Walker's pace!

  - *Stay relevant*—Explain your goals, what you're doing, and how it relates to the Walker's expertise and area of responsibility. While all the detail may be important to you, a Walker doesn't need to know *everything!* Try not to overburden a Walker with too much information.

- ◦ *Slow your roll*—Manage your tendency to move too fast for others. Slow down and take a breath. Leverage the power of pauses to allow people to catch up, think, and absorb things.

- ◦ *Keep it manageable*—Plan ahead and engage in short, productive spurts to avoid being overly demanding, overwhelming, or energy-sucking.

- ◦ *Ask questions*—Build on what you learn by asking leading questions to help draw out the opinions, feelings, and expertise of the Walker.

- ◦ *Follow instead of lead*—Walkers are subject-matter experts. When you position them to lead you on a tour through their territory, they can better explain the of the lay of the land. Remember, they know their assigned areas far better than you!

- **Stay focused**—Remember, it may be a stretch for others to track with you. Staying focused will help you get what you need and preserve people's willingness to engage in the future.

- ◦ *Plan ahead*—Walkers want to remain productive and efficient. Plan meetings to establish what you will and *will not* cover. Keep discussions manageable and focused.

- ◦ *Stay on track*—Picture in your mind the Walker's focused path of expertise, well-defined territory, and unique perspective. Focus probing inquiry, discussions, and activities within that territory, and lane of expertise. If you have to diverge in discussion, explain why.

- ◦ *Break it down*—Find ways to break down discovery or collaboration into manageable pieces to help preserve the Walker's energy—and schedule!

- ◦ *Narrate your process*—Explain your thought process. For example, when you transition from high-level vision to a dive into detail, explain what you are doing. This will help the Walker follow your train of thought.

- ○ *Check in*—Pay attention to whether a Walker is tracking with you. Remain sensitive to people who hit critical mass and need a break or to regroup later! Don't push ahead when others are signaling "too much." Take a break! Demonstrating sensitivity will encourage Walker engagement.

- ○ *Demonstrate progress*—Make sure the Walker knows *how* their input is being used and has benefitted you, your project, or progress.

CLIMBER/WALKER DYNAMICS

It is very common for strong bonds to develop between Climbers and Walkers, especially when their roles and functions are highly compatible. For example, my Walker friend Marie and her boss, Marcus, enjoy a tight and productive relationship. While Marie reports to Marcus, she often feels like his equal, and the trust they have built is strong. They have a natural way of working together that is ordered and comfortable: Marcus knows he doesn't have to worry about anything Marie is working on because she's an admirably proficient overachiever. He remains busy establishing strategic industry relationships and setting up deals, and is available to support Marie or break down barriers when needed. Marie doesn't just kick butt at her work in sales; she is hyper-observant and connected inside the organization. She keeps Marcus abreast of the happenings, drama, and gossip at work. They schedule regular "eat our feelings" lunches and talk through deals, concerns, and office drama (though Marcus would never admit his interest in the gossip). They stay in touch constantly via text and by phone, and together, manage to stay two steps ahead of the competition. If Marcus needs something that falls outside of Marie's responsibility, she'll handle it, as his "key" person. Marie knows Marcus will always support her and she is determined to do the same.

In reporting relationships, remember that Walkers may serve in a right-hand capacity to a Climber or vice-versa. It is not uncommon for Walkers and Climbers to form bonds that lead to them advancing through corporate ranks alongside one another. In the case of particularly strong relationships, it's not unusual for the compatible individuals to "follow" each other in job shifts between companies. Walkers and Climbers can also function relatively well as peers at any rank inside a company. Both Walkers and Climbers tend to respect clarity, focus, and structure, and when there's a strong level of respect and trust, the relationship usually works well. Both have a natural propensity to manage and delegate well, although doing so takes experience, practice and, some coaching or training—and typically gets better with experience.

Both Climbers and Walkers have the tendency to become protective or territorial over areas of responsibility, knowledge, resources, and relationships. Tensions can be magnified by a competitive nature on both sides of the relational fence. Problems also tend to arise when a Climber demonstrates a lack of appreciation or respect for a Walker's boundaries and systems, or tries to tell a Walker how to do his or her job. This makes the Walker feel disrespected, undermined, used, taken advantage of, and other related feelings. In turn, the Walker's schedule, methodical way of getting things done, and emphasis on procedure may be frustrating for Climbers, who like to plough through things with ruthless efficiency, and may exhibit a lack of patience and understanding that can be perceived as disrespectful. Collectively, these areas are where conflicts commonly arise.

Tips for Walkers Working with Climbers

The Climber's natural propensity is to treat work relationships with guarded professionalism and to leverage those relationships to achieve objectives. To Climbers, this may be "all business" and this can work with a focused Walker with compatible goals. To the Walkers who fall in and out of the "light of favor," the Climber's approach can make a person feel used. Depending on the individual and level of emotional intelligence, Climbers are more likely to avoid emotional displays, drama, admitting fault, or apologizing. Finally, a Climber's ambition can often undermine relationships with Walkers, as Climbers are often not aware of how their maneuvers may slight or offend people. Climbers can be dictatorial and project a superior attitude, and depending on the individual's convictions, they may even take ownership or credit of jointly-developed work or ideas, if they don't take full credit (implied or expressed), in order to advance professionally.

- **Understand the Agenda**—Getting a handle on the agenda (goals and objectives) of a Climber is key to helping you work more effectively together and foster an alliance.

  - *Build your relationship*—Break through defenses to earn a higher level of trust and openness by keeping a cool head and mastering your area effectively. Building trust takes time, as Climbers tend to be guarded and reticent to share openly, engaging most when they need something, and keeping their agenda and information close-to-chest.

  - *Identify the agenda*—As you build a relationship, pay attention to the Climber's mandate, areas of authority, role, and tasks. Listen to expressed or implied goals and ambitions to get a better sense of the agenda, priorities, goals, and objectives they strive to accomplish.

  - *Resonate with the agenda*—Identify ways to align or position your role, function, and activities in a way that supports or complements the Climber's agenda. This is especially important for direct reports, but for peers, agenda alignment will help the Climber understand that you share goals and objectives, creating common ground.

  - *Foster an alliance*—Make it clear you support a Climber's priorities, goals, and objectives and prove your usefulness in helping the Climber "reach the summit." However, as you do this, be sure to find ways the Climber can help *you*, too—creating a partnership instead of a one-way, overly subservient relationship.

- **Match strength with strength**—Climbers can assume too much, come across as authoritarian, dictator-like, and/or attached to their ideas and objectives, often at a Walker's expense. Stand strong in your position, knowledge, responsibility, and authority or you may lose respect and be "run over" in the name of "progress!"

  - *Clarify your role*—Make sure there's no misconception about your authority, role, and territory, as it relates to engaging with a Climber. Clarify misunderstandings about what you will and will not do.

- *Use caution in extending favors*—Climbers can be very persuasive and charming when they want or need something, and are resourceful in delegation. Doing favors and/or bending the rules should be a nice, flexible exception, *not the rule!* Otherwise favors may be expected often.

- *Stand your ground*—Asserting and reinforcing your boundaries is critical to maintain Climber respect and protect yourself from unreasonable demands. Push back if needed. Say no when necessary.

- *Clear the record*—If you are being treated unfairly, feel as if you are being taken for granted, or having your work or ideas commandeered, try to find the most firm, unemotional, and pleasant way to confront bad behavior. A sense of humor helps. Respond in a positive manner that's appropriate to your relationship.

- *Choose your battles*—Remember that Climbers don't like to be confronted, but won't usually back down easily in an argument. A Walker friend once confessed that while it was sometimes hard, the only way she had found to work with her Climber boss who was heavily attached to his own ideas, was to *convince him that her ideas were his own.* When she did this, she got the outcome she wanted, and her ideas got the traction required to become reality. This wasn't easy for her on an ego-level, but it was *her way* of choosing her battles. Think through how to choose your own battles with the Climbers in your workplace, so you find yourself with an end result with which you feel content!

- *Leverage authority*—If you find yourself being taken advantage of, dumped on, or directed by a Climber who doesn't have authority over you—and you can't reset the behavior yourself—ask your management to help reset the Climber's expectations.

- **Depersonalize behavior**—Climbers are wired differently than you. The Climber's rather perfunctory focus and drive may result in insensitive behavior. However, this focus and drive also make a Climber effective at hitting milestones and objectives.

- *Consider the context*—Climbers tend to be (and are not always) more prone to leverage relationships to get things done—to have a utilitarian view of people and situations and a focus on driving to an end-goal. Walkers are highly relational.

- *Don't be easily offended*—Some Climbers will rub you the wrong way. You can't change this, but you can take comfort in the fact that it usually isn't personal. Try not to be hypersensitive. Address offenses when absolutely necessary, but remember that Climbers don't like confrontation or "drama."

- *Minimize emotional response*—While emotional themselves, Climbers often associate displays of emotion from others as weakness. Don't allow yourself to be triggered into an emotional response. If necessary, take a breather to maintain objectivity and a professional demeanor.

- *Don't spin on negativity*—Avoid the urge to replay offenses or complain to others about a Climber. Feeding negativity can fuel the fire of gossip and contention, and make things worse. Where you can, take a deep breath, move on, and forgive. Where you can't, deal with things outright.

Tips for Climbers Working with Walkers

Walkers adhere to the adage, "Trust is earned in drops and lost in buckets." Walkers want to feel respected, protected, acknowledged, and included. Climbers that violate a Walker's trust, disrespect a Walker's role or boundaries, and/or take credit (indirectly or directly) for a Walker's ideas will lose trust and ruin a relationship. This is also true when a Climber excludes or fails to consult a Walker in a discussion or decision that impacts the Walker's assigned area(s). Further, Walkers may be offended by a Climber's more utilitarian approach to getting things done. Due to the "light of favor" effect, when interacting with Climbers, a Walker may feel valued, needed, and respected one minute, and disregarded or ignored the next. Walkers dislike dictators and heavy-handed demands. They also become angry when Climbers repeatedly undermine their established systems—instead asking for exceptions, favors, privileges, or deadline extensions. Walkers who feel "run over," "dumped upon," or undermined by a Climber are likely withdraw, to the extent they can, from a relationship. They can also become barriers instead of helpful allies. To avoid conflict, consider the following tips:

- **Respect roles & boundaries**—The best way to foster a good relationship with a Walker is to demonstrate regard and respect for their roles and boundaries, with sensitivity to demands, priorities, and schedule. Maintaining structure and balance are paramount to Walkers, and Climbers that disrupt may incur wrath! As a respectful advocate and supporter, you can earn your way into the circle of trust.

  - *Understand role and job function*—Make sure to obtain a clear understanding of the Walker's role, purpose, tasks, and responsibilities to ensure the requests you make are *appropriate*.

  - *Be sensitive to demands and schedule*—Choose your timing and approach with sensitivity to the Walker's schedule, demands, and bandwidth. If it's a bad time, muster up some patience and wait. Remember, Walkers typically deal with a lot of dependencies within and across departments.

  - *Ask, don't demand*—Walkers dislike heavy-handed requests. It's often better to make your needs known along with any pressing deadlines that exist, and allow the Walker to figure out how to accommodate you in light of other demands. Advance notice is critical, and encouraging the Walker to work with you consultatively is likely to incur more favor and less ire.

- **Demonstrate sensitivity**—While it may feel overly "touchy feely," it's important to be sensitive to a Walker's feelings and triggers. Think of it this way: Upsetting even one Walker can have a trickle-down effect, as repeated offenses and/or behavior become a topic of discussion in the Walker Grapevine. This may damage your reputation, power base, and ability to work with others.

  - *Communicate well*—Walkers hate being left in the dark, being blindsided, and surprises that disrupt the balance of things. Make a concerted effort to proactively communicate in a manner that helps the Walker sufficiently anticipate what's coming. Shine a light on the path ahead.

○ *Work inclusively*—Climbers have the tendency to include "only those necessary" in a discussion because it feels more efficient and helps drive a desired outcome. To the Climber, this feels efficient. To the person excluded, it feels offensive and is likely to draw hostility. Walkers dislike being left out of discussions or decisions that impact them or the areas for which they are responsible. Where possible, give a Walker the option to participate, and offer to stand in if you think it's more efficient.

○ *Express gratitude*—Praise, appreciation, and gratitude will leave anyone—but especially a Walker—feeling positive about working with you. Extra thanks when warranted is also advisable. Gifts may be in order for going the extra mile!

· **Be a mensch**—A mensch by definition is a person of integrity and honor. These traits help balance out the more hard-charging traits of the Climber. In reality, there are three "ropes" that keep a Climber safe on the incline: 1) natural talents and abilities; 2) ability to deliver and scale; and 3) integrity and reputation. When one or more fail, a Climber can be subject to a crushing fall. Consider the legacy you want to leave as you:

○ *Manage perceptions*—The Climber way of working may feel natural and efficient to you. However, it may be perceived or experienced differently by others. Manage the perceptions of others. Develop empathy by putting yourself in the Walker's shoes (stylistically and individually) and remain sensitive to emotions and triggers.

○ *Model good ethics*—Climbers can behave shrewdly on the incline when threatened, grasping for opportunity, or attempting to get leverage. Use caution in your choices! Whether you are hitting a deadline, removing an adversary, or obtaining a promotion, remember that *business is personal to others*. Think of the implications of your choices on others, as well as your reputation. Always give credit where credit is due, and refrain from even indirectly accepting credit for the work of others.

- *Don't just manage, lead*—There are a ton of managers in the world and comparatively few leaders. Pulling rank to dictate the actions of others is easy, but that won't win hearts and minds. Consume books about good leadership. Develop more emotional intelligence. Practice goodness. When you lead by example and influence, you will garner a bigger support base that can make you unstoppable!

- *Finish the right way*—It's a fallacy that nice guys finish last. When you take time to really understand and value others, you can finish first with a clean conscience and a powerful army of colleagues that believe in your abilities.

CLIMBER/FLYER DYNAMICS

There are many natural tensions that can occur between Climbers and Flyers because of the very different ways in which they think and function. In many respects, Climbers and Flyers are polar opposites. This is why building understanding and establishing common ground are critical to relational success. When Climbers and Flyers work well together and develop a respectful bond, it can be a powerful and effective partnership. The best relationships are garnered from mutual respect, trust, and a clear understanding and appreciation for what each party brings to the table. When Climbers and Flyers do find common ground, the focused, driven nature of the Climber, combined with the strategic, innovative work of the Flyer, can produce business-altering results.

Tips for Flyers Working with Climbers

It's important to realize that the unique, out-of-the-box, boundary-less vision and perspective offered by a Flyer often feels like "too much" for a Climber. All that passion, ideation, and vision can be overwhelming and distracting—even threatening. In approaching collaboration, it's best to keep things high-level to start—leading with facts, data, and proof with your gut, and keeping interactions short, focused, and manageable. When a relationship is successfully forged, Climbers can be instrumental in helping Flyers become "unstuck," simplify, and prioritize.

When Flyer's ideas misalign with a Climber agenda, a Climber may feel threatened, overwhelmed, or that their authority is challenged or disrespected, and may be prone to strong reactive behavior. Climbers may attempt to exert control—even trying to shut down, box in, suppress, restrict, or "wing clip" the Flyer. It's important to manage this tendency, as it can result in behavior that leads to conflict. Here are some ways that a Flyer can create better understanding and common ground with Climbers:

- **Resonate with the Climber's agenda**—Understanding the agenda of the Climber can help you position your ideas, communication, and work effort in an aligned and complementary manner. This will help minimize threats and make a Climber more willing to engage with you.

  - *Identify the agenda*—It won't always be evident, so ask a Climber to clarify their priorities, goals, and objectives. Listen to what is expressed or implied and stay observant. When a Climber disengages, bring things back around to their priorities to stimulate reengagement.

  - *Align to the agenda*—Find ways to either position or practically align your expertise, your role, the work you are doing, and/or your ideas to the Climber's agenda. For example, when making a point you may say, "This, for example, helps answer a need to improve (insert name of area), which was one of the goals you mentioned, Joe." Actions like this go far in establishing common ground.

  - *Remove any real or perceived threat*—Flyers naturally put Climbers on the defensive. Approach with a calm energy that speaks to alignment and find ways to disarm and/or remove any real or perceived threat.

  - *Call attention to broader goals*—The Climber's agenda isn't the only one in the room, and Flyers excel at assimilating and identifying stakeholder needs across functional areas. Build context for the Climber, and identify common goals, issues, and challenges to bring people together. Help the Climber understand context as you seek to serve others and point the way to the future.

- *Understand the power of leverage*—Everything is leverage for a Climber. It's important to find ways to get your own leverage with a Climber and help the Climber leverage your strengths, too. Highlight people in authority that support or sanction your ideas, or the traction you have gotten working with people the Climber respects. Demonstrate how supporting you will help a Climber meet goals or objectives. Communicate "what's in it for me" to garner extra support, traction, and credibility.

- **Minimize "wing flapping"**—As with a Walker, it's advisable to land quietly to avoid being overwhelming or threatening to a Climber. This will have a disarming effect and make the discussion feel more grounded. Your calm energy will also give the Climber a willingness to "come your way" or even turn around "on the incline" to consider the expanded vision, perspective, or ideas you wish to present.

  - *Plan your approach*—Plan Climber interactions in advance, keeping your thoughts and ideas focused and high-level. This will help you manage the propensity to dive too deep, be too broad, or to overwhelm with too much detail. Communicate things in digestible bites (e.g. challenge, solution, key considerations, recommendations, costs, and benefits). Be prepared to give detail but refrain from diving deep unless the Climber is willing to go there.

  - *State your objective*—Clearly present why you're there and what you wish to accomplish up front. As you do so, try to demonstrate how it complements the Climber's present realities, goals, and objectives to motivate participation.

  - *Avoid overcommunicating*—Saying too much won't just overwhelm but is likely to result in a Climber tune-out or shut down. Focus your communication. Try to say more using *fewer* words. Think about what your Climber needs to know, and focus on that. Again, planning helps.

  - *Be factual*—You may have a great gut instinct, but to win over Climbers, you'll need facts, data, backup information, and/or case studies to prove your case. Be ready to be asked questions, grilled, and/or challenged. Tell stories with data. Prove your point. Make any sense of urgency believable and real.

- *Shorter is better*—Engage in shorter, efficient spurts to avoid taking too much time, being perceived as high maintenance, being overwhelming, or posing too much of a distraction.

- *Slow down*—Manage your Flyer tendency to move too fast for other people. Slow down, take a breath, and leverage the power of pauses. This will allow a Climber to catch up, think about, and absorb what you are saying.

- *Ask for feedback*—Don't leave the room without gauging the Climber's initial input, as it will help gauge initial thoughts, and prepare to respond.

- *Make room for processing*—Climbers often need time to process, which is inconvenient juxtaposed with a Flyer's desire for almost immediate validation and input. Give it time. It may be unclear whether they will have the cognitive "bandwidth" to complete this process, so try to set a deadline for feedback provision and loop back to prevent "spinning."

- *Set next steps*—To avoid losing traction, establish next steps and conduct follow up within a reasonable timeframe.

- **Stand strong and confident**—Climbers are attracted to confidence, strength, and power. Managing your emotions and matching strength-for-strength is important if you want to be perceived as an equal and an ally.

  - *Remain composed*—Control your energy level to avoid seeming emotional, which *may* be a sign of weakness and/or a turnoff to a Climber. Flyers are passionate, which is often tied to a sense of mission and purpose. Be sensitive to how your passion may be perceived.

  - *Be polished and professional*—Climbers often dress to impress and pay attention to external appearances. To increase your credibility, maintain a professional demeanor: look sharp, sit tall, and speak clearly, articulately, and professionally.

- *Leverage like a pro*—Taking a lesson from a Climber, find ways to leverage the support you have already garnered from other departments and individuals—especially those the Climber respects. This will up your cache with a Climber instantly.

- *Protect yourself*—Climber's advocacy can help a Flyer gain traction and broader organizational support. However, the inclination for a Climber to assume a kind of co-ownership of the ideas of others is both a compliment, and something that needs to be monitored. Establish boundaries, and be mindful of the fact that Climbers often under communicate, fail to be transparent, may attempt to ally fault or blame when things go wrong, and not admit to fault or make apology. Keep communication open, and be optimistically cautious in what you share, who you trust, and what you relinquish in collaboration!

- *Watch your back*—Hope for the best, prepare for the rest. Climbers are highly competitive and if threatened by someone, they can (depending on the individual) undermine another person's position to secure their own. Due to natural tensions that can exist with Climbers, you may be surprised to find a target on your back. Be prepared for this, and work to disarm your opponent.

- *Don't try too hard*—Don't try too hard to ingratiate yourself with a Climber. Climbers have trouble respecting individuals who try too hard or appear weak. Stand tall in your strengths and tell the truth with sensitivity and confidence. Do great work and you will earn respect from those who matter.

- *Deliver beyond expectations*—Climbers are drawn to individuals who deliver reliably and without delays or excuses. By delivering well, you demonstrate your value, worth, and potential.

Tips for Climbers Working with Flyers

Flyers are relatively unconcerned with hierarchy, power, position, and politics. They feel very comfortable crossing boundaries and speaking their truths, even if they may challenge others in an attempt to make improvements or problem solve. This is part of the Flyer's gift. The challenge is, a

Flyer will inevitably hit close to home when they freely criticize or make recommendations in areas that fall within your purview. This can feel threatening and even personal to a Climber—especially when a Flyer challenges a Climber in a public setting. Remember that the Flyer has a heartfelt interest in doing the right thing, and in seeking to problem solve. While it may feel like you are being targeted, it's not necessarily the case. Flyers tend to be equal opportunity critics. Resist all defensive, knee jerk reactions.

Furthermore, the Flyer's process can seem overwrought, undisciplined, and a questionable use of time to a Climber. In contrast to a Climber's "top-down," more fact-based approach, Flyers rapidly vacillate from high level to excruciating levels of detail, examining the interconnections between things, looking at many angles in a way that's hard for others to follow. Flyers that have a salient point to make, may take a while to get there—and this is likely to drive a Climber nuts. Climbers often have difficulty tracking, staying tuned in, and managing the Flyer's unwitting overcommunication with patience.

When a Flyer behaves in ways that threaten, overwhelm, and frustrate Climbers, the natural tendency is to want to tune out, or even shut down the offender. However, in doing so, a Climber may do him/herself a great disservice. A Flyer's job is to open an organization's eyes to new vision, perspective, and paths to the future. When Flyers are shut down or prevented from doing what they do best, Climbers lose the inside track on new vision and opportunity that may be profitable. So, where there may be an inclination to control, box in, or force your perspective on a Flyer, it's important to resist this urge. Climbers working with Flyers may benefit from these tips and recommendations:

- **Drop the scissors**—The Climber's natural instinct to control, silence, shut down, filter out, or clip the wings of a Flyer is an attempt to minimize distraction, diversion from the agenda, and/or and feeling overwhelmed. However, attempts to control and/or treating a Flyer like a "problem person" indicate disrespect and erode what could be a powerful partnership. Instead of clipping, caging, controlling, or crippling the Flyer, it's more productive to find ways to "tame" or focus the energy and help a Flyer be more grounded in goals, objectives, and priorities.

- ◦ *Check your attitude*—When you approach with an attitude, judgment, or preconceived notions, you will likely shortchange yourself along with undermining the Flyer you're working with. Don't discount the incredible strategic edge a Flyer can bring. Stay patient and stay positive!

- ◦ *Broaden your perspective*—While at times, engaging with a Flyer may feel like a distraction you don't have time for, Flyers bring you the gift of a bigger map—a picture of what's over the next ridge—and a view of the summit to take on next. This bigger-picture perspective is absolutely critical to paving the way to the future. Open yourself to new ideas, try to take the time periodically to turn around and see the vision the Flyer is painting with an eye toward opportunity identification, risk mitigation, market insight, and more.

- ◦ *Redirect the flight path*—When a Flyer is going in a direction that is confusing or doesn't map to your objectives, asking questions to bring clarity or redirect focus back to priorities at hand can help. By expressing your priorities clearly and asking the Flyer to speak to those, it's possible to redirect the Flyer.

- ◦ *Paint the target*—Climbers excel at understanding priorities and the goals, objectives, and milestones to hit, and can be instrumental at crystalizing the short-, mid-, and long-term objectives. Flyers are motivated by having a mission, and giving them one can be a powerful way to establish a productive alliance. When you highlight or issue a clear challenge (e.g. scope, milestone, objective, or problem to solve) you can motivate decisive action and partner together to hit that target and drive mutual wins.

- • **Engage with intention**—A Climber's natural inclination is to get in and get out of an interaction in the most effective and strategic way. Flyers need periods of more intense interaction and engagement (this especially true in reporting relationships) to support ideation, validate ideas and direction, review and provide input to recommendations, and to help determine next steps. To streamline engagement:

- *Make your needs and interests clear*—Up front, state your interests, objectives, and goals and ask the Flyer to consider and speak to these. This will help make the interaction more relevant and manageable.

- *Set boundaries*—Make your parameters clear. Specify the time you have available; clarify the agenda for a discussion or meeting. Ask for the high level without diving into detail first. Help add structure by encouraging the Flyer to break down information in understandable, digestible pieces. For example, saying "Can you just give me the bulleted version?" can streamline interaction. As you do this, you're setting the boundaries within which the Flyer can deliver.

- *Be patient*—Just like you need time to process information against your agenda and priorities, Flyers have a process, and it's usually very inclusive. While it may sometimes feel it consumes more of your time than it's worth, it's fairly critical to have your input inform their points and perspective to ensure there's alignment between you. Flyers naturally assimilate feedback to improve their ideas and solutions. So, by taking the time to engage, you benefit yourself in the long run.

- *Stay tuned in*—Participate, provide feedback, and most definitely avoid checking out, getting sucked into your phone, and becoming distracted by other concerns. This will undermine results and cause later rework. If you're dying in a meeting, ask for a break. When a Flyer needs to dive deep, you may want to resist, but sometimes, it just may be necessary to get to a decision or key determination.

- *Provide feedback*—Flyers work well without structure, but they dislike ambiguity and not knowing where someone stands. After a Flyer provides an "output" they feel much better receiving some kind of input. Provide as much feedback as you can, being honest about questions or concerns. When needed, let the Flyer know you need time to process things—but to ensure things aren't "left hanging," indefinitely (which will be a temptation because engagement can be laborious). Instead, establish next steps so that there's a clear path forward for the Flyer.

- *Suppress the competitive urge*—Climbers and Flyers can be equally competitive. However, the styles are typically motivated by entirely different rewards. This makes room for collaboration and partnership. By defining roles and establishing a clear picture of the win angle for both parties, Climbers and Flyers can support each other and work to ensure both parties obtain just recognition and meaningful rewards.

- **Work inclusively**—A Climber's perfunctory way of streamlining discussion and "ploughing through" to an objective can make a Flyer feel disregarded and run over. Flyers remain sensitive to having anyone speak for them, or being excluded from communications or discussions that impact them. They may react strongly to having tasks or work taken over by someone without a discussion or agreement to that fact. To avoid eroding trust:

  - *Approach as an equal*—To a Flyer, what you can do is much more important than your title. Flyers appreciate people who treat others as equals, regardless of rank or position. Leave the titles, posturing, and/or ego at the door, and be prepared to roll up your sleeves as a contributor.

  - *Assume a role*—Establish roles and agree on tasks that will be managed by each person to synchronize activities and minimize overlaps and toe-stepping. If there will be an imbalance in contribution, acknowledge it up front to properly set expectations.

  - *Be a champion*—Climbers can be instrumental in helping a Flyer gain broader traction, creating a platform for worthy ideas, work, or projects. Climbers make great champions and advocates—helping "sell" ideas, securing internal support and resources, removing barriers, and providing input and coaching when needed. Your greatest contributions may lie in those contributions. So, be a champion, and as great things happen, be sensitive about assuming too much ownership or credit as you move ahead.

  - *Stay reasonably transparent*—A Flyer's moves are rarely concealed, and they expect the same from others. For example, if there's a meeting where you feel a Flyer's involvement may be unproductive, don't exclude the Flyer and attend by yourself. Instead, address the meeting, invite the Flyer—and offer to attend and report back. Making your moves known with a reasonable amount of transparency will help maintain trust.

- *Communicate well*—Under-communicating is prone to backfire. Flyers are natural over-communicators and don't do well without details and context, or when they are left hanging without required information or necessary feedback. Again, make a strong effort to keep communication open!

- *Don't micromanage*—Flyers need latitude to do their best work. Micromanagement reduces latitude and creates stress under which Flyers have trouble performing. When managing a Flyer, you'll have to fight your urge to control and dictate, and instead find ways to check in and build in accountability without overdirecting. No cages, and no wing clipping!

- *Model good ethics*—Climbers may behave shrewdly on the professional "incline," especially when threatened, grasping for opportunity, or attempting to get leverage. Use caution about how you proceed. Flyers take work very personally and may draw a hard line on principles and ethics. Whether you are solving a problem, removing an adversary, obtaining a promotion, accepting an award, or winning a new contract, treat others how you wish to be treated.

- *Request, don't demand*—Asking for insight, favors, and handoffs with sensitivity and kindness is a much better way to get what you need and is likely to garner less ire and more favor from a Flyer.

- *Share the love*—Express gratitude and appreciation. Always give credit where credit is due to preserve your reputation and manage perceptions.

CHAPTER 14
STYLE BIAS & BALANCE

Diversity is the key to any healthy ecosystem. Establishing an appropriate balance of operational styles, based on organizational needs, growth phase, and focus should be a key consideration for any OST-practicing manager. However, like the dynamics that occur within an ecosystem, managing style dynamics to create a balance of operational styles is complicated. Operational styles directly impact and shape organizational culture, morale, communication, collaboration, relationships, and productivity.

STYLE BIAS

Within organizations and teams, Style Bias, which occurs when one or two styles shape the collaboration of a group *rather* than all three, is very common. A natural outcome of many factors, Style Bias typically isn't necessarily problematic—as long as the organization, as a whole, is appropriately infused with the presence of all three operational styles.

At an organizational level, I've noticed the following trends in Style Bias across the organizations for whom I have worked:

- **Organizations with a Walker Style Bias** naturally tend to have a more ingrained operational process and function with more mature protocols than other types of organizations. This creates a predictable pace, helps coordinate activities, and ensures teamwork and productivity. Walker organizations might include, but are not limited to, government organizations, non-profits, and organizations or companies that are well-established.

- **Organizations with a Flyer Style Bias** are often entrepreneurial enterprises, rapid-growth companies, and/or organizations with a creative focus. These organizations tend to thrive on less structure, fewer rules, processes, and poor boundaries. They operate in a somewhat "grassroots" manner and are typically marked by a frenetic pace and activity, with an ever-changing agenda and an atmosphere of passionate ideation and creation. Flyer-biased organizations may include new ventures (e.g. startup companies), product development companies, creative or development agencies, and other similar organizations.

- **Organizations with a Climber Style Bias** have a well-established power structure, and a well-articulated roadmap for the future. These organizations are typically driven by strong leadership in a very "top-down" manner, with a focused agenda, clearly established goals, objectives, and metrics in place. You are likely to find Climber Style Bias in sales-driven organizations, financial institutions, investment and venture firms, and similar organizations.

Style Bias can occur on any team and often impacts business divisions, as people with the same operational style congregate within teams. For example, you might find a Climber Style Bias in business development or the sales arm of a business. In contrast, you might find a higher concentration of Walkers in divisions like HR, contracts, payroll, or marketing. While Style Bias can occur anywhere, it's very common and typically easy to identify because it impacts organizational culture. As bias manifests, the traits of the dominant style impress themselves into groups, teams, or organizations as a whole. Over time, those traits can become well-ingrained.

This is one of the reasons why, when I work with a new client, the first thing I try to do is understand the operational style of the person I'm working with. The second thing I try to do is to identify whether there is Style

Bias is within the organization or group I'll be working with. Doing this can be powerful in helping me tailor my approach, anticipate how people are likely to respond to me—and position myself and my work in the best possible way.

A Case of Style Bias & Balance

I once worked with a pioneering startup. When I was hired, the company had about twenty-five full-time staffers with a style-balanced leadership trio. The company was led by a Flyer CEO; a highly-connected, Climber vice president; and a rock steady, wise, seasoned Walker president. The company was in active development mode and poised to launch with anticipation of an initial public offering.

At the start, there were several Flyers, some Walkers, and only a few Climbers. It was, without question, a Flyer-biased environment. The company structure was flat, and there was little hierarchy in place. It was easy to get permission to do something and to get the resources we needed. The Flyers regularly overwhelmed the Walkers, as we flew around in vision land and actively experimented in building new products and services. We worked insane hours, pulling all-nighters, and working ourselves into regular coffee-infused stupors. The constant flow of creativity, building, and learning was magnetic and energizing for us—though I sense it exhausted everyone else!

As we gained traction, we became more profitable and the company grew. Within eight months, we expanded from twenty-five people to about sixty people. We were the healthiest, organizationally, at this point, with a nice balance of Walkers, Climbers, and Flyers. The Flyers kept building, enjoying latitude and freedom. The Walkers began establishing the critical infrastructure, process, and technology required to make the place run smoothly, producing a more ordered, stable environment. Climbers were busy making deals and establishing plans for an initial public offering, and largely kept to themselves. It was a highly productive period of growth marked by incredible flow, innovation, and revenue. The company was well structured and smartly focused, and probably the most style-balanced at this stage of development.

About nine months later, the company doubled in size to about a hundred people. As we prepared for an initial public offering, a new board of directors had been put in place. The board was Climber-dominated, and their first action was to replace our Flyer CEO with a Climber CEO tasked with establishing more focus and discipline. The new CEO was a hard-charging leader with an extensive corporate resume. He realigned our Flyer/Climber development team under a Walker COO, and brought on more staff. While he added more Walkers, he added a significant number of Climbers who were given some rather intimidating titles—within every department. The company culture shifted to a Walker/Climber-biased culture, where Flyers became squarely outnumbered. The new leadership continued to map out business development, finance, and acquisitions plans, and prepared to take the company public. They pushed hard for sales revenue to build working capital and positioned to secure our initial round of venture funding.

As we grew to 135 people, we shifted to a Climber-biased culture. While other styles were present, many people didn't feel they had a voice. A very staid approach governed product development, and new checks and balances were put in place to govern resources, development, and purchasing, clipping the wings of Flyer innovators. The development team (a balanced mix of Flyers and Walkers) was split up and reassigned to manage existing products and services. The era of free-wheeling innovation was over. We continued to provide great service, and sales increased. However, at the same time, growth began to slow. Company goals focused on reaching investment milestones and driving profit.

Shortly after a successful IPO, growth stalled. Leadership became intently focused on responding to pressures from investors. The board placed pressure on leadership to take on work that fell outside of the company's strike zone. An internal divide opened up over the focus and future of the company. Climbers were fixated, with good reason, on driving the company to hit key milestones and "keeping the lights on." Walkers were frustrated with the stress of conflict and heavy demands. Flyers, who had their wings clipped, felt disenfranchised and disconnected from leadership's future vision for the company (something they had previously driven). The company's Style Bias became strongly Climber-biased.

It's important to note that during this phase, Style Bias wasn't necessarily the biggest problem at this company, although it did impact the future direction of the organization. The real problem seemed to be that the team became divided and conflicted internally about how to work together and move forward in a unified way. This was naturally exacerbated by style dynamics. However, at the same time, the company faced problems that were not easy to solve. When I felt I could no longer contribute my best, I made a painstaking decision to pursue a new opportunity. Over the next eighteen months, I watched from a distance as the company began to radically downsize, finally to be acquired by a large conglomerate in a transaction that was positioned as a good financial move. In the end, only three to five people were left, and none of them were original staffers.

STYLE IMBALANCES

While Style Bias isn't a bad thing, a style *imbalance*, in which one or two styles become dominant to the exclusion of other styles, can be problematic. Style imbalances are caused by a total absence or exclusion of at least one operational style at an organizational level. This typically results in compromised momentum, culture, and teamwork.

For example, within a Flyer-dominant organization, you'll find a dizzying amount of ideation and vision casting combined with active experimentation and development work. It is likely to be an undisciplined, passion-driven, creative, and visionary environment, where people are free to think big and build new things without a lot of discipline or boundaries. *Without* Climbers and Walkers on board, however, it may be challenging to order, organize, and streamline production, establish a reliable framework for it, and move the needle on funding, production, and operations to create a sustainable business model.

Typically, style imbalances take root over time, and the problems they trigger often take years to manifest. As the pros and pitfalls of the dominant style (or styles) become deeply ingrained an organization's culture, it will gradually lose pliability. This can result in a culture with a status quo mentality that becomes closed to change or becomes subject to other pitfalls. When there is a lack of infusion of one style there will inevitably be consequences:

- **Without Flyers,** there may be ideas for the future, but there will generally be a lack of cohesive, high-level perspective and broad vision that harnesses and prioritizes ideas to create a future vision that can fuel ongoing development, growth, and innovation.

- **Without Climbers,** there may be a lack of structure and discipline to hit organizational and/or financial milestones, which can especially impact the financial performance of the organization.

- **Without Walkers,** there is likely to be an immature operational infrastructure and crippled ability to deliver with reliability, quality, and consistency.

The specific problems that result will depend on which styles are missing, the organization's context, phase of growth, and more. As dominant operational style(s) become well-ingrained, blind spots will inevitably emerge that complicate teamwork and collaboration.

For example, I once managed a transformation initiative within a government agency that serviced an arm of the US Military. The first day, it became clear that the culture was Walker driven, and the Style Bias in the organization favored Climbers and Walkers. In fact, I was hard pressed to find any Flyers in the organization at all! When I talked to the person in charge, it became clear to me that this was part of the reason I'd been brought in.

For decades, the organization's Style Bias had worked well for a military organization with a strong hierarchy. As a Walker-run organization, they got things done, cutting through red tape and doing their work with patriotism, conviction, and heart. A lot of things worked well in that organization. However, when it came to building out the "next generation" of service, the team found it difficult to see the forest for the trees. There was a mixed bag of ideas, some high-level vision casting, but the ideas weren't bound by a clear, big-picture vision or roadmap that the organization could rally around for future development, and they had been stuck for a decade.

We were brought in as a catalyst. Our job was to leverage our expertise against the deep knowledge already present to identify opportunities for the future. While we came in gently, we had to work through some well-ingrained change resistance, territorialism, and attachment to the status quo. Slowly and methodically, we worked with the organization to infuse some Flyer perspective and develop a new, big-picture vision—identifying a solid point on the horizon to which they could navigate, and developing a roadmap that would help them get there, step-by-step. My firm then stayed on to help that organization mobilize to realize that vision over a period of several years.

Correcting a Style Imbalance

Assuming all individuals are properly skilled, there are typically three causes for a problematic style imbalance.

1. Absence on the team of one or more operational styles
2. Under-participation from one or more operational styles
3. A single operational style dominates collaboration

In cases where a style is underrepresented, it's important infuse the team with a missing operational style. This may mean mixing up the team by bringing in a new person—or it may mean shaking things up by bringing in some new talent. Be prepared, however, as the status quo may not welcome change with open arms!

In organizations with Style Bias, consultants are often useful for filling style gaps and infusing teams with new perspective and skills. For example, you might need a strong Walker subject-matter expert with deep experience and authority to help you dig deep to improve, organize, and properly maintain a core area of operations. You might need a highly focused Climber to help establish priorities, objectives, and key milestones that will drive productivity and momentum. As mentioned, a Flyer can come in handy for introducing change, new vision, or future-focused ideas. As you infuse your culture with a missing or absent style, it's important to make sure to create an environment that is hospitable to them, and provide support as they struggle to acclimate.

Style imbalances can also be created when there is a lack of participation from certain individuals, or when individuals dominate and drown out the voices of other team members. While anyone can dominate, it is not uncommon for Flyers and Climbers to be the culprits here. This, again, is where leadership comes in. It's important for team leaders to remain sensitive to style dynamics and behaviors, and establish mechanisms and ground rules that help ensure balanced representation in cultures that may be inclined to resist others. Creating a safe, constructive environment where underrepresented individuals (and operational styles) have a voice is essential to balanced collaboration.

I once faced a situation where an outspoken Climber dominated a collaborative project and shut down other voices among her peers. She had the same level of authority as the others, a much larger ego, a selfish fixation on her own goals and objectives, and a disregard for the priorities of others. To combat the problem, I asked a competent Walker to be formally in charge of the team and the project, and sent an email notification to the team. As an introvert who felt uncomfortable around the dominant Climber, she initially protested. However, I instructed her to institute some simple rules of engagement to help ensure everyone had a voice, and to ensure that no individual dominated the discussion moving forward. By putting the Walker authority over the team and establishing ground rules, she was instantly empowered to speak and be heard, and balance out the Climber's input against the input of other team members. This opened up the project for greater participation and helped the team work more productively.

In truth, the solution to a style imbalance is going to be unique to each situation and often involves creativity. Managing problematic style imbalances involves an understanding of situational, style, and team dynamics as well as creativity around managing and resourcing teams. It also requires coaching as we encourage team members to listen proactively, work with empathy, arrest their headspaces, and neutralize pitfalls. There's no magic formula here, and you'll probably experiment a bit. However, when leaders are armed with an understanding of the pros and pitfalls of each style, it can become easier to correct problematic style imbalances for the benefit of collaboration and better outcomes.

TIPS FOR CREATING STYLE BALANCE

While areas of Style Bias are certainly acceptable, as a general rule, leadership should work to ensure the presence and participation of all three styles within an organization, at some level, across departments. The challenge remains that there is no magic formula for creating style balance. The balancing of operational styles in a group can be likened to balancing the ecosystem in a saltwater fish tank. The bigger the team, the bigger the tank—and the more complicated the ecosystem!

My friend Avery has a 500-gallon saltwater fish tank in his family room. It is filled with beautiful fish, colorful coral, crustaceans, and more. It's mesmerizing to watch. However, almost every time I come over, Avery seems to be working on that fish tank—measuring the PH balance and salt content, adjusting the filtration, cleaning the tank, and making sure it has the right mix of creatures help keep things in balance. Watching Avery manage this work of art, I saw patience, experimentation, learning, trial and error, and sheer dedication in action. I believe attaining style balance requires a similar kind of diligence. This said, here are some key recommendations that can help managers as they attempt to create style balance:

Get Everyone on the Same Page

It's easier to create style balance and manage style dynamics when teams are working from the same playbook. By encouraging teams to leverage a common framework to understand each other, like the OST, it's easier to inspire a unified approach to collaboration.

Customize for the Company

Is your company a high-growth company? A creative agency? Is it an investment firm? An established blue-chip behemoth? A non-profit? Something else? What kind of culture do you have today, and what kind of culture do you want to create for the future? Do you have a current Style Bias? What pitfalls are active in your culture? Take the time to study the style traits and position gravitation of Walkers, Climbers, and Flyers to identify "best likely candidates" for various positions or teams.

Leverage an Appropriate Mix of Styles

While it's not uncommon for there to be bias to hire individuals with a certain operational style, it's important to seek a mix of operational styles to help your organization remain agile, balanced, and efficient. Pay attention to operational styles in the hiring process, taking note of pros and pitfalls you see active in the people you hire. Help people acclimate to your culture, and in doing so, shift your culture for the better.

Anticipate Shifts and Transitions

There will be seasons within your organization that create demand for one style over others. For example, if you are in startup mode, you may benefit from Flyer bias. When you move into maintenance mode, you may need more Walkers and Climbers, and when it's time for reinvention, Flyer bias comes in handy again. It's important not to develop tunnel vision and embed a dominant style that may not be able to help your company transition to the *next* phase. Always think ahead and align teams with an eye toward growth. As you transition into new phases, make your employees partners in your evolution, helping them understand the shift and redefine their roles in moving the company forward, in solid alignment with their operational design.

Consider Authority, Voice & Volume

As you assemble teams, it's important to consider factors like authoritativeness, position, outspokenness, openness, honesty, and extroversion as you attempt to balance the voices of individuals with different operational styles. For example, a single, extroverted Flyer may go a long way in a culture of introverted Walkers. Style balance helps ensure the proper resources are in place to help the organization address current needs, anticipate the future, and respond to support the changing organizational needs. At times, balanced teams come together miraculously. However, most of the time they are the result of hard work and experimentation. It takes time, practice, and emotional intelligence to get things right. However, when balance is attained and style dynamics are on point, everyone benefits!

PART FOUR

PLOTTING A NEW COURSE

CHAPTER 15
MANAGING TOUGH TERRAIN

Survivalists must know how to use their skills and the resources around them, along with an understanding of their environment, to solve problems with confidence in a vast wilderness. They must be *prepared to manage* challenges, obstacles, and even crisis—whether it involves finding food or a source of water, keeping warm, crossing a chasm, or weathering a violent storm.

The same is true for you, as you work to navigate within your Workplace Wilderness. As you face the terrain ahead, you'll manage an onslaught of demand, overcome challenges and obstacles, build bridges of understanding with people, and weather the storms of style clashes and interpersonal conflict. Like getting your bearings in a natural wilderness, it may feel overwhelming. It can be easy to assume a position of powerlessness when you feel overwhelmed, insignificant, or threatened. However, it's critical to remember on this journey that you carry much more power than you realize! Understanding operational styles makes it easier to focus your power and take a proactive stance in shifting your position, your relational stance, the way you relate to others, and confront challenge. The following story underscores this point:

WAR AND PEACE

Over a decade ago, I was working on a massive project for a Fortune 500 company, under a project lead I'll call Charles. He had risen quickly within the corporate ranks, without the experience to bolster him in a senior role. While he was good at working with company leadership and great at schmoozing with our client leads, it became clear on this project that he was in over his head.

Afraid to push back against mounting client requests, Charles's response to out-of-scope requests was to promise the world and then squeeze extra, out-of-scope work out of our team at night and over weekends. As a result, our team had been working late into the night and on weekends for a months without a break or an end in sight. Every time Charles walked into our office, it was like my team was braced for an ice bucket challenge! There was a physical reaction: people tensed up with clenched jaws, hunched shoulders, furrowed brows—just *waiting* for more work to be dumped on their heads.

As the functional lead responsible for seven people, I had a strong protective impulse to advocate for and protect my team. I tried different approaches to addressing problems with Charles. However, he had a "my way or the highway" demeanor and responded by making it clear he did not want any input from me. His snarky, authoritarian, dismissive, and rude behavior—along with his management style—infuriated me. Along with the rest of the team, I quickly lost respect for Charles. I tried to maintain professionalism, but as our interactions became more public and heated, the tension became difficult to hide. To triage the situation, I scheduled a meeting with Charles to clear the air.

This meeting became one of the ugliest, closed-door professional exchanges I have ever experienced. It started positively and politely. Right out of the gate, he seemed closed off. I started with positivity—yet the minute I expressed concerns about the team, scope, and project, Charles cut me off claiming he had "no time for this." I pushed back respectfully saying that I really felt we needed to get on the same page. Charles then accused me of being subversive. I calmly explained that, if I'd wanted to be subversive, I would have gone over his head rather than trying to meet to resolve things. I then added that, if we couldn't resolve things one-on-one, that perhaps it *would* be better to get management involved.

This triggered a red-faced, explosively hostile, profanity-laced diatribe in which he threatened, in highly specific terms, to "F*ing bury" me and professionally ruin me if I went to management. Hackles up, I looked him in the eye and cut to the chase, describing in precise detail what I really thought about his poor management abilities, rotten communication skills, lack of inclusion, deep insecurity, immaturity, passive-aggression, and raging ego. I underscored that he'd be hard pressed to find a team member that didn't agree with me. There was a lot more to the exchange, and I can't remember how it ended except that we both left the conference room enraged.

That night, I went back to my hotel room, head throbbing, and replayed the scene several times in my mind. I was convinced my feedback had been accurate and on target. The big question was where to go next. Going directly to management wasn't a great option. The executive in charge of the project didn't like bad news and *loved* Charles. He was slick, smooth, and sociable and had painted a rosy picture of the project, keeping me and our (equally frustrated) development lead out of briefings and client inter-actions. The client liked Charles, too, but why wouldn't they? His lips were firmly affixed to the backside of our client lead, and he handed out free development work like a high-tech Santa Claus!

While I knew I was right, we were at a stalemate. I could leave the proj-ect on principle alone, fairly confident that due to a stellar track record, I'd come out relatively unscathed. However, I had made a commitment, and the work wasn't done. My team would suffer without my support and might not be able to deliver. Further, if I left, I was absolutely certain Charles would cover his tracks by blaming me when things unraveled.

My thoughts intensified into hatred. How dare he threaten to damage me when I was trying to HELP him? Who threatens to ruin someone? I sat there in shock. I had never wanted to physically harm someone so much in my life! In fact, I was shocked at the feeling of pleasure that washed over me when I envisioned planting my fist in his face. I let out an exasperated muffled scream into the bedspread.

"GOD!" I cried. "You have got to help me! I HATE him!" Pulling my head out of the cover, face plastered with tears, I reached for a tissue. "He is literally my enemy," I thought, with a sudden level of fascination. I'd never had an enemy before. Suddenly, a childhood Sunday school lesson replayed in my mind. I recalled instruction to bless your enemy instead of cursing him. I remember something about refusing to repay evil with evil, and a verse from the book of Romans that said: *"If your enemy is hungry, feed him; if he is thirsty, give him something to drink. In doing this, you will heap burning coals on his head."*

The idea of *burning coals* on Charles' head thrilled me. However, *blessing* him? Showing care or concern for him? Nope. I had no love for Charles. I had *nothing* for him but contempt. My conscience challenged me with a new thought: if I embraced a Christian worldview, where God loved everyone— even jerks—wouldn't that mean that God loved Charles as much as me? The thought of this actually made me angry: this guy was patently *unlovable*. Like a hysterical lunatic, I balled up my fists and said out loud: "Okay God, if you are listening, I *hate* this guy. I have *nothing* to give. No blessings, no love. Nothing. If you want me to *bless* him, then you're going to have to help me see Charles with *your eyes*."

Now, let me stop here for a moment and underscore that belief in a Christian God or a higher power is absolutely not a prerequisite for finding this book helpful or useful. However, I would not do justice to this story if I did not tell you how I arrived at a pivotal realization about Charles and where it led. I would be lying if I did not tell you with all assurance, that in my frustration and desperation that night, I received a rather miraculous answer in response to yelling at God like a nut job in my hotel room.

As I held my throbbing head with one hand and wiped my puffy eyes with the other, eight disembodied words drifted gently through my conscious mind, seemingly disconnected from all I was feeling or thinking. They were full of empathy, grace, and an understanding that was not my own:

"Can't you see? This is all he has."

It was like the atmosphere shifted: In a split second, I became empathetically aware of both Charles's insecurity *and* desperation. He had come back to my firm after leaving to build a startup that failed within a year. Upon his return, he was promoted from consultant to senior manager, jumping two levels, without the experience or training to back this advancement. He had a huge ego and a lot of pride and couldn't admit he was in over his head. He was also terribly insecure and paranoid about having his weakness discovered. Good or bad, Charles was managing to the best of his ability—as I called attention to every weakness. To Charles, I was nothing but a *threat*.

"*Can't you see? This is all he has.*" At the time, I didn't know how true that statement was until months later. I will pause for a moment to explain that I later learned that Charles had not only been forced to return to my company after his startup failed. During his one-year absence, his fiancée also left him for his business partner and he lost almost everything he owned. He was sick all the time and had been placed on antidepressants. In all seriousness, Charles was about one dead dog and a beer short of a bad Country Western song. His professional reputation was all he had left—and he was legitimately convinced that I was trying to ruin him.

That's why he went for the jugular! Ironically, he threatened me with the *one thing he most feared for himself!*

The thing is, as furious as I was, I wasn't out to ruin anyone. Sitting in that hotel room, I didn't need to know more of the backstory to figure out what came next. As I thought about our problems rationally, I realized that even *if* I was ninety percent correct in my assessment of Charles, I had a "ten percent problem" to deal with, and it was this: I didn't like Charles. I didn't respect him, and my attitude had shown to the team.

I thought about how I'd feel in a similar position: undermined, humiliated, and embarrassed. As I wrestled with what came next, I realized one thing: regardless of whether I stayed or left that project, to maintain a clear conscience, I had to *own* my part in our conflict.

Without question, Charles had run our team into the ground. He gave away work for free, and undermined our profit margin. He excluded me and others with a condescension and disrespect that was infuriating. He was aggressive, self-centered, short-sighted, and authoritarian. He was a bad manager. He didn't need a lot of help looking foolish. He was his own worst enemy. All of this was true. *However, I wasn't responsible for Charles. I was responsible for me.* I knew what I needed to do.

The next day, I mustered up the courage to approach Charles as we exited a meeting. "Can I talk to you for a minute?" He sucked in a deep breath, crossed his arms, pursed his lips, and scowled. As people disbanded, I took a deep breath. "Listen," I said, "This won't take any time. I reflected on yesterday's discussion, and I want to quickly address one thing you said that stood out to me."

"Okay..." Charles responded, suspicious and guarded.

"You said you feel that I disrespected you in front of the team." I said. Charles nodded.

"Well, I think you are right. I have had an attitude of disrespect toward you. While it wasn't intentional, I believe it has shown to the team."

Charles eyes widened as a genuine wave of compassion washed over me.

"Look," I said, maintaining his gaze and swallowing hard. "I would never, *ever* want anyone to treat me that way. So, I want to apologize. I hope you'll forgive me."

Charles's jaw literally fell open. He stroked his goatee furiously, clearly confused, and looked around as if to see if he was being "punked." All he could muster was, "Okay. Wow. Uh, thanks."

I dismissed myself, leaving Charles in a stupor and went on with my day—immediately aware of a total sense of freedom. The feelings of anxiety, abject hatred, and animosity I had carried for months *vanished*. I went back to managing my team with a spring in my step. I managed just like I had before with one difference: moving forward, I squashed the urge to roll my eyes or pass a snarky comment when Charles pulled a dumb stunt. I didn't feed the negativity. With only eight weeks remaining on the project, I just wanted to lead well and muscle through to deliver good results.

I could never have anticipated the enormous impact the simple act of owning my part in our conflict would have on the project and in our relationship.

While Charles never once apologized or admitted any fault, his attitude toward me completely shifted from that point on. Almost immediately, he stopped skulking and became curiously cheerful. While he didn't apologize or acknowledge *anything* I had said, there was no doubt he'd heard me loud and clear. His shifty, exclusionary, and dictator-like behavior changed. He began consulting me, instead of telling me how things would be. He began including me in discussions and seeking counsel on how to better handle project, scope, client, and team issues. Much to my shock and amazement, he brought me (and later with my encouragement, the development lead) into executive meetings and client discussions! Trust blossomed and we became a team.

Together, we pushed back on the client and landed a lucrative scope adjustment. The project became more manageable and extended four more weeks. The changes didn't just benefit me or Charles, they benefitted the entire team, our company, and our client. My team went home on time and did work we were proud of. Morale shifted. *Everything shifted.* We even won an award for our work!

OWNING YOUR POWER

Looking back, I had set up that meeting with Charles to try and establish some common ground, not knowing how badly it would backfire. A colleague who had witnessed the rotten way Charles had treated me and the team expressed disgust and disbelief that I would "lower myself" to apologize to him for anything. Free of bitterness, I couldn't help but smile in response. I admitted that, while the apology was humbling, I'd also found it liberating and empowering. It gave me a clear conscience, and released me from being a prisoner to anger, anxiety, drama, hostility, *and* any sense of being a victim.

Owning 100 percent of my responsibility in the conflict with Charles was the right thing to do, and it opened the door to reconciliation. In truth, I only have God to thank for the wisdom to do this. I didn't have any magical, unicorn-like relationship powers of my own. I was only trying to do the right thing. My apology wasn't about weakness, or covering my butt, or kissing up to Charles, or even manipulating him. Also, I did not feel the need to apologize for the very truthful, unabashed feedback I'd given him. My apology was simply about *owning the role I'd played in creating a toxic relationship dynamic.*

I was blown away by the beautiful restorative power it had and the power one person can wield in a bad situation. It instantly built a bridge between us that led to common ground. When we finally came together, Charles was shocked to find what an invaluable ally I was: I supported his agenda, helped him manage and lead better, and achieve critical goals.

This incident also flipped a switch in my brain about style dynamics and the natural tensions that can occur between people with different operational styles. While at the time, I had been searching for a new way to understand people at work, some of what I learned working with Charles informed the development of the visual framework for OST. Shortly thereafter, I laid out my theory about Walkers, Climbers, and Flyers on a napkin in a New Jersey diner!

WEATHERING STORMS OF CONFLICT

One of my favorite "The Far Side" cartoons by Gary Larson depicts God in the kitchen making the earth. The world sits on the counter in a giant baking pan, and he is sprinkling "spice containers" over the planet, labeled "Birds," "Reptiles," "Insects," "Medium Skinned People," "Light-Skinned People," and "Dark Skinned People." In the picture, God's face looks contemplative as he holds his arm over the earth with a spice container labeled "JERKS." His thought bubble reads, "*Just to make it interesting.*"

There's no escaping the fact that the modern workplace seems to have more than its fair share of jerks. The Oxford Dictionary online defines the word, "jerk" as "a contemptibly foolish person." However, when you think about it, a jerk is merely a triggered person with a lot of very active pitfalls. Jerks certainly can be contemptible and stir up conflict at work. By nature, however, there may not be a whole lot you can do about a jerk, besides manage that behavior and choose the right responses.

Most often, workplace conflict is more complicated than this. Conflict is almost always a two-way street, fueled by the natural tensions, clashes, misunderstandings, and miscommunications that occur between people with different operational styles. These tensions are compounded when people become triggered and pitfalls become active, which can set off chain reactions.

This book provides ample resources that can fuel your ability to work adaptively, anticipating and navigating the natural tensions that occur between operational styles. This can improve your ability to neutralize and diffuse conflict and help you avoid stepping on landmines as you work with others. It can also help stop the chain reactions that magnify misunderstanding and escalate conflict to impact other people. Collectively, this can make you a better communicator, collaborator, and manager that weathers the storms of interpersonal conflict well.

However, this isn't enough. As you navigate the twists and turns of interpersonal relationships and workplace conflict, there's one more key ingredient necessary for success. If you can really "get this" I believe you will become more than a good manager who knows how to handle people well—you will become a transformative force for good in your workplace.

We talked before about keeping your headspace in check. However, doing this involves more than just controlling your thoughts and emotional triggers. It involves owning *100 percent of your responsibility in creating positive or negative outcomes everywhere you go*. In our modern society it's so common to point fingers, assign blame, and "right fight." This behavior dominates the workplace, too. It's very easy to try people in the court of our own opinions and expect the "guilty parties" to assume responsibility for their behavior, while we fail to take responsibility for our own. The problem is, *we are very often the guilty party too*! It doesn't matter *how guilty* we are. It doesn't matter if we have good intentions. It doesn't matter if we are mostly right. Even if we only play a small role in contributing to a negative outcome or inadvertently trigger someone—our thoughts, judgements, words, insensitive behaviors, and actions carry weight and impact and we are responsible for them!

In my conflict with Charles, he was probably about ninety percent at fault. However, I had a "ten-percent problem" to deal with. If I hadn't dared to own my responsibility—regardless of how big or small it was—that entire situation would have ended *very* differently. When I decided to own my part, I not only set myself free of all the negative "stuff" that accompanied that conflict—I became a powerful catalyst for change in that environment. The same can be true for you. As you navigate the twists and turns of the emotional landscape of your Workplace Wilderness, demonstrating a high level of responsibility and accountability for the outcomes you create can help you step into your power and transformative potential.

UNDERSTANDING THE NATURE OF THE BEAST

I live on the Pacific Coast, and my surfer friends accept sharks with full knowledge of their natures and what they are capable of. They know what kinds of environments to avoid and even what gear to wear in the water, to minimize the chance of a shark attack. However, they also realize they are sharing the water with an apex predator. To a seasoned surfer, a shark bite may be a scary thing, but it's nothing personal because they understand the "nature of the beast."

People are without question, very different than animals and driven by a more complex array of situational, intellectual, emotional, and instinctual drivers. However, in the same way that it makes sense for a hiker to know how to handle an encounter with a cougar—or even a bear—it makes sense for you to develop a firm understanding of the potential "natures" of the individuals you will encounter in your Workplace Wilderness.

When we encounter traits in others that may be confusing, difficult, or uncomfortable to deal with, there is a natural human tendency to want to label them as bad or good. However, those judgements can be off-base and increase our inclination to become offended or triggered by people. OST can help you more objectively understand the traits that naturally accompany each operational style. Leveraging this insight, it becomes easier to understand how people function and depersonalize behavior that might seem aggressive, ambitious, possessive, territorial, defensive, insensitive, threatening, or overwhelming. This can help you better appreciate others and manage interactions and confrontations in ways that drive positive outcomes.

ADDRESSING CHALLENGES & OBSTACLES

It's common to encounter obstacles of every size and shape on your professional journey. There are many practical obstacles that can be imposed by our employers, like having a difficult boss, being laid off, being denied a promotion, undergoing a difficult reorganization, or not having the budget or resources you need. You may grapple with professional development challenges, such as the need for a particular skill set, or the need to secure additional education or training. You might struggle with personal issues that impact work, such as depression or health issues, or the need to care for a special-needs child or an aging parent. Self-employed individuals often grapple with the practical challenges of running a business, like finding qualified help, managing growth, and keeping the business pipeline full. As you navigate ahead, taking the time to identify the challenges and obstacles that impact you and/or block paths of opportunity is important.

EXERCISE 10
CHALLENGES & OBSTACLES

OBSTACLE BRAINSTORMING		
Take a minute to write down the unique challenges and obstacles you face. Describe the impact or limitation they impose on you. Take some time to consider ways you may remove, work around, or eradicate those obstacles. Do they seem insurmountable? Why? Is it possible to prioritize them?		

OBSTACLE	DESCRIPTION/IMPACT	PRIORITY
Example:		
• *Raise/bonus promotion challenge*	• *Company financial challenges feel like an excuse. Need to have a hard talk with manager – met objectives!*	*1*
• *Health & burnout*	• *Need to find a way to work out and see if I can obtain comp or vacation time.*	*3*
• *Apartment*	• *Apartment isn't healthy for me. Too far from work. No gym nearby. Noisy and can't rest. Dark and depressing but hard to move without the raise/bonus.*	*2*
• *Commute*	• *Long commute is killing my time for rest, workouts and fun. Waste of time.*	*2*

As you consider these challenges and obstacles, it may be encouraging to remember that very often, difficult times can serve a positive and important purpose! C.S. Lewis once said "Hardships often prepare ordinary people for an extraordinary destiny." When we encounter trials and obstacles, they can form a kind of training ground, where we learn to be more patient and flexible, develop new strengths, and discover what we are made of. They can also become catalysts that motivate us to problem-solve, develop important new skills, and pursue new paths that lead to a better future.

CHOOSING YOUR BATTLES

From interpersonal conflict to practical business concerns, to taking on competitors: The ability to choose your battles is a mark of a wise leader. Depending on the situation, it's not always necessary to engage. Sometimes, it's better to ride things out. It's important to realize when the cards are stacked against you and resistance is futile—and when to fight. As you journey forward, you'll have to make decisions about when to stand your ground or eat humble pie, put your foot down or be flexible.

Working with greater understanding of others can help you battle smarter, rather than harder. With an understanding of operational styles, you will work with greater empathy and adaptivity while depersonalizing attitudes and behavior. You will also learn to make decisions that help ensure you can do your best work, without paying a price that is too high.

My team once completed a web redesign for a firm led by a very focused, demanding executive. As a Climber, I knew he'd have a strong agenda, which turned out to be taking over both the digital and social teams. He was very focused on moving past maintenance-type projects to very high-profile projects that would "move the bar" for his company. We tailored our pitch to him—keeping it bulleted, clear, concise, no-nonsense, and addressed his agenda directly with options for timing and pricing. We won the phase one project, did a beautiful job, and delivered on time and on budget.

After Phase 1 completion, the executive immediately invited us to do a smaller second phase, which involved building a new component of the website for another business unit. However, when we looked at the scope of the job, it became clear that it was a poorly conceived idea that was unlikely to drive desired results. Further, we felt it would create usability problems, confusion, and potentially make everyone look bad.

As I predicted, when we raised these issues to our Climber executive, he didn't want to hear about the problem—even though we presented our case well. He shut us down, making it very clear that "fixing this project" wasn't a priority for him. He explained that it was for another group, and he simply wanted to "check it off my list and get it done." He continued, "Look, they think this fills a purpose, and if I can give them what they ask for, they'll get off my back." He had bigger plans and just wanted it "done." The problem was, we couldn't put our name on that project.

Rather than right-fighting, I came up with a plan to gracefully bow out. The next morning, I sent him a full-price, very padded proposal. I thanked him for the opportunity, explained that our dance card was very full (which was true), and apologetically I explained that we would be unable to start the work for five weeks. He not only choked on the bid, but the timing. He rushed out and hired a cheaper agency, which did the work without question. Our plan worked well. There were no hard feelings on either side.

Eight months later, we were brought back to clean up the disaster that ensued. This paid off in many ways: the executive ended up having more respect for us and our boundaries. By the time we addressed the work, we were positioned to not only do it properly, but to expand the scope, preserving our stellar reputation. Further, we were paid a mint to do it.

CHAPTER 16
FINDING TRUE NORTH

We've talked a lot about embracing and recognizing our operational styles, mitigating weakness, and working adaptively. I'd like to come back now and talk about your journey through the Workplace Wilderness and where you will go from here.

It wasn't until I found myself totally burned out and sick in the Virgin Islands that I realized how far off course I was. I certainly didn't look "off course" to most people. I had a lot of what people would associate with success, on the surface. However, while I had a lot of what I thought I wanted, I had very little I needed. I felt completely sapped of energy, I was physically ill and could not heal.

As I began to question things, I started making incremental changes. I reduced travel hours. I really focused on improving my health, too. I stopped eating out of vending machines and started carrying protein bars with me. I increased my water intake and began taking the stairs instead of the elevator. At night, rather than going out to meals with my project teams, I worked out in the hotel gym and ate protein and vegetables afterward. I managed to drop twenty pounds.

With each success, I found myself feeling stronger and healthier. Yet, even with all these positive changes, I continued to struggle with my firm's culture, which seemed more focused on the bottom line than on taking care of people. While I had helped secure millions in annual revenue, a pending reorganization—combined with market corrections, fiscal challenges, and a possible acquisition on the horizon—meant the promotion I'd been promised wasn't likely to materialize. It was clear the organizational culture would continue to be a battle zone—potentially worsening under market pressure. I had to decide whether I wanted to make the best of it—armed with my resolve and daily triple-shot lattes—or dare to make a bigger change.

As I mentioned before, I had been fortunate to secure a very demanding, local, eight-month project, but after it ended, I had gone back out on the road. While I changed the way I worked and was feeling better, I still grappled with health concerns, and with more tests ordered by my doctor, I did not want to lose traction in making healthy life changes. So, I mustered up the courage to ask my boss for a three-month personal leave of absence, which was granted. I needed time to figure out what was next, and was blessed to be able to live off my savings, as well as the equity I had built in my home.

The first month, I "rested and nested," slept in every day, lived in my jammies, stayed home, watched chick flicks, and had girlfriends over. The second month, I reconnected with family, attending two out-of-town family weddings, spent time with precious people in my life, did projects at the house and even started going on dates after a serious drought. I also got a trainer and beefed up my workouts. The third month, I began to explore my options and plot a new course. I started a blog and was soon approached to do some writing and consulting work for another company.

As my leave of absence came to an end, I found myself conflicted and anxious: I had wrestled with the urge to go out on my own for a decade, and now had a clear entry point, with a client waiting in the wings. While I was more at peace about the idea, I was terrified of taking the leap. The loss of job security and benefits frightened me. I began to lose sleep as I battled my fear as well as the nagging idea that it was time to take "the leap."

THE IMPORTANCE OF ENERGETIC ALIGNMENT

A few days before my scheduled return to work, I had an appointment with my endocrinologist, Dr. Susan Rogacz, to go over some of my test results.

Sitting in the exam room, my eyes welled with tears. I explained to her that my leave of absence ended the next week. I was dreading my return, worried about the impact on my health and well-being—and totally afraid to do something else. Dr. Rogacz's response was a catalyst that literally changed my life—and continues to influence my journey today.

"Leigh," she sighed, "my job is to study the impacts of stress on the body's endocrine system." She looked at me intently. "What I have learned is this: When you are fulfilling your purpose in life, you expend your energy and it *returns to you*. It comes back to regenerate you in body, mind, and spirit. However, when you *abuse* your purpose in life, you expend your energy and it *doesn't return,* and you find yourself depleted. This always results in "disease"—whether it is physical, spiritual, or mental."

She paused, looked at me gravely, and went on. "Now, I'm not going to tell you what your purpose is, but I am going to tell you this job is *not* your purpose in life." As I swallowed the giant lump in my throat, Dr. Rogacz encouraged me to dig deep and consider my purpose, and to be brave in doing so. Then she gave me a big hug and wished me luck in making my decision. I bawled on the way home, not in self-pity but in full realization of the truth of what I needed to do. That same day, I called my boss and told her it was time for me to go. It was time for a more serious course adjustment.

GOING AROUND IN CIRCLES

Outdoor enthusiasts and survival experts will attest that, when a person becomes disoriented in an unfamiliar place and doesn't understand how to navigate using fixed landmarks like rock configurations, mountains, elements on the horizon, or even the stars, they often find themselves walking in circles. This happens due to the natural human inclination to bias your course toward your dominant hand. As a result, most right-handed people will have a natural directional bias to turn slightly right, and left-handed people will have a natural propensity to go left.

As many hikers can attest, the circles may be big or small, but if you're not navigating properly to keep yourself on-course, it's possible to walk for days hoping to make progress only to find yourself frustratingly close to where you started at the beginning—wasting time, resources, and burning valuable energy. In a similar manner, it's possible to allow your natural instincts—as well as "career autopilot"—to run you in proverbial circles when it comes to your profession, like I did, for years.

Perhaps you've tried to plot a new course before, by changing jobs, roles, locations, titles, or even professions. Maybe you've found yourself, after trying to make a positive change, in a job situation that feels eerily familiar to one from your past. The reasons we repeat patterns are likely to be deeply rooted in our psychology, situation, and choices. However, the root cause is likely to be rooted in two things: a lack of stewardship of your own career journey and a busted career compass!

TAKING THE HELM OF YOUR CAREER JOURNEY

Again, it's silly that we spend years preparing to have a job or career, and almost no planning for the professional journeys we will embark on. Sure, some of us set goals for the future. Many of us have ideas about where we'd like to be in five or ten years. Some of us may even have a minds-eye view of what success should look like. However, when I ask people to raise a hand to indicate that they can give me a clear, articulate vision of how they define success, I don't see many volunteers. Most of us carry a more esoteric sense of this thing called "success." It can be a stretch for many of us to articulate what we believe success should really look like, feel like, and the kind of "fruit" we believe it should produce in our lives. More often than not, we press along on our professional journeys, managing things as they come up, leveraging our successes and grasping at opportunities as they present themselves—and hoping we'll be happy and satisfied when we "arrive."

Unfortunately, this is a bit like taking a canoe ride down a swift river without a paddle. Imagine yourself sitting in a canoe, traveling through a system of branching streams, creeks, and rivers. The current, especially a strong one, can easily pull you along this journey, directing your course, pulling you through the rapids and pushing you out into calmer estuaries that let you rest before facing the challenges found around the next bend. Currents can build quickly and can take you by surprise, pushing you past critical turns and taking you in directions you didn't anticipate. You can unwittingly find yourself swept down a new branch with very little notice.

Fail to pay attention, and you may also find yourself on a collision course with the rocks or caught up in Class III rapids, where the current can sweep you along, pull you under, and even drive you over a steep edge.

So many people take on this career journey without ever picking up the proverbial paddle—without ever taking charge! The thing is, you weren't meant to coast along like this. You were never meant to have your career path dictated to you by a corporate machine or to persist on a form of career autopilot, subject to the whim of your career current. As the sole traveler on your particular career path, there isn't anyone else who can steward this journey for you. It's up to you!

If your assets, talents, and natural gifts represent the canoe you ride in, your smarts, self-awareness, and leadership skills are what you'll need to steer. However, you must make a choice: will you ride along, banging off the rocks and canyon walls—or will you take the helm and purposefully navigate the twists and turns of this journey, so that you arrive in a more thriving, hospitable place?

For those who are ready to lead, carrying the following things in your backpack can prepare you to navigate well:

- A strong understanding of your operational style
- A clear understanding of the things that energize and motivate you
- A meaningful, individualized definition of professional success

Understanding your operational design is like packing the proper shoes, clothing, and shelter. Doing things that align to your skills, talents, and abilities forms an insulating layer that can protect you from the harsher elements of the Workplace Wilderness. Understanding what energizes you is like packing proper food as well as some matches to start fires: consider it "fuel for the journey!" Finally, establishing a meaningful, individualized definition of professional success is like packing a really good "career compass"—calibrated against your operational style, values, dreams, hopes, beliefs, and plans for the future. Together, this "gear" can prepare you for the journey ahead and can help you navigate to a more hospitable destination where it's easier to thrive!

A Busted Compass

Danielle, a Walker, is a wife and mother of two who worked as a technical writer for the same company for a decade. Her job wasn't terribly demanding or stimulating, but for many years, it fit the bill, providing the flexibility she needed as she raised two kids, and the stability of the paycheck enabled her to float their family while her husband stood up a small business.

Later in life, after her children left the nest and her husband's business became stable, Danielle struggled with boredom and isolation at work. She longed for more challenge, creative pursuits, and human interaction. She disliked feeling "chained" to a computer all day long. When she asked to be transitioned to an open position, her boss responded by giving her a fat raise with a promise to make things better. Danielle was glad for the raise, but the promise for improvement proved hollow. She soon learned that her boss, who relied heavily on her, had blocked her transition to the other, more creative position. In response to this news, Danielle resigned.

She found herself, after fifteen years, lost in the middle of a career wilderness, not knowing where to turn. A year before, she'd started a new hobby refinishing furniture. Working with her hands and exercising her creative muscle had a therapeutic effect on her. It also turned out that Danielle had a gift for turning garage sale finds into masterpieces that looked like they belonged at swanky uptown boutiques. As she brought these masterpieces to life, she wrestled with questions about her professional future. As she began selling pieces online and at a local antiques mall, it became clear that parlaying this into a sufficient paycheck was unlikely. Facing the grim reality that she still required a job, she reached out to me.

After numerous job interviews, she was struggling with vision and motivation. Danielle knew what she was good at: she was a terrific writer with deep experience and understanding of the publishing process. She also had a keen understanding of people and a masterful eye for detail. She delivered on time and was imminently reliable. In probing into why Danielle struggled to move forward professionally, it wasn't a lack of self-understanding. Her problem seemed to be that her definition of success wasn't at all grounded in *anything* that energized her!

Danielle's definition of success was a throwback to the era when her family was young and they were deep in survival mode. She was fixated on having a job that paid and provided benefits and became "stuck" at that destination. When I asked if that gave her energy, she said, "Energy, no. Peace of mind, yes." When I asked what she really longed for, that's when the passion poured out. She confessed she had been dying on the vine for years. She had more to offer, she wanted to be with people, she wanted to do new things and feel like her work mattered. Yet, her definition of success contained no criteria that emphasized these things! Further, as we retraced her journey, it came to light that her deeply ingrained emphasis on pay over passion was rooted in an impoverished upbringing and the fear of not having enough, which she'd carried into her own adult life.

I drew her attention to the new season she was in and complimented her on the sacrificially awesome job she had done to provide for her family. I pointed out that while she still needed a paycheck to support the family, she didn't really have to sacrifice all her heart's desires in the name of a higher salary anymore: Her husband's business now provided more steady income. Further, she was no longer raising kids or in "startup mode" on a family business.

Danielle had entered a time of freedom and greater latitude and it was time to define what success should look like. We worked on her definition of success together. We balanced pay and benefits with the need to find challenging and creative work that wasn't isolating, a work culture that was more fun and rewarding, and freedom to do new kinds of work. Paying attention to her Walker design, we also prioritized a shorter commute that would allow her to attend to other pursuits and interests, such as her love for travel and her furniture hobby.

A few months later, Danielle began a new job as a senior writer in the marketing department for a major consumer packaged goods company. The writing work was more creative, and she had more latitude to work on a variety of projects. The team culture was innovative, fun, and team-oriented. A reduced commute gave her back an hour in her day. Her salary was competitive and included a benefits package with some great perks. She enjoyed flex time and work-at-home days, too. Collectively, this increased flexibility gave her more time to pursue the furniture hobby, care for her family, and start an entirely new phase of her career.

Today, Danielle's countenance is different. Instead of feeling stuck, bitter, and despondent, she has a lightness and ease about her. I think she's even found some joy. The job is going well—offering sufficient stimulation, challenge, and creativity while remaining manageable. Her furniture venture remains a profitable hobby that helps her work off the stress of the day. She has embraced a new normal and can attest that taking the time to reprioritize and reset her career compass helped her align to work that is energizing, satisfying, and gratifying.

RECALIBRATING YOUR CAREER COMPASS

In chapter 2, I asked you to write down your definition of success. Go back quickly and re-read what you wrote. Consider now that what you wrote down is technically "True North" on your own career compass. It guides the direction for your professional journey and impacts nearly every area of your life. It's time to think about how your current perceptions and definition of success have brought you, on some level, to where you are today.

It's important to realize that our definitions and ideas about success don't just form when we enter the workforce—they begin to form when we are very young, shaped by many influences. Consider the role your parents or guardians played in your understanding and attitudes about work, finances, materialism, money, and this notion of success. Consider the role educators, coaches, and authority figures played along the way. Think about how the attitudes and opinions carried by friends, neighbors, and community influenced your ideas about what a successful person "looks like." Beyond those close to you, your definition of success has also been shaped by your socio-economic status, ethnicity, geographic upbringing, the media, and popular culture!

Our definitions of success are also shaped by what we accept to be true about ourselves and the world we live in. Is your world full of abundance and opportunity, freedom and choice, or is your world a place of fear, hostility, scarcity, and/or poverty—like Brad, Marie, and Danielle's were? These factors tend to condition our views on money, power, influence, and ambition. They tend to impact how we view ourselves as individuals, and what we expect out of life. Do you believe you are strong, able, well-equipped, capable, and an overcomer, or do you believe you are in some way disadvantaged, poorly equipped, weak, or a victim?

Finally, the institutions we serve also have a profound impact on the way we view "perks" and define success. If you think about it, much of what we find acceptable, in terms of compensation and benefits, have been normalized by the industries that employ us. In truth, many of the conventions around *how* we work and *what* we receive in compensation for our labor are artifacts of an Industrial Revolution that gave us conventions like three meals per day and an hour for lunch. As fixed as our employers may seem, it's important to realize that much of what we accept as "givens," today—like two weeks' paid vacation, may not be as fixed as we think! Today's workforce is enjoying more flexible ways of working, from telecommuting to four-day work weeks, to job sharing, and more.

All of these factors serve as the "magnetic forces" that influence our ideas about hard work, success, rewards, and more. Over time, these forces have influenced your course, pulling you down pathways and motivating your decisions. They have pounded and shaped our concepts and ideas about success into what we believe to be true today. However, as Danielle discovered, our definitions can be insufficient, outmoded, and/or outdated, throwing us way off course. Perhaps your definition of success was immature to start with—or maybe it just hasn't grown with your needs and desires. Maybe your thinking is off base or poorly informed and you're stuck in the weeds.

EXERCISE 11
REDEFINING SUCCESS

As you attempt to set a new course for yourself, taking the time now to revisit how you define success will be instrumental for course correction. As you weigh the magnetic forces that brought you to where you are today, it's important to challenge what you accept as truth and make sure your definition of success aligns to your operational design and aspirations for the future. By challenging everything, you can reset your career compass and set a course to a new destination, full of promise.

RESETTING THE CAREER COMPASS

This exercise focuses on taking your definition of success to a new level. For many readers, this may be the first time you've done something like this. However, I hope it won't be your last! This is a great way to do a "course check" and identify areas for correction.

A. REVIEW

Go back to the definition of success you wrote down in the chapter 1 exercise and review it. Take some time to critique what you wrote and answer the following questions:

1. Is it leading you in the right direction?
2. Does it emphasize the right things?
3. Is it sufficient, substantial, and clear?
4. Does it align you to things that are motivating, energizing, and aligned to your operational style?
5. Give yourself a grade!

Go back to the exercises in chapter 2. Examine the things you have always loved to do. Consider the questions below and record your notes.

1. Does your work involve doing things you love to do?
2. Can these energizing pursuits be woven into your work?
3. Do you feel your energy returning to you, even if work leaves you tired at the end of the day?
4. How often do you feel a sense of satisfaction, gratification, or accomplishment? Is it enough?
5. In the course of reading this book, what have you learned you need to feel more energized in your work?
6. What should meaningful accomplishment success and gratification look and feel like on the journey ahead?

B. CHALLENGE

Take some time to completely challenge your definition of success. Think long and hard about your operational design and what's most important in your life. Think about how your definition of success should point you to "what matters most." Ask some tough questions:

1. Is your definition shaped by fear or insecurity? How?
2. How do cultural or societal norms and popular culture sway your ideas about what you need to have to "feel" successful?
3. How does your definition ensure you are always growing and learning?
4. How does your definition of success accommodate the needs of your family, friends, and loved ones?

5. How has your definition been impacted by influential people in your life, and has that that influence worked in your own best interest?

6. Have Discouragers and Dream Killers influenced your ideas about your destiny?

7. How do you prioritize money and material gain against other rewards?

8. How do you prioritize your need for rest, quality time with people who matter, and the need to "play?"

9. What lies or past labels have influenced your thinking? How can you remove negative labels, fear-driven criteria, etc.?

10. How can you align your work to tasks and activities that inspire, motivate and energizes you?

11. How does your definition of success encompass your role in your community and/or larger society?

12. What things would better position you to feel gratified and satisfied?

13. Is there anything else that's missing?

C. REDEFINE

Leveraging all the thought you have put in so far, begin to revise, expand, adjust and correct your earlier definition of success. Think about all the considerations above. Reach into your pocket and pull out the precious pieces of the past that you have dropped along your career path—things that made you special, things you love to do and filled you with energy. Construct a new definition of success, considering the list of considerations below. *Note: You'll probably need your notebook journal, paper, or word-processing document here.*

- Position, rank or advancement
- Type of work, tasks, etc.
- Type of company
- Type of workplace
- Workplace culture
- Working arrangements
- Income level
- Benefits and perks
- Vacation time
- Paid leave
- Flex time
- Industry positioning
- Reputation & exposure
- Health/physical wellness
- Lifestyle/quality of life
- Energizing work
- Accomplishments
- Ethics, values, spirituality
- Amenities and possessions
- Workplace relationships
- Family life, relationships
- Geographical preferences
- Professional growth/challenge
- Extracurricular goals
- Retirement objectives
- Short-/long-term goals

I'm a fan of conducting course checks frequently, reviewing and challenging myself, and tweaking things as needed. This can be incredibly useful in helping me stay on course, face obstacles, and weather challenges as I attempt to stay on course to a meaningful and rewarding destination. Remember, the key to adjusting your definition of success properly is refusing to accept any idea at face value—and *resisting* any force that compromises the following:

1. What's best *for you*—Your mental, physical, spiritual and financial well-being

2. The best things *about you*—Your own unique talent, skills, purpose, likes, values, and more

3. The *people* you care about—Your significant other, spouse, children, family, friends, etc.

What I found, myself, in doing this—and what I've witnessed in clients and colleagues—is that on the surface, coming up with a definition of success seems like it might be an easy task. In reality, creating a personalized, customized definition of professional success is a rather involved, intense exercise for those who take it seriously. As you start redefining what success means to you, it may put you in a place that requires you to reframe or challenge some of the truths you've accepted—about you, your life, your calling, your future, what's feasible, and what you should be willing to settle for.

I strongly encourage you to spend at least an hour on this now but to take as much time as you need to *complete* this important exercise. Take as much time as you need, and feel free to stop and think, and come back as needed to tweak and adjust. When I first did this, I locked myself in a cabin at the top of Mt. Hood in Oregon for a couple of days. Because your definition of success will help you navigate the journey ahead, it is important that it be carefully conceived, calibrated, cohesive, comprehensive, and aligned to your operational design.

A Shift in Mindset

As I did this exercise, I was forced to reframe a lot of my ideas and expectations in *several* areas, and it resulted in a radical alteration in my thinking on many levels. One simpler example of the shift I made had to do with my perspective about vacation time.

I used to count my ability to take a pretty lavish vacation each year as a mark of my own success. In addition to being a reward for really hard work, I suppose these vacations were a kind of status symbol, too. In reality, they served as a totally insufficient treatment for burnout and became stressful in their own right because they required more planning and travel (the *last thing* someone who is time-starved with a travel-intensive job might need). As a result, I *rarely* used all my vacation time, and while I took some nice vacations, they never did much to recharge me because I lived in a perpetual state of exhaustion.

In recalibrating my career compass, I realized that, because I work intensively, what I need most is *quality time off for recuperative rest*. That time can't be isolated to two or three weeks out of the year, and often should *not* require travel. I also recognized that what made vacation powerful for me was spending time "unplugged" in beautiful, inspiring places. I tend to recharge in nature, and as a high-tech worker, unplugging is a way for me to get more grounded. These realizations shifted my view of "time off" and years later, motivated a move to the central coast of California.

Today, I intentionally live in a beautiful place where I can get out to recharge in the woods, beach, or take a drive down the coast, or take in a sunset at a moment's notice. We enjoy living here because a lot of friends come to stay with us, giving us company and companionship without the need to travel extensively. I also try to take six to eight weeks off per year to rest, pursue learning, writing, and spiritual or personal growth.

Another area where I changed my perspective related to the way I prioritized financial security. As I grappled with leaving my company, I was confronted with incredible anxiety over financial concerns. This had a strong, magnetic impact on me. In retracing my steps, I recalled how my own parents struggled financially. Early in life, I had determined not to have that kind of financial stress in my life. As I traced many career compromises that threw me off course, I found many of them were driven by money. Because I didn't place doing purpose-driven, style- and energetically-aligned work on an *equal level* with financial achievement, a focus on financial security gradually pulled me away from work that energized me!

As you modify your definition of success, it's important to consider that even small changes and adjustments can make a big difference in your final destination, leading to a richer and more fulfilling life. It may not seem like it, but while a *one-degree* adjustment will only change your course by about five feet per hundred yards, over the course of one mile, that same change would make you miss your original target by ninety-two feet. If you went sixty miles, you would miss your original target by one mile! In like manner, the thoughtful adjustments you make to *better align your professional life to your new definition of success*—and a vision for the destination at which you wish to arrive will really matter—physically, spiritually and mentally.

CHAPTER 17
KEYS TO COURSE CORRECTION

Course correcting isn't just about situational change. It's about rolling up your proverbial sleeves and doing some really hard work to reorient your entire approach to work. A Discovery Channel show called *Homestead Rescue* comes to mind. In each episode, veteran homesteader, craftsman, and survivalist Marty Raney and his tough, able, adult children, Misty and Matt, sweep in to help struggling homesteaders who are trying to live off the grid and find themselves in crisis. Marty and team arrive on the scene to listen, observe, and begin to fix problems by hitting the basics: shelter, water, food, and safety. It isn't uncommon to find them building or reinforcing structures, installing solar generators, digging wells, and putting in water filtration systems. They also teach willing homesteaders how to grow their own food, hunt, and fish, so they can become more self-sustaining. They also deal with threats, pests, and predators.

In nearly every episode of *Homestead Rescue*, homesteaders are confronted with the uncomfortable reality that they are off the mark. They must grapple with their own shortcomings, weakness, mistakes, denial, and even blind spots that test their resolve to make it independently in harsh conditions. In similar fashion, in the Workplace Wilderness, we must grapple with areas where we may be weak or living in denial. You may identify with some of the pitfalls that stand as traits of your operational style, or struggle with issues, obstacles, or challenges as you face your own professional territory—and some are perhaps more challenging than others. You may be aware of areas where you simply lack the skills and abilities needed for a certain role, function, or job. The good news is, these weaknesses present immediate opportunities for course-correction.

One of the things I like about the Raney team is that while they call homesteaders to be accountable for their shortcomings, they don't offer condemnation for their failures. They'll challenge people who resist positive change—and work very patiently with anyone who is willing to learn and embrace improvement. In like manner, we need to take a positive and more kind approach to ourselves as we attempt to alter our own course.

While your weaknesses and shortcomings will be unique to you, how you feel about the challenges you face—and your deeply rooted attitudes, beliefs, and behaviors—are the determining factor for whether you will overcome them. It's very easy to taint your professional journey with "can't do" thinking, negativity, and/or false assumption, especially if you've had a hard time, to date. Changing course requires a pragmatic recognition of weakness as well as a dedication to address and remove as many potential stumbling blocks from your pathway as possible. When it gets tough, getting a little help in the form of a mentor, counselor, or a life coach might help!

As you journey forward, it's important to embrace and celebrate what's great about you while acknowledging and readily accepting the areas where you remain challenged. As we seek to improve, correct negative thinking, behavior patterns, and weakness, it's essential to be kind—and maybe a little gentler with ourselves. Further, we must also offer this same kindness to others! After all, we are all just travelers, trying to find our way!

GET READY

Once you have taken the lead of your own career journey and have recalibrated your career compass by challenging and redefining what success means to you, course correction becomes easier and a lot more natural. However, be warned: the minute you try to align your professional life to a new course, you are very likely to have your resolve tested!

The minute I announced my intention to leave my overdemanding job, my manager was ready to counter. She tried to lure me back with a long-term local project, highlighting an immediate opportunity for me. Her appeal was almost seductive. "You owe it to yourself to come back and at least check it out, Leigh," she said. "You are in line for a promotion!" She argued that coming back could do no harm. "Just come back for a week or two," she cooed. "Even if you don't stay, you can recharge your bank account a little." The icing on the cake was: "We've got projects for you and are looking forward to your return." There were the magnetic forces again: stability, financial provision, being accepted and validated, being needed—tugging at me and mocking me.

I agreed to return for two weeks. My mistake became evident the minute I walked into my company's lobby. After six years of employment, it felt like a foreign place. I walked into the café to get some coffee. I was shocked to find that the Red Bull coolers in our café had multiplied like rabbits. I grabbed my coffee as time seemed to slow down. I was lost in a sea of suits and serious faces, hurried and focused, preoccupied on their mobile phones. I saw people furiously heads-down, engaged intently behind laptop screens. I heard the native language of consultants, which mostly involves buzzwords and acronyms, from the "ROI on the CRM solution..." to the "meeting with the DOD on ICT." For a moment, it was funny.

The mood was intense and pressured—a rude awakening after three months of rest. I felt my blood pressure rise. I followed a crowd to the elevator. Everyone was going up with eyes down, either looking at their phones, sipping their coffee, or contemplating the crumbly carbs they held, dressed in recycled paper jackets. The silence was broken by the ninth floor "ding." I walked to my barren desk, finding it equally foreign and sterile. I saw no one familiar. It was hard to focus. I felt like a fish out of water, with a tightness in my chest. I didn't belong there anymore.

While I kept my obligation to my boss, I confirmed my departure date within days. I resigned with a spring in my step, with my head high, two weeks later—feeling empowered, emboldened, and just slightly terrified. Looking back, I had considered leaving that job for four years. I had been making small course-adjustments for two years. It started with my wake-up call in the Caribbean. It continued as I searched for a better way to work and continued when I discovered how operational styles work and began establishing better boundaries with the intention of thriving where I was planted. As I took the helm of my journey, I was repeatedly tested as I faced difficult situations. I grappled with my pitfalls, made a few mistakes, and had a few successes. I did a lot of soul-work to filter through the lies and labels I had embraced over the years—about myself and my identity. However, as I began making better choices, I became bolstered and strengthened by every new success—one degree, one step at a time.

Starting my own consulting practice was exhilarating and exciting—and scary. But I was motivated and filled with a calm sense of assurance that I had found the right path. I was guided by a clear picture of what I wanted success to look like—to nourish me in body, mind, and spirit. I hung reminders on my desk to keep myself on course. I dug deep into stimulating work and chose clients with missions I could get behind. I worked from home. I traveled when I chose to do so. I continued to heal and work out five days a week. I became social again, and felt my health, energy, and vitality returning to me.

The benefits of these changes weren't just work related. While I wasn't sure it would ever happen, just three months after I left that job, I met an amazing guy, and we were married just six months later. I moved from the East Coast to the snowy Midwest, and found myself working from a little home with a warm Labrador retriever at my feet. I had married my best friend and was developing a great relationship with an amazing, fourteen-year-old step daughter, doing life in a way I'd never done it before. Just five months after that, I became pregnant with a miracle baby. I worked from home and got to snuggle with him and watch him grow every day. We brought in far less money than I had made in the past, and we didn't take lavish vacations or drive fancy cars. My life was a huge departure from what I'd experienced for decades, and on some counts, about five times harder. However, it was also ten times more fulfilling, gratifying, and energizing! It was, in every way, *worth it!*

When I changed my definition of success and began to realign my life to it, I couldn't have anticipated where it would take me. It has radically altered my course and moved me into a much more thriving, abundant, and purposeful existence. We moved to the West Coast in 2010 to continue our adventure as a family, and continue to live there today. As for the journey, there is no end in sight. I continue to adjust my course as I press forward. In fact, writing this book is another one of those gut wrenching, wing-stretching, uncomfortable leaps of faith. I am so very far from perfect, and still working on talking too much, working too much, and overwhelming people in all my Flyer glory—but I am filled with joy, happiness, and gratitude, and amazed by the blessings and miracles that surround me every day. This is me, thriving.

When you realize you've been working the wrong way for a portion of your life, it may feel overwhelming to course correct. However, the best way to begin is to make incremental, meaningful changes. Remember the power of a one-degree shift! The same is true in life. Making iterative adjustments takes resolve, discipline, courage, sacrifice, patience, time, and hard work. You may have to adopt some new behaviors. You might have to come to terms with bad thinking or even make amends with people. The people closest to you may or may not understand. However, every change that begins to align you toward "True North" will be empowering, energizing, and infuse you with additional resolve and confidence and boldness to go beyond survival to a thriving professional existence that makes you feel truly alive.

GET SET

As you begin your own course correction, here are some admonishments to keep in mind.

Reset Course to Thriving

Always start with redefining success. Then take the lead, grab your pack, pick up that compass, and set a course to a more design-aligned way of working. By changing the way you perceive success and manage yourself within your workplace or business, you can positively impact your situation, adapt to face pressures and challenges, make a positive impact on others, and drive better results.

Be Strong!

Address weakness from a position of strength. Focus on what *can* change, first, making meaningful adjustments one by one. This will empower and strengthen you. As you build gradual momentum and see the fruits of small changes, you will be emboldened to press ahead and make more. With some wins under your belt, you'll begin to enjoy a greater sense of victory and find joy in your journey.

Prepare to Be Tested

As I mentioned previously, the minute you resolve to change things, you must be prepared to have your resolve tested. Author Steven Pressfield wrote a great book called *The War of Art* that addresses the force of resistance that comes against us any time we attempt to do anything expansive, creative, bold, or good for us! If you find your new resolve tested, you are on the right path! Stay the course. If you need a shot in the arm, grab Steven's book for some inspiration and encouragement!

Kick Fear in the Teeth

Fear becomes your enemy the minute it plays a role in keeping you stuck, paralyzed, co-dependent, or captive. If your fear is not keeping you safe, it's not a good excuse for phoning it in or failing to live up to your potential. Life is too short to spend the majority of your waking life cowering and afraid. Kick fear in the teeth! Seize the day!

Own Your Power

Course correction is empowering, and so is owning 100 percent of your responsibility in creating success or failure, collaboration or conflict. You may not always feel like you are winning, but with ownership, you will always have power. As you own your successes, you shine. As you own failure and your mistakes, you walk with dignity and with a clean conscience, humble and learning. As you demonstrate a high level of accountability in your workplace and encourage others to do the same, you can help put an end to bad behavior, blame-games, and finger-pointing. Beyond the benefits to yourself, the good this can do for others and your workplace can be immeasurable.

Step out with Confidence

As the small changes mount, the confidence grows. You may even arrive at a place where you sense it's time to take a bigger professional leap. I believe the desires of your heart have been put there for a reason. You are meant for more! Plan well, and bring in good counsel, starting with the people who know you best and matter most—especially your significant other, spouse, and immediate family. Big leaps are hard and impact everyone, and you'll need each other as you move further outside your "discomfort zone."

GO FOR IT

EXERCISE 12
QUICK COURSE CORRECTIONS

PLOTTING SOME MEANINGFUL CHANGES
In Exercise 10, you identified obstacles and challenges that you face. In Exercise 11, you redefined success. Using material from both exercises, take twenty minutes to map out at least three meaningful course corrections you can begin to act on immediately. Start by thinking about realistic adjustments you can make today that calibrate with your new definition of success. Make your changes actionable, and set timing!

EXAMPLE	
NEW PRIORITY	**CHALLENGES & OBSTACLES**
• Move back into design work	• My job has pushed me out of doing the design work that energizes me, forcing me to take on too much paperwork and project management work. • I need refresher training for AutoCAD and other programs in order to be able to step back in at the level I had before (and to grow).
TIMING	**THE PLAN**
• Immediate	• Immediate: Find ways to engage more in the design process, mentoring team and proofing/reviews.
• July 30th	• Investigate course opportunities and costs. (By end-of-month)
• August 2 review	• Meet with boss to discuss increased involvement in design process and secure approvals, input and feedback on trajectory, training, etc. in review.
• August 30th	• Enroll in first class.

YOUR ENTRIES	
NEW PRIORITY	**CHALLENGES & OBSTACLES**
TIMING	**THE PLAN**

A CASE STUDY IN COURSE CORRECTION

Amanda was an extraordinarily driven Climber. Growing up, her parents, both hard-charging executives, were equally hard on her. From a young age, she was expected to deliver with a level of perfection. From the age of four, she was enrolled in dance, language immersion class, sports, and more. While she excelled in her overscheduled life, play was almost always focused on learning or performance. She was never given much time just to be a kid.

Her parents' marriage was contentious, and her relationship with them was too short on affirmation, affection, and the words "I love you." She often felt like an obligation. When she was sixteen, her father left her mother for a twenty-three-year-old intern, triggering a contentious divorce. Despite the stress, Amanda managed to maintain her position on the honor roll, as well as serving as captain of the Lacrosse team and president of the student body. Her parents acknowledged these accomplishments with a smile and a head nod—having become immersed in new relationships— both marrying and starting new families shortly thereafter. Amanda felt like an outsider in both families and was relieved to graduate and leave home to attend college.

She was accepted at Columbia where she became the head of her sorority. She graduated *summa cum laude* with a degree in communications. She went on to obtain her MBA from Wharton with a specialization in business finance, and with several internships under her belt. Armed with a load of recommendations, Amanda entered the workforce with determined ambition, and her choice of job offers.

Amanda went to work for a venture capital firm and, in true form, rose quickly through the ranks. After just four years, she was promoted to director, followed by rumors of a romantic tryst with a married, senior VP. Despite the rumored impropriety, no one could deny Amanda's performance: She knew how to recognize a good investment prospect. She maintained a network that helped her secure the inside track on deals that translated to millions in revenue. In a male-dominated company, she was one of few women that rose quickly to the top, having ingratiated herself to upper management through relentless hard work.

Outside of being a high performer, Amanda was perhaps the most feared person in her company. She drove herself hard and expected others to do the same. She demanded loyalty, confidentiality, performance, and 24/7 availability from her direct reports. She ignored birthdays, anniversaries, weddings, and baby showers for peers and colleagues—unless the person celebrating happened to be someone in the power structure she wanted to impress. Her dutiful admin, Stacey, created the illusion of Amanda's "soft side." She knew who mattered most and managed the gift-purchasing and card-sending for Amanda.

On the positive side, Amanda was smart, eminently resourceful, and knew how to hire good people and delegate tasks. She was excellent in using her powers of persuasion to rope in support when necessary. On the negative side, she had problems on her team, including some turnover and poor morale. Amanda's self-ambition was transparent to her staff. She seemed to care only about herself, building a power base and her own accomplishment. She was protective of her relationships and contacts to the point of being territorial. She exceled at crushing the competition and winning. She wasn't afraid to call out, or even to slight, a colleague or competitor who got in her way. She let her team do the heavy lifting while assuming most of the credit as she managed negotiations, politics, and strategic relationships herself. She pushed her people the way her parents had pushed her, developing a dictator's reputation. She felt emotions had no place in the workplace. She was all business, and never seemed happy, satisfied, or connected in a meaningful way to the people around her.

Five years in, her CEO retired, and the firm's leadership changed. Her new CEO was a seasoned Climber with a high emotional IQ, who was well regarded by the people who had worked with him. He had a hands-on way of working with teams. While the numbers at the firm were good, he entered the company concerned about some negative feedback he'd received across the board regarding leadership, morals, and ethics in the firm. He hired an organizational consulting firm to probe more deeply into the leadership, culture, and morale of the firm as he planned for future growth. The team conducted interviews all over the firm.

Amanda had recently been thrust into the spotlight for blowing a deal by trying to crush the competition in a questionably ethical way. As a result, she lost the deal. It was an embarrassing gaffe for her, but with a track record so impressive, the backlash was minimal. When the results came back on the corporate leadership assessment, however, more issues with Amanda emerged. While her performance largely impressed her CEO, her conduct horrified him. The feedback that was provided by peers and direct reports served as a source of deep concern. While she delivered outstanding results, it was clear to the CEO that Amanda posed a risk to her company, and this required action.

The CEO personally conducted a performance review with Amanda, during which it was made clear that her future advancement would hinge not just on her ability to land deals and manage investments, but to change the perceptions about her within the firm *and* to better manage the people with whom she had been entrusted. Much to her horror, her CEO expressed strong reservations about his ability to promote her to the next level—or keep her with the firm long-term—without knowing she could demonstrate the kind of leadership and ethics that were critical for a senior executive to have. To do this, he said, she'd need to shift from dictator to one who leads; she'd need to inspire and motivate, rather than manage by threats and intimidation; and she'd need to find ways to share more credit, reward performance, and celebrate success with her team. This wasn't just about improving her *reputation*—it was about improving her *relationships*. To help her out, her CEO assigned Amanda a career coach for a six-month period.

Amanda was mortified, humiliated, and concerned. This ended up being a very good thing, however. This humiliation, bolstered by the 360-degree feedback provided by her team, painted a clear picture of a problem that was hard to deny. Because her ability to advance hinged on her improvement, Amanda had no choice but to feel motivated to participate. It took time for her to abandon a defensive posture and engage freely with her coach. In time, they began to dive deeply into how she worked, and traced many of her behaviors to the rigidity of her upbringing.

Amanda did not put much stock in the "touchy feely" aspects of her coaching. She was surprised to be confronted by her coach about her lack of ability to build and sustain interpersonal relationships and encouraged to begin reaching out to build relationships with her people. Amanda didn't want to go out to lunch with peers or direct reports, engage in occasional banter or water-cooler conversations, or hang out at happy hour after a win, just for celebration or socialization. Her personal life was rather unremarkable and largely centered on activities that supported her professional life. She worked out, belonged to a club, and engaged in professional networking. She kept her family at arms' length. Her sorority chums were busy raising families. She had a number of fair-weather friends and relatively shallow, sporadic dating relationships with emotionally unavailable men, much like her father. When Amanda pushed back against her coach's assertions about her lack of human engagement, saying, "Look, this is a bit too much," her coach presented her with a list of offenses that showed just how socially out of touch she was with her team.

For example, she once threatened to fire a staff member who failed to finalize a financial analysis because he left to attend to his wife who had gone into premature labor with their first baby. She had once castigated Stacey for crying at the office after her grandmother died, telling her to "get ahold of herself" at work. She discouraged her direct reports from taking a few hours to go to school events for their kids during the day. Because she was all business, it was easy for Amanda to tune out others' life situations—illnesses, challenges, life events, family emergencies, etc. She had zero tolerance for "whining" and felt uncomfortable with people who expressed emotion—even on a "down" day.

Her coach helped open her eyes to these matters and more. She helped Amanda confront the utilitarian view she had of people. She made her see that she only really paid attention to people who were in a position to help her. Amanda was floored by the perspective of a peer who quipped, "If Amanda doesn't need you, you are dead to her." She was embarrassed at how she failed to express gratitude. While Amanda did feel grateful, she had never been taught to show it!

Amanda may have behaved as an ice queen, but she was far from being unemotional. To protect herself, she established walls between herself and other people that made her feel safe. Her coaching was breaking those down, and she found herself in tears behind closed doors much of the time. The truth was, no matter how much she accomplished, it never felt like enough. She never felt good enough, or truly gratified or satisfied. She was paranoid about losing her job. She felt as if she were slowly suffocating, under three feet of water, and breathing through a straw. She knew people didn't like her and tried to tell herself it didn't matter. She tried to ignore it when a laughing group of coworkers quickly disbanded when they saw her coming down the hallway—or when they went to lunch without inviting her. When she started trying to become more social, people responded with suspicion and concern. It was awkward and depressing.

Amanda trudged home each day after work feeling alone, disliked, and lost, trying to tell herself she didn't care. She didn't like herself very much, either. Despite her financial success, she really worked around the clock as a way of hiding from the world. She deprived herself of rest and episodically binged and starved herself to maintain a trim figure. Her drive to "prove herself" and "win" had completely overshadowed everything else. In reality, she felt miserable, off course, and confused.

At her coach's suggestion, Amanda found a good psychologist and leveraged an ample amount of unpaid vacation to take some time off. During that time, her coach encouraged Amanda to consider the long-term legacy she wished to leave, and to itemize the skills, achievements, and abilities that would be necessary to realize that legacy. Having come to the end of herself, Amanda did just that.

In the course of rest and therapy, Amanda realized that, even as an adult, she was still trying to prove herself to her parents. Her past disappointments had created an internal belief that people were not safe and could not be trusted, resulting in defensive isolation. Her counselors helped make her see how her thoughts and behavior made others feel and served as stumbling blocks on her way to advancement. She began to authentically empathize with the longsuffering people who worked for her, like dutiful Stacey and other people she had crushed. To her credit, Amanda began issuing apologies and making amends. She sent flowers to Stacey and a gift certificate for a spa day. She began to see the truth of how important her journey was. Sacrificing people for the outcomes she wanted had led her down a dark and lonely path—and they were all worthy of better.

With light at the end of the tunnel, her coach also helped Amanda redefine what success looked like to her. Amanda had acknowledged that her long-term desire was to run her own venture capital firm. It followed that without the ability to lead and motivate others, this could never happen. She marveled at how wise her CEO had been in providing her with coaching. He had taken a father-like interest in Amanda and began to mentor her. She responded positively, fascinated at how he motivated and influenced people, building his own success by building people up. She studied and read management books he recommended, realizing her need to be able to do more than just oversee, manage, and delegate. Under his encouragement, she even agreed to participate in volunteer work for Habitat for Humanity in Mexico City with her firm. She was unprepared for the flood of emotion that overwhelmed her during that experience. In fact, she found it so gratifying, she became a regular volunteer and leader.

About six months into her transformation, Amanda was introduced to OST and was intrigued to see someone had laid out a framework for course correction that was very similar to the one she had followed. Identifying strongly as a Climber, her pros and pitfalls seemed to align rather neatly. She leveraged OST and style dynamics to build strong bridges with others. With the help of her coach and her therapist, she began to address her emotional scars and heal. She began to arrest the negative internal dialogue and emotional triggers that made her defensive, cold, territorial, and closed off. As she learned to work adaptively with others, she began to connect in a more authentic and meaningful way with people in her workplace. Fostering authentic connections with people no longer stimulated career-damaging rumors, either! She began to build trust with the people who served under and alongside her.

Amanda's challenge was never the mechanics of her job. She could put together deals with her eyes closed. Her challenge was placing an equal emphasis on developing people and helping them succeed. Amanda made this her mission. With a different view of success, she began to allocate time and personal attention to her direct reports. She rewarded them with praise and credit. She celebrated their accomplishments as her own. As she became more focused on the journey and less obsessed with the destination, her reputation began to change. A softer Amanda emerged as she transitioned from being a sledgehammer into what her boss called "the velvet hammer."

Today, she is an EVP. She is still tough, but she's human. She hits hard and doesn't pull punches. However, she no longer does this as a defense mechanism. She no longer throws people under the bus unfairly or defines their worth based on how useful they are to her at the moment. She is building stronger and longer-lasting, healthy relationships. She is laughing more and having more fun. Her social life has improved, and she's in a long-term relationship. She's mentoring with a startup incubator and has respect and the regard of others. Having learned how to arrest her emotional triggers and work more empathetically with others, Amanda is focused on the legacy she wants to leave. She has become a better leader and better person as a result.

Course correction like Amanda's is a time-consuming process, and often, it requires peeling back the layers to reveal what's really driving us and influencing our behavior. When we change our perspective and begin to work with greater empathy, it can lead to radical shifts in the way we approach our work. As you learn to embrace your style, minimize your pitfalls and emotional triggers, and work adaptively with others, you can move from mere career survival to a thriving, professional existence, as we'll discuss in the conclusion.

PART FIVE

MOVING FROM SURVIVING TO THRIVING

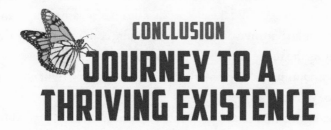

CONCLUSION
JOURNEY TO A
THRIVING EXISTENCE

Back when I was really struggling in my abusive job and trying to figure out what I would do next, I called my mom in tears. I poured my heart out describing the challenges I faced, lamenting how stuck and abused I felt. I complained about how confusing it was to figure out what was next—especially as I grappled with the idea of self-employment, which terrified me.

"Leigh," she said, thoughtfully, "do you know what a mother eagle does when she wants her baby eaglets to leave the nest?"

"No," I said.

"She stirs up the nest," Mom said.

She went on to explain that an eagle's nest is originally lined with soft downy feathers and soft leaves, placed to cushion and insulate the eggs, and eventually the eaglets. It's warm, cozy, and safe. However, when the babies are sufficiently grown, the mother eagle stops bringing food to the nest, and starts removing the down and leaves, bringing in sharp sticks, twigs, thorns, rocks, and anything else that might render it inhospitable. *She knows the eaglets will not leave the nest unless they are hungry and uncomfortable.*

To escape the discomfort, the eaglets will step out onto the edge of the nest or onto adjacent rocks or branches, to perch. There, they begin to get their balance, stretching and strengthening their wings and catching breezes to "hover" above the nest. When the mother eagle determines it is time, she simply nudges them off the edge, one at a time. Down the eaglet tumbles, shocked and confused, until the mother flies up underneath to catch and lift it to a new height. She then drops the eaglet again, coming up underneath it and repeating the move until the eaglet catches the wind and flies.

My mom continued. "I believe that's going on with you right now, Leigh. It's time for you to fly."

Her analogy couldn't have been more apropos: I was a Flyer who was afraid of heights. The thing was, after wasting so much time being afraid, it began to feel simply absurd not to take the leap. Fear was keeping me stuck; it wasn't keeping me safe. Fear was my enemy. My nest was no longer comfortable, and I was hungry for something more. It wasn't much later that I made that very worthwhile leap!

About two years ago, I recalled my mom's story as I watched a mother hawk teach her baby to fly from a friend's back deck. It started from the top of a Redwood tree on a hillside in the Santa Cruz mountains. I saw the poor baby hawk tumbling from the top of the tree, and the mama hawk fly up underneath it, catch it with wings spread, using her back and talons to carry it up to a higher point and drop it again, calling to it. The poor little hawk tumbled again, trying to spread its wings, as the mama hawk completed another harrowing rescue move and repeated the drill. This continued several times. After about five minutes, the air was filled with tiny cries as the baby hawk began to catch the breeze and soar. It was frightening and beautiful—kind of like my journey. Perhaps like yours, too.

Whether you are a Walker, Climber, or Flyer, it often takes time to alter your course, carve a new path, take a leap, or spread your wings to fly. Sometimes, like a hawk or an eaglet, you may get a nudge. They come in many forms. You may be sitting in a stirred-up nest. Perhaps you have experienced a job loss, defeat, challenging life event, or even illness—or your life has changed through marriage, divorce, death, the birth of a new baby, or the need to care for an aging parent. Perhaps you are self-driven! Nudges can come from a boss, mentor, family member, or a friend offering encouraging or chastising words—or from a book, like this one. The catalyst for change and actions that follow will be uniquely your own and can radically alter your course and your destination.

The thing is, if you never venture out, you'll never know the exhilaration or joy of flight, of reaching new heights, or the beauty of treading where few have ever gone before. It's okay if you need to "perch and hover" first, like the young eagles do. Heck, that's progress! Embrace the season you are in! Grow first where you are planted. Embolden yourself by making those meaningful changes that better align your work with your design, and keep on walking, climbing, or flying. Take courage, and remember the power of small, one-degree changes!

My friend Dan, a Walker, called me last spring feeling really down, unmotivated, and stuck in his job. On one hand, he had job stability, a very nice paycheck, and benefits with an easy commute. On the other hand, his employer was stuck in the Stone Age. His work had become boring, and he was no longer challenged. Dan felt a deep dissatisfaction, restlessness, and impatience to move on to a job that was more tech-enabled and leading-edge. We talked about his current job, the opportunities on the horizon, and the implications of changing jobs for Dan and his family.

I learned that Dan's wife, a former school teacher, was at home with their four-year-old daughter and eighteen-month-old son. Dan's present job and a fifteen-minute commute made it easy for him to go home on time, be supportive of his wife, and to enjoy family time. He felt good about the ability to give his wife the opportunity to be home with his children, as well as the flexibility be home as a present, engaged father.

While he had the opportunity to make an immediate job change, it wasn't his only opportunity. We talked through Dan's career timeline, goals, and desires, and how he defined success. We celebrated the incredible freedom and power he had in his situation. He was in an uncomfortable place, in a good position. We talked about the window of time he had with his children at home and how miniscule it was in comparison to the time he had to develop in his profession. I recalled how fleeting the time was when my own son was young, and how precious that time was. Then, we reviewed the challenges that might be introduced by a new job, new commute, new demands, a new schedule, and employer expectations.

I suggested to Dan that perhaps the best opportunity in front of him was to slow his roll and just enjoy this precious and short season with his family. That didn't mean he had to ignore what was wrong at work. We discussed some very practical ways he could shift things with a determination to thrive where he was planted. We also talked about how to plan intentionally so that when he did make a move, it would be a strategic one. As we laid out these options, Dan got a burst of new energy, and became suddenly relieved and excited. "Wow," he exclaimed, "you have no idea how much better I feel! I was putting so much pressure on myself to make things happen all at once!"

Dan's story demonstrates the importance of patience, weighing our options during different seasons of life, and making changes that make sense. Sometimes, it just takes time to ready ourselves for bigger moves. Heck, it took years for me to take a leap. Dan's story also illustrates the power of smaller changes. Today, he's still with his company—and thanks to our planning, helping them adopt new technology in ways he didn't anticipate. Plus, he's home in time for dinner, bedtime stories and snuggles every night!

At the beginning of this book, I asked you to plot your position on the surviving to thriving continuum. It is my hope that, armed with the information provided in this book, you now feel better equipped to embrace your design, understand and adapt to others, and plot a course in the Workplace Wilderness to a place where you can thrive. As you make your way with new tools and awareness, I'd like to leave you with the following admonitions:

BE PATIENT WITH THE PROCESS

We all travel at our own pace. Don't compare yourself to others. Make changes that are right for you. You didn't get where you are overnight, and you're not likely to shift everything in a day. The best journeys aren't completed overnight, anyway! By taking the helm of your professional journey, aligning work to your own design, and setting a course for your own "True North," you can begin to establish a more harmonious relationship with this thing called work. In time, and with course correction, you can arrive at a much better destination.

MAKE MEANINGFUL, INCREMENTAL CHANGES

I've referred to this a few times now, but I can't stress it enough. You can wallow in the negative and feed that spinning Headspace Hamster, or you can take the helm and start making empowered, incremental changes that build empowering momentum. You can be part of the problem or choose to be part of the solution. By changing your mindset, establishing boundaries, and choosing action over apathy, you can begin to drive wins now that strengthen you and energize you for the path ahead.

MEASURE YOUR R.O.E.

Remember the wisdom of Dr. Rogacz: When you are fulfilling your purpose, your energy returns to you, regenerating you in body, mind, and spirit. When you are abusing your purpose, it will not return, resulting in dis-ease. It's okay to get tired, if you can recover quickly and feel good about what you are doing. It's okay to go through seasons of working hard and sucking it up, if it leads to a fruitful harvest and a season of rest and recuperation. However, when you find yourself depleted, look out! It's a warning sign on the pathway to burnout. Pay attention to your Return on Energy as you journey forward!

FIND JOY IN THE JOURNEY

In our modern society, there's a whole lot of emphasis on "arriving" at a successful destination, as well as an ongoing romance with professional achievement. However, it's also important to find joy in the journey you are on each day and celebrate the meaningful achievements that happen at the intersection of work and relationships. Take the time to acknowledge your progress. Take in the view. Get happy with other humans. Be an Encourager who brings out the best in others. Celebrate achievement. It's not only a great way to extract a greater sense of joy, gratification, and satisfaction from your work—it's an incredible way to lead and inspire others.

GO WITH GRACE

My Southern Mama once asked me what I thought the definition of grace was.

"Elegance?" I stuttered.

"No, honey," she replied. "Grace is the art of making anyone feel at home."

That definition has always stuck with me. We all desperately need grace. We all need to feel safe, at home. Grace does honor to others by understanding, embracing, and accepting people for who they are. Grace forms natural bridges to human relationship and wholehearted communication. As you encounter people on the path ahead, I wish you an increased measure of grace. May you be the kind of person that embraces your design, seeks to understand and adapt to others, establishes common ground, and makes people feel at home in this wilderness of work. May you thrive in your potential and encourage others to do the same!

REFERENCE
RESOURCES

CHAPTER 1

Ben Wigert and Sangeeta Agrawal, 2018. "Employee Burnout, Part 1: The 5 Main Causes." Gallup Research. Accessed online, https://www.gallup.com/workplace/237059/employee-burnout-part-main-causes.aspx

Gallup Research, 2017. "State of the Global Workplace Report." Accessed online, https://www.gallup.com/workplace/238079/state-global-workplace-2017.aspx?utm_source=link_wwwv9&utm_campaign=item_231668&utm_medium=copy#formheader

Jim Harter, 2018. "Employee Engagement on the rise in U.S." Gallup Research. Accessed online, https://news.gallup.com/poll/241649/employee-engagement-rise.aspx

Ben Wigert, 2018. "Talent Walks: Why Your Best Employees are Leaving." Gallup Research. Accessed online, https://www.gallup.com/workplace/231641/talent-walks-why-best-employees-leaving.aspx

American Psychological Association, 2017. "What is Stress." Accessed online, https://www.stress.org/daily-life/

Korn Ferry Institute, 2018. "Workplace Stress Continues to Rise." https://www.kornferry.com/institute/workplace-stress-motivation

Daniel Cable, 2018. "There's a Biological Reason You're Bored at Work." *Quartz*. Accessed online, https://qz.com/work/1237505/why-youre-bored-at-work-and-what-to-do-about-it/

Ultimate Software and Generational Kinetics, 2017. "New National Study Conducted by Ultimate Software Reveals Need for Greater Focus on Manager-Employee Relationships." Accessed online, https://www.ultimatesoftware.com/PR/Press-Release/New-National-Study-Conducted-by-Ultimate-Software-Reveals-Need-for-Greater-Focus-on-Manager-Employee-Relationships

Gallup Research, "State of the American Manager Report," 2017. Accessed online, https://www.gallup.com/services/182138/state-american-manager.aspx

Korn Ferry Institute, "Workplace Stress Continues to Mount," 2018. Accessed online, https://kornferry.com/institute/workplace-stress-motivation

Gary Burnison, 2018. "Breaking Boredom: What's Really Driving Job Seekers in 2018." Korn Ferry Institute. Accessed online, https://www.kornferry.com/institute/job-hunting-2018-boredom

Robert Half and Cynthia Kong, 2017. "Bored at Work." Accessed online, https://www.roberthalf.com/blog/management-tips/bored-at-work

ibid., Daniel Cable, 2018. "There's a Biological Reason You're Bored at Work."

Covestro LLC, 2018. "A View from the Top: US Fortune 100 CEOs and C-suite Executives on Social Purpose and Its Impact on Business."

Gallup Research, 2017. "State of the American Workplace Report." Accessed online, https://www.gallup.com/workplace/238085/state-american-workplace-report-2017.aspx

Working Families and Bright Horizons, 2018. "Modern Families Index 2018, How Employers Can Support the UK's Working Families." Accessed online, https://www.workingfamllies.org.uk/publications/mfi2018_employer_summary/

Udemy, 2018. "Udemy in Depth: 2018 Workplace Distraction Report." Accessed online, https://research.udemy.com/research_resport/udemy-depth-2018-workplace-distraction-report

Radius Global Market Research, 2018. "Nearly Half of American Workers are Bullied According to Survey." Accessed online, https://radius-global.com/news-relese/nearly-half-of-american-workers-are-bullied-according-to-survey

Jeffrey Arnold and Michael Hughes, 2018. "Companies are Overlooking a Primary Area for Growth and Efficiency: Their Managers." West Monroe Partners. Accessed online, https://www.westmonroepartners.com/Insights/Newsletters/Productivity-Imperative

Execu|Search Group, 2018. "2018 Hiring Outlook." Accessed online, https://www.execu-search.com/~/media/Resources/pdf/2018HiringOutlook

Korn Ferry Institute, 2018. "Workplace Stress Continues to Mount." Accessed online, https://kornferry.com/institute/workplace-stress-motivation

Bright Horizons and Working Families, 2018. "Modern Families Index 2018: How Employers Can Support the UK's Working Families." Accessed online, https://www.workingfamilies.org.uk/wp-content/uploads/2018/05/UK_MFI_2018_Employers_Report_A4_Summary_FINAL.pdf

World Health Organization, "Problems related to life-management difficulty: Z73.9, Burn-Out." ICD-10 Version: 2016. Accessed online, https://icd.who.int/browse10/2016/en#/Z73.0

ibid., Ben Wigert and Sangeeta Agrawal, 2018. "Employee Burnout, Part 1: The 5 Main Causes."

ibid., Gallup Research, 2017. "State of the American Workplace."

Gallup Research, 2018. "Work and Workplace Poll." Accessed online, https://news.gallup.com/poll/1720/work-work-place.aspx

Michele Hellebuyck, et al, 2017. "Mind the Workplace." Mental Health America and Fass Foundation. Accessed online, http://www.mentalhealthamerica.net/sites/default/files/Mind%20the%20Workplace%20-%20MHA%20Workplace%20Health%20Survey%202017%20FINAL.PDF

Bureau of Labor Statistics, 2018. "American Time Use Survey." Accessed online, https://www.bls.gov/news.release/pdf/atus.pdf

Robert Smith, 2018. "This Country Works the Longest Hours in Europe." World Economic Forum. Accessed online, https://www.weforum.org/agenda/2018/02/greeks-work-longest-hours-in-europe/

G.E. Miller, 2018. "The US is the Most Overworked Developed Nation in the World." 20 Something Finance. Accessed online, https://20somethingfinance.com/american-hours-worked-productivity-vacation

Robert Half, 2018. "More Money Same Problems: Firms Often Counter With Higher Salaries to Keep Departing Employees, but Staff Leave in Less than 2 Years Anyway." Accessed online, https://rh-us.mediaroom.com/2018-07-17-MORE-MONEY-SAME-PROBLEMS-Firms-often-counter-with-higher-salaries-to-keep-departing-employee-but-staff-leave-in-less-than-2-years-anyway

Yoh, 2018. "Yoh Survey: Excluding a Raise, Flexible Work Environment and Better Benefits Top the Reasons Employed Americans Would Accept a New Job Offer." *Globe Newswire*. Accessed online, https://globenewswire.com/news-release/2018/04-11/1468489/0/en/Yoh-Survey-Excluding-a-Raise-Flexible-Work-Environment-and-Better-Benefits-Top-the-Reasons-Employed-Americans-Would-Accept-a-New-Job-Offer.html

Valerie Bolen-Barrett, 2018. "Survey: 'Work Perks' are Gaining on Traditional Benefits." HR Drive. Accessed online, https://www.hrdive.com/news/survey-work-perks-are-gaining-on-traditional-benefits/532350

National Sleep Foundation, "How Much Sleep Do We Really Need?" Accessed online, 2018. https://www.sleepfoundation.org/ecvessivesleepiness/content/how-much-sleep-do-we-really-need

CHAPTER 2

James Lipton, Dave Chappelle, 2006. *Inside the Actor's Studio*. In the Moment Productions Ltd. Accessed online, https://www.imdb.com/title/tt0850928/

CHAPTER 4

A.H. Maslow, 1943. "A Theory of Human Motivation." *Psychological Review*, 50(4): 370–396. http://dx.doi.org/10.1037/h0054346

CHAPTER 9

ibid. Jeffrey Arnold and Michael Hughes, 2018. "Companies are Overlooking a Primary Area for Growth and Efficiency: Their Managers."

CHAPTER 10

Jeff Hayes, 2018. "Workplace Conflict and How Businesses Can Use It to Thrive." CPP Global Human Capital Report. Accessed online, https://shop. themyersbriggs.com/Pdfs/CPP_Global_Human_Capital_Report_Workplace_ Conflict.pdf

CHAPTER 12

Neel Burton, M.D., 2016. "What is Emotional Intelligence." *Psychology Today.* Accessed online, https://www.psychologytoday.com/us/blog/hide-and-seek/ 201608/what-is-emotional-intelligence

Daniel Goleman, 2005. *Emotional Intelligence.* Bantam Publishers.

Daniel Goleman, 2000. *Working with Emotional Intelligence.* Bantam Publishers.

Travis Bradberry, 2009. *Emotional Intelligence 2.0.* TalentSmart; Har/Dol En edition.

Oxford Living Dictionaries. Accessed online, https://en.oxforddictionaries.com/ definition/humble

CHAPTER 15

Oxford Living Dictionaries. Accessed online, https://en.oxforddictionaries.com/ definition/jerk

CHAPTER 16

Antone Roundy. "A Mere One Degree Difference." The White Hat Crew: The Art of Ethical Persuasion. Accessed online, https://whitehatcrew.com/ blog/a-mere-one-degree-difference/

CHAPTER 17

Steven Pressfield, 2012. *The War of Art.* Self-publish, 47716th edition.

ABOUT THE AUTHOR

LEIGH DURST is a recognized authority in business, operations, and digital transformation. For twenty-five years, she has advised the global Fortune 100, startups, nonprofits, and businesses across sectors, including 1-800-FLOWERS, American Express, AOL Time Warner, Bristol-Myers Squibb, Chevron, IEEE, Walmart, and the US Army Reserve. Leigh is a change agent who helps people work smarter to produce exceptional outcomes and has presented at events like SXSW, New Media Expo, and MarketingProfs B2B. She has been featured in media outlets like *Fast Company*, CNN, CNET, ABC News, *National Geographic*, CustomerThink, the feature documentary *Social Good in a Digital Age*, and three bestselling books.